The Sports Stadium as a Municipal Investment

Recent Titles in
Contributions in Economics and Economic History

United States–Japan Trade Telecommunications: Conflict and Compromise
Meheroo Jussawalla, editor

Pacific-Asia and the Future of the World-System
Ravi Arvind Palat, editor

Development versus Stagnation: Technological Continuity and Agricultural
Progress in Pre-Modern China
Gang Deng

Commodity Chains and Global Capitalism
Gary Gereffi and Miguel E. Korzeniewicz, editors

Global Telecommunications Policies: The Challenge of Change
Meheroo Jussawalla, editor

The State and Capitalism in Israel
Amir Ben-Porat

The Economy of Iraq: Oil, Wars, Destruction of Development and Prospects,
1950–2010
Abbas Alnasrawi

The Economy in the Reagan Years: The Economic Consequences of the
Reagan Administrations
Anthony S. Campagna

Prelude to Trade Wars: American Tariff Policy, 1890–1922
Edward S. Kaplan and Thomas W. Ryley

Projecting Capitalism: A History of the Internationalization of the
Construction Industry
Marc Linder

Recent Industrialization Experience of Turkey in a Global Context
Fikret Senses, editor

The Chinese Financial System
Cecil R. Dipchand, Zhang Yichun, and Ma Mingjia

The Sports Stadium as a Municipal Investment

Dean V. Baim

Contributions in Economics
and Economic History, Number 151

Greenwood Press
Westport, Connecticut • London

Library of Congress Cataloging-in-Publication Data

Baim, Dean V.
    The sports stadium as a municipal investment / Dean V. Baim.
      p. cm.—(Contributions in economics and economic history,
ISSN 0084–9235 ; no. 151)
    Includes bibliographical references (p.) and index.
    ISBN 0–313–27816–4 (alk. paper)
    1. Stadiums—Economic aspects—United States—Case studies.
2. Urban economics—United States—Case studies. 3. Sports—
Economic aspects—United States—Case studies. I. Title.
II. Series.
GV415.B35   1994
796'.06'91—dc20   93–21501

British Library Cataloguing in Publication Data is available.

Library of Congress Catalog Card Number: 93–21501
ISBN: 0–313–27816–4
ISSN: 0084–9235

First published in 1994

Greenwood Press, 88 Post Road West, Westport, CT 06881
An imprint of Greenwood Publishing Group, Inc.

Printed in the United States of America

The paper used in this book complies with the
Permanent Paper Standard issued by the National
Information Standards Organization (Z39.48–1984).

10 9 8 7 6 5 4 3 2 1

To Shelli

27 March 1981(?)–12 July 1992

You were always there with a warm heart and a cold nose

Contents

Tables   ix

Preface   xv

1. Introduction   1

Part I: Financial Data

2. Milwaukee County Stadium   21

3. Baltimore Memorial Stadium   29

4. Buffalo War Memorial Stadium   41

5. Denver Mile High Stadium   47

6. Dodger Stadium   53

7. Robert F. Kennedy Stadium   61

8. Anaheim Stadium   75

9. Atlanta–Fulton County Stadium   83

10. Oakland–Alameda County Coliseum Complex   91

11. Jack Murphy Stadium   101

12. Cincinnati Riverfront Stadium   109

13. Foxboro Stadium   121

14. Rich Stadium   127

15. Louisiana Superdome   135

16. Minneapolis Metrodome   149

Part II: Data Analysis

17. Summary and Analysis of Financial Data   157

18. Non-Financial Data and Analysis   175

19. Comparison of Public and Private Stadiums   195

20. Conclusion   217

Bibliography   223

Index   235

Tables

2.1   Milwaukee County Stadium
Capital Improvements (1953–1976)   26

2.2   Milwaukee County Stadium
Operating Profits (Losses) (1956–1985)   27

2.3   Milwaukee County Stadium
Direct Municipal Inflows (Subsidies)
(1971–1985)   28

3.1   Baltimore Memorial Stadium
Operating Profits (1954–1982)   34

3.2   Baltimore Memorial Stadium
Direct and Indirect Outlays (1954–1985)   35

3.3   Baltimore Memorial Stadium
Direct and Indirect Outlays Using Alternative
Property Tax Assumption (1954–1985)   36

3.4   Baltimore Memorial Stadium
Tax Revenues (1954–1985)   37

3.5   Baltimore Memorial Stadium
        Accumulated Net Present Value
        of Stadium Investment (1954–1985)   38

3.6   Baltimore Memorial Stadium
        Accumulated Net Present Value of Stadium
        Investment Using Alternative Property Tax
        Assumptions (1954–1985)   39

4.1   Buffalo War Memorial Stadium
        Operating Profits (Losses) (1960–1985)   44

4.2   Buffalo War Memorial Stadium
        Municipal Outlays (1960–1985)   44

4.3   Buffalo War Memorial Stadium
        Estimate of Bills' (Subsidy)
        over "Baseline" (1960–1979)   45

5.1   Denver Mile High Stadium
        Direct and Indirect Outlays (1968–1989)   51

5.2   Denver Mile High Stadium
        Accumulated Net Present Value
        of Stadium Investment (1968–1989)   52

6.1   Los Angeles Dodger Stadium
        Net Municipal (Outlays) or Receipts
        (1958–1991)   59

7.1   Robert F. Kennedy Stadium
        Revenues and Expenses (1962–1968)   70

7.2   Robert F. Kennedy Stadium
        Revenues and Expenses (1969–1972)   70

7.3   Robert F. Kennedy Stadium
        Revenues and Expenses (1973–1979)   71

7.4   Robert F. Kennedy Stadium
        Revenues and Expenses (1980–1990)   72

7.5   Robert F. Kennedy Stadium
        Present Value of Cash Flows (1962–1990)   73

8.1   Anaheim Stadium
       Operating Profits (1967–1990)   80

8.2   Anaheim Stadium
       Direct and Indirect Municipal Outlays (1967–1991)   81

8.3   Anaheim Stadium
       Profit and Losses and Present Values
       (1967–1991)   82

9.1   Atlanta–Fulton County Stadium
       Direct and Indirect Municipal Subsidy
       (1966–1985)   88

9.2   Atlanta–Fulton County Stadium
       Present Value of Stadium Investment
       Cash Flows (1966–1987)   89

9.3   Atlanta–Fulton County Stadium
       Present Values of Stadium Cash Flows
       with Alternative Property Valuation
       (1966–1987)   90

10.1   Oakland–Alameda Coliseum Complex
       Operating Revenues, Expenses, and Taxes
       (1967–1991)   98

10.2   Oakland–Alameda Coliseum Complex
       Present Values of Cash Flows from Stadium Investment
       (1967–1991)   99

11.1   Jack Murphy Stadium
       Operating Profit (1968–1990)   105

11.2   Jack Murphy Stadium
       Municipal Outlays (1968–1990)   106

11.3   Jack Murphy Stadium
       Present Value of Cash Flows
       from Stadium Investment (1968–1990)   107

12.1   Riverfront Stadium
       Operating Profits and Losses and
       Direct Municipal Subsidy (1969–1989)   115

12.2   Riverfront Stadium
       Direct and Indirect Property Tax Expenses
       (1969–1988)   116

12.3   Riverfront Stadium
       Tax Revenues Derived from Stadium Operations
       (1970–1988)   117

12.4   Riverfront Stadium
       Total Profit (Subsidy) from Stadium
       and Present Value of Cash Flows (1969–1988)   118

12.5   Riverfront Stadium
       Present Value of Cash Flows Using
       Alternative Property Values (1969–1988)   119

13.1   Foxboro Stadium
       Foregone Property Taxes (1971–1990)   124

13.2   Foxboro Stadium
       Admission Tax Revenues and Present Value
       of Cash Flows from Stadium Investment
       (1971–1990)   125

14.1   Rich Stadium
       Direct and Indirect Municipal Outlays
       (1977–1986)   131

14.2   Rich Stadium
       Municipal Receipts and Present Value
       of Cash Flows from Stadium Investment
       (1977–1986)   132

14.3   Rich Stadium
       Present Value of Cash Flows Using Alternative
       Development Assumption (1977–1986)   133

15.1   Louisiana Superdome
       Operating Revenues (1977–1984)   143

15.2   Louisiana Superdome
       Operating Expenses (1977–1984)   144

15.3   Louisiana Superdome
       Non-Operating Revenues and Expenses
       (1977–1984)   145

15.4   Louisiana Superdome
        Foregone Property Taxes (1975–1990)   146

15.5   Louisiana Superdome
        Accumulated Present Value
        of Cash Flows (1975–1990)   147

16.1   Minneapolis Metrodome
        Operating Profits, Cash Flows, and
        Present Value of Cash Flows (1982–1991)   154

17.1   Projected vs. Actual Stadium Construction Costs   169

17.2   Summary of Present Value Calculations   170

17.3   Accumulated Present Values of Stadium
        Investments Using Alternative Development Assumptions   172

17.4   Per-Capita Subsidies   173

18.1   The Relationship Among Service Employment,
        Population, Baseball, and Football Franchises
        (1958–1984)   192

18.2   The Relationship Among Non-Agricultural
        Employment, Population, Baseball,
        and Football Franchises (1958–1984)   193

18.3   The Relationship Among Crime, Population,
        Baseball, and Football Franchises (1958–1984)   194

19.1   Construction Costs of Publicly Built Stadiums   204

19.2   Construction Costs of Privately Built Stadiums   209

19.3   Public Stadiums: Number of Days Used in 1984   211

19.4   Private Stadiums: Number of Days Used in 1984   211

19.5   Capacity: Parking Ratios
        Private Stadiums Used for Football   212

19.6   Capacity: Parking Ratios
        Public Stadiums Used for Football   212

19.7   Attendance: Parking Ratios
        Public Stadiums Used for Baseball   213

19.8   Attendance: Parking Ratios
        Private Stadiums Used for Baseball   213

19.9   NFL Stadiums
        Capacity: Parking Ratios by Ownership Category   214

19.10   Major League Baseball Stadiums
        Average Attendance to Parking Ratios
        by Ownership Category   214

19.11   Parking Capacities by Ownership Category   214

19.12   Independent Rating of Baseball Stadiums   215

19.13   Franchise Moves, 1953–1985   216

Preface

Rarely in life does one get a second chance. The proverbial writing finger passes on, and what one has written is pretty well left for the ages, with all of its strengths and weaknesses. This book originates from my doctoral dissertation, *Home Field Advantage: Municipal Subsidies to Professional Sports Teams*. While that work was well received, shortcomings arose in the pressure to get it completed. This volume represents, I hope, one of the rare opportunities to maintain the strengths of one's work and to strengthen the weaknesses that inevitably arise when one is attempting to complete something like a doctoral dissertation.

ACKNOWLEDGMENTS

As anyone who has ever undertaken a study of this magnitude understands, it is by using only the most strict (fraudulant?) interpretation of property rights that my name appears as the sole author. The list of those who have contributed is long and includes more than those mentioned here.

Chronologically, the list begins with George W. Hilton, who suggested the dissertation topic more than a decade ago. His suggestions for material and prompt reading of manuscripts allowed me to avoid the delays so frequent in the dissertation process. Professor Gary Dunbar's contributions of editorial and factual comments were above and beyond the call of duty for an outside member on a dissertation committee.

Gratitude is extended to Pepperdine University, which provided me with valuable computer and personnel support. The personnel came in the form of student workers who helped with the original dissertation. Penny Pribble contributed with research in the formative stages, and Anne Fortney performed an exhaustive newspaper search on New York, Chicago, and Washington. While this edition does not include the work she did on these first two cities, the results of the Washington citations remain. Gretchen Everett put much of the accounting data into a format that I could understand, and Lory Lees put much of the statistical data into a format that the computer could understand. Sharon Ellers provided helpful typing and proofreading skills.

Moral support was plentiful from several generations of my family. My parents deserve special recognition. My wife, Karen, has been patient for all the time spent on the rewrite, and I hope, Pat and Erin have not resented the time that their father has spent on his work. Now, at least, Erin will be able to make it to Disneyland before her third birthday.

I will be able to return the economic impact studies to Gerry Swanson of the University of Arizona. They were lent to me eight years ago with the understanding that I would return them promptly. Beverly Firestone, while she was at the International Association of Auditorium Managers, also provided me with economic impact studies and information concerning stadium lease terms. Apple Computers in general, and Linda Featherstone in particular, went more than the extra mile to fill computer needs while on the road and helped this manuscript get finished only a year behind schedule.

Sally Scott, former production editor at Greenwood Press, and Glenn Briggs of the Pepperdine University word processing department, improved the final product by their helpful suggestions during the last stages of proofreading. Ms. Scott's contributions were surpassed only by her, and Greenwood's, patience during the final stages of production.

The original dissertation was dedicated to Shelli, the only creature with me on a daily basis during the entire dissertation process. Her unconditional love and companionship were a credit to the Golden Retriever breed. Had she not had to say good-bye in July 1992, she would have made it through the rewrite process as well. She is sorely missed, and this study is once again dedicated to her. Unfortunately this time, the dedication is to her memory.

The Sports Stadium as a Municipal Investment

Chapter 1
Introduction

By opening Union Grounds in Brooklyn on 15 May 1862, William Cammeyer is credited with being the inventor of the enclosed ball park. The invention of the closed field was a natural progression as baseball became increasingly professional. The enclosed park not only excluded non-paying spectators, but as local teams began to pay exceptional players in an effort to attract or keep them, the enclosed park was a way of impressing these players. It was also a way of attracting the attention of baseball promoters. When the National Association was established in 1871, owners of enclosed parks, including Cammeyer, had a distinct advantage in receiving franchises.

In some ways, not much has changed since the formative days of professional sports. Today, one of the common ways of demonstrating an interest in hosting a professional sports franchise is to possess a facility in which the team can play. In many respects, however, much has changed over time. In most cases since 1953, the facility used to attract a franchise is not owned by a private entrepreneur but rather by a government agency.

This change is not trivial. No longer is the decision to build a stadium made by a private individual who has his personal wealth rising or falling with the worthiness of the decision. Recently, most new sports facilities are constructed by government entities that have goals less clearly defined than the proprietor's or that conflict with one another. Maintaining taxpayer wealth may be one concern of government decision makers, but it competes with other goals, such as the promotion of civic pride and the local economy. If having a big-league sports team in the city contributes to civic pride and causes the local economy to grow, how far does one go in sacrificing taxpayers' wealth to promote civic pride?

Many cities and recently, some states, often with voter support through referendum, have decided that providing a facility for a professional sports team is a legitimate function of government. This reasoning has led cities and states, many of them in dire financial situations, to spend an aggregate of more than

$1.2 billion to build or renovate sports arenas and stadiums occupied by professional sports teams between 1975 and 1990.

The question this book addresses is whether the cities are getting their money's worth from investments in sports facilities. Are the cities building the stadiums in hopes of attracting a major league sports franchise and finding the competition so vigorous that a team can only be secured by charging rents insufficient to cover the stadium's costs?

The negotiations between Los Angeles and the National Football League's (NFL) Raiders franchise serve as an example. In July 1982 the Los Angeles Coliseum Commission entered into a lease with the then Oakland Raiders, allowing the Raiders to play their home games in the Coliseum. The agreement would return professional football to the Coliseum after an absence of two seasons and followed a celebrated antitrust case between the Raiders and the Los Angeles Coliseum Commission on one side and the NFL on the other.[1] Both sides of the case spent millions of dollars for legal services. The dispute entered into state politics when Los Angeles mayor Tom Bradley commented to an Oakland audience during his 1982 gubernatorial campaign that Los Angeles should abandon its pursuit of the Raiders and seek an expansion team from the NFL.

The impact on the Los Angeles Coliseum Commission of this hard fought victory was ironic. On 16 December 1982—about five months after the agreement between the Raiders and the Coliseum—Los Angeles city controller James Hahn reported that the Coliseum was on the brink of bankruptcy because of the terms of the lease with the Raiders.[2] Hahn estimated that in the first two years the Coliseum would realize a total net gain of $6,000, while during the third year of the contract, the Coliseum would run a $4 million deficit.[3]

---

1. *Los Angeles Memorial Coliseum Commission v. National Football League*, 484 F. Supp. 1274 (C. D. Cal. 1980), *rev'd*, 634 F.2d 1197 (9th Cir. 1980). The lower court's ruling in favor of the Raiders and Coliseum Commission was overturned because no agreement between the Raiders and the Coliseum Commission had been signed, hence, no damages could be claimed. The Raiders and the Coliseum then signed an intent agreement for the team to play in Los Angeles, which precipitated a 22–0 vote to deny the Raiders permission to move to the Coliseum. This brought about *Los Angeles Memorial Coliseum v. National Football League*, 519 F. Supp. 581 (C. D. Cal. 1981), *aff'd*, 726 F.2d 1381 (9th Cir. 1984). The latter decision, upheld in appeal, awarded the Raiders permission to move to Los Angeles. This will subsequently be called the "Raiders' Case."
2. "Danger of Coliseum Going Broke Seen," *Los Angeles Times*, 17 December 1982.
3. Ibid.

A QUESTION OF SUBSIDIES

The negotiations between the Raiders and Los Angeles is a highly publicized example of negotiations between a government entity and a sports franchise that are being performed in many cities around the country.

Early in their academic training, economists learn about the mechanics of mutually beneficial trade. If two parties differ as to the relative value of two goods, both parties can benefit if some mid ground value can be found as a price to trade the goods. There is an area of indeterminacy concerning the terms of trade that will be determined through negotiation. Each party will attempt to bargain for a price that will be to their advantage. In the case of stadium lease negotiations, the area of indeterminacy is quite large, and perhaps it is difficult for the parties to determine when they are not receiving a benefit.

League rules place a city that recruits a major league franchise at a disadvantage. All league by-laws exclusively allocate territories to one league member. Although league officials argue this restriction is necessary to protect a team that has cultivated an interest in the sport, it also means that the city is forced to deal with only one consumer per sport as a tenant of its facility.

In addition to the league rules, there are few alternative uses for an outdoor stadium. The city often is put in the position of having to accept an offer that does not fully cover the costs of building and maintaining a stadium, or to see the facility stand empty and pay the debt service from even fewer receipts. The result is that franchise owners frequently are able to rent a municipal facility for less than they would have to pay if the market more clearly followed a "perfectly competitive" model, or if the franchise were to build its own facility.

The leverage provided by the league's rule on geographic exclusivity appears to have been used by the Raiders during their negotiations with Los Angeles. Howard Daniels, one of the negotiators for the Coliseum, reported that Al Davis, the Raiders' managing partner, told Los Angeles that he was considering remaining in Oakland or moving to New York if he could not get the terms he wanted. Daniels concluded that, given this background, the Coliseum Commission got the best deal possible from the Raiders.[4]

JUSTIFICATION FOR SUBSIDIES

By itself, the existence of a shortfall of rents relative to costs does not indicate that the team is costing the city more than it benefits the city. In 1776 economist Adam Smith recognized that a legitimate role of government is to provide "those public institutions and those public works, which, though they may be in the highest degree advantageous to a great society, are, however, of such a nature, that the profit could never repay the expense to any individual or

---

4. Ibid.

small number of individuals, and which it therefore cannot be expected that any individual or small number of individuals should erect or maintain."[5]

Proponents of sports facilities argue that the city benefits from added tax revenues and other positive externalities, which cannot be captured by the proprietor of the stadium but may make up for the shortfall of rents relative to costs. Since decisions are made by weighing costs and benefits, an individual considering the construction of a sports facility will have a tendency to ignore the social benefits if he or she is unable to capture them. Such an underestimate of benefits would lead to an "under production" of sports facilities unless the government was to provide or subsidize these services because it realized the full advantage to society of the facility. Thus, looking only at the stadium's cash flows may understate the social benefits received by sports facility investment.

Increased Tax Revenues

Cities grow influential, and economically, by capturing and holding capital and financial assets. A new assembly plant means more people work, live, and spend their income in the city than before the assembly plant was constructed. A stadium investment is viewed not only as a way of providing employment, but it may attract funds from non-residents, as well.

To the extent that a professional sports team draws fans who would otherwise spend their entertainment dollars outside the city, the city's economy benefits from the increased economic activity, and the city's government benefits from increased sales and income tax receipts. Estimates of the additional sales tax and income tax revenues are often large, and possibly inflated, but there is little doubt that a city treasury receives increased tax revenues when a sports franchise moves into town.

Income and sales tax income will increase since sports teams will hire people to work at the games and the team offices. If these people are unemployed, or in lower paying jobs, before the arrival of the team, the city will realize an increase in employment tax revenues.

Finally, cities frequently impose taxes on attendance of a sporting event. If these admission tax revenues are only on sporting events, then the sports fans are directly contributing to any deficit that arises by hosting a sports franchise. A subsidy will exist, however, if patrons of events other than those held at the sports facility are asked to help finance the structure.

Most estimates published by a team or a city when projecting the economic impact on a stadium investment are overestimates. Typical errors include assuming that everyone who attends a sporting event would have spent their money outside the city limits, if the stadium is not built. In all probability, if there was no sporting event to attend, a fan would go to some other

---

5.   Adam Smith, *An Inquiry into the Nature and Causes of the Wealth of Nations*, ed. Edwin Cannan, vol. 2 (Chicago: University of Chicago Press, 1976), 244.

entertainment event, such as a play, concert, or movie. While there would be no employment at the stadium, there might be more jobs at the alternative entertainment providers.

Positive Externalities

Economists, following the lead of Smith, recognize that when property rights are poorly defined or unenforceable entrepreneurs may benefit others, but the benefit is of such a nature that they cannot charge the beneficiaries for their increased good fortune. Smith argued that when this occurred to the extent that it prevents the undertaking of a project that has a positive net benefit to society, a legitimate role of government was created.

To the local government officials, one attraction of hosting a major league sports team is the instant elevation of the city to "major league" status. There appears to be no limit to the number of times this argument can be used in one city. Los Angeles mayor Norris Poulson was able to chide opponents of the deal he made with the Brooklyn Dodgers as wanting to keep the city "bush league," despite the fact that Los Angeles had been the home of the NFL Rams since 1946.[6]

If this increased civic pride accrues only to those who follow the sport, the externality could be small. Fans who derive satisfaction from knowing their city is now a "major league" city will display this civic pride in the form of ticket and concession expenditures. The team owner would benefit directly from these transactions, so little externality would seem to exist. If, however, non-sport fans have a more positive image of their city because of the sports team, then an external benefit, albeit one that is difficult to measure, would exist.

The almost free advertising received by "second tier" cities such as Portland and Buffalo during sports reports may give these cities an advantage, at least subliminally, over other cities in the region when competing for convention business and the location of regional offices. This elevation in the minds of others may create a powerful externality.

Another suggested positive externality is reduced crime among area youth. Sports, says this argument, provide legal alternatives to criminal behavior, teach the virtues of living by rules, and present positive role models for the youngsters. While this last argument may be tarnished with the increasing number of revelations of substance abuse and sexual misconduct among athletes, positive role models such as the one-handed baseball pitcher Jim Abbott, basketball center Kareem Abdul-Jabbar, and football player Marcus Allen are not difficult to find.

When computing external benefits, the wages paid to those employed by the team should not be included. Those wages are payment for the services the team owner received. If the employees reside within the city, the wages may increase

---

6. "L.A. Council Votes Dodger Deal, 11–3," *Los Angeles Times*, 17 September 1957.

city income, but they do not represent an external benefit unless a multiplier is applied.

OTHER ISSUES

The "Hold-up" Potential

Once a team locates in a city, the city becomes vulnerable to what economists call a "hold-up" situation, in which the team engages in threats to leave the city if it does not receive new concessions on the contract or improvements on the facility. One study showed that in the two years after the Raiders' case at least thirteen of forty-two host cities were asked to provide tax incentives or improve the facility to prevent the team from moving.[7] Even when a city has reached an agreement with a team, it may not be long before it will be asked for concessions. Hold-up situations appeared in New York (in baseball with the Yankees, Brooklyn Dodgers, and in football with the Jets and the Giants), Buffalo (with the football Bills, the National Hockey League Sabres,), Washington (with two sets of baseball Senators), and Baltimore (with the football Colts and baseball Orioles).

Wealth Transfer and the Subsidy

When a subsidy exists, a question arises of who ultimately pays and who benefits from this municipal largess. The most likely beneficiaries are the owners and the fans, if the subsidy is passed on in the form of lower ticket prices. A further complication arises when the wealth transfer leaves the city in the form of lower ticket prices to an out-of-town fan or an increase in wages or profits for an out-of-town player or owner.

The Comparison of Privately and Publicly Owned Facilities

Economists often theorize that decisions made by a private entrepreneur differ from those made by a government employee. No normative statement is implied here, just a theory that the incentives for the two types of decision makers differ. The existence of privately owned and publicly owned arenas and stadiums provides an excellent laboratory to test this hypothesis. In short, are there significant differences in the number of resources used to build private and public facilities? Are amenities better under one form of ownership than another? Is one type of ownership conducive to intensive use of the facility or

---

7. Arthur T. Johnson, "Municipal Administration and the Sports Franchise Relocation Issue," *Public Administration Review* no. 6 (November/December 1983): 519–529.

to team loyalty? These are questions for which the answers, if they are definitive, should be observable.

REVIEW OF THE LITERATURE

The literature divides into two topics that match the division of this book. They are, respectively, the economic aspects of sports and the private and public production of goods.

The Economic Aspects of Sports

The economics of sports is a relatively new field that is growing steadily. This growth may reveal the researchers' interests and, as such, is partly a consumption good.

More important, as leisure activities command a larger share of consumption expenditures, more of society's resources are being devoted to sports. For example, in fiscal year 1938 the Los Angeles Coliseum's operating expenditures were $58,269.40.[8] This is less than the average salary of each of the NFL players who now play at the Coliseum. Even after allowing for the roughly 750 percent increase in prices between 1938 and 1987, the resources spent on running the Coliseum fifty years ago appear minuscule by today's standards. Since sports is a growth industry, it is not surprising to see the increasing level of interest in the field.

In the United States, serious study of the economics of sports began during the 1950s. In 1956, Simon Rottenberg's article on the professional baseball labor market that promoted the concept of free agency for baseball players was one of the earliest academic endeavors in the field of sports economics.[9] Rottenberg modeled a league in which the output was the team's profit and the production function exhibited diminishing marginal product to increases in player salaries. A team that added too many star players would experience lower net receipts because fewer fans would attend games without league balance. With an incentive for no team to monopolize talent, league balance could be maintained even if players were allowed to move freely. This led to Rottenberg's conclusion that team owners should not fear free agency.

Congressional hearings in 1958, which investigated the wisdom of exempting professional sports from antitrust laws, provided some additional exposure for those performing research in the area.[10]

---

8. Los Angeles Memorial Coliseum Commission, *Annual Report for Fiscal Year 1938–1939* (Los Angeles, 1939), 2.
9. Simon Rottenberg, "The Baseball Player's Labor Market," *Journal of Political Economy* 64 (June 1956): 242–248.
10. U. S. Senate Subcommittee on Antitrust and Monopoly of the Committee on the Judiciary, *Organized Professional Team Sports*, 85th Cong., 2d sess.

The only major work during the 1960s was done by Walter C. Neale.[11] He argued that traditional economic models did not apply to professional sports because the teams' profits were based more by the "on the field" competition, than by the economic competition among franchises.

By 1970, the anomalies and barriers to free trade that exist in professional sports were recognized as a fertile ground for research. Like Rottenberg's article, most of the work concentrated on the reserve clause in every professional athlete's contract. El-Hodiri and Quirk developed an economic mathematical model of professional sports in 1971 that embodied Rottenberg's concept of league balance in a cartel.[12]

Harold Demsetz's conclusion on free agency was similar to those previously mentioned, but by using the Coase Theorem, he could explain why owners rejected free agency even if league balance were not threatened.[13] To Demsetz, the same teams would receive the players by outbidding other teams for the players' services in either a reserve or free market. The difference is that in a reserve market, owners can capture the players' economic rent.

In 1974, Gerald Scully attempted to estimate baseball players' marginal revenue product to a team.[14] Scully's model was suspect, however, when the sum of the marginal revenue products estimated by Scully exceeded the revenues received by the franchise.[15]

By the mid 1970s several authors were developing models for professional sports leagues to address issues other than the labor market. Henry Demmert used Neale's structure of a league to build a mathematical model of professional sports.[16] Demmert used his model to develop a demand for seats to a major league sports event, among other things.

Government and the Sports Business, published in 1974 and edited by Roger Noll, was a landmark of sports economic thought.[17] While it did not ignore the

---

(Washington, D.C., 1958). The same subcommittee met again under the same name in the first session of the 86th Congress as well.

11. Walter C. Neale, "The Peculiar Economics of Professional Sports," *Quarterly Journal of Economics* (February 1964): 1–14.

12. Mohamed El-Hodiri and James Quirk, "An Economic Model of a Professional Sports League," *Journal of Political Economy* 79 (November/December 1971): 1302–1319.

13. Harold Demsetz, "When Does the Rule of Liability Matter?" *Journal of Legal Studies* (January 1982): 13–28.

14. Gerald W. Scully "Pay and Performance in Major League Baseball," *American Economic Review* (December 1974): 915–930.

15. Private conversation with Bruce Johnson, Department of Economics, University of California, Santa Barbara, California, in February 1979.

16. Henry G. Demmert, *The Economics of Professional Team Sports* (Lexington, MA.: D.C. Heath and Company, 1973).

17. Roger Noll, ed., *Government and the Sports Business* (Washington, D.C.: Brookings Institute, 1974).

antitrust issue, this book was not preoccupied with the topic, unlike any study published previously. The topics covered a wide range of subjects from broadcasting[18] to the taxation of franchises.[19]

The matter of team location and relocation also became an issue in the early 1970s after a decade of what many felt to be rash franchise moves inspired by greed. Quirk used the model he and El-Hodiri developed to analyze professional sports franchise relocations.[20] Quirk concluded, "Application of the antitrust laws to baseball offers the only practical possibility of control of the abuses of franchise moves, since the record indicates quite clearly that organized baseball is incapable or unwilling to reform either its revenue-sharing arrangement or its rules governing location of franchises to put an end to such abuses."[21]

Frank Jozsa, Jr., studied the economic rationale and factors motivating team relocation of National Basketball Association (NBA), NFL, and Major League Baseball franchises in a 1977 doctoral dissertation.[22] Jozsa modeled a profit maximizing team owner within a model of a cartelized sports league. From this set of equations, he set out to identify the decision variables used to relocate an existing franchise or expand the league. Jozsa also studied the factors leading to a league's decision to expand as well as site selection once the league decided to expand.

For each decision, relocation, and expansion, Jozsa developed and tested two equations. The first model considered the likelihood of a team relocating or a league expanding. The second model attempted to identify the characteristics that a team or league looks for in a city when the decision is made to move or expand.

Jozsa's findings are intuitively comfortable.[23] The likelihood of a team relocating was inversely related to average attendance for the previous four seasons. Perhaps related to the attendance variable, team performance was also inversely related to the chance that the team would move. As might be expected, the more competition the team has for patrons from other sports teams, the higher the probability the team will seek a new site.

Jozsa's findings regarding the demand for new cities contained few surprises. Team owners preferred larger population centers and cities with higher per capita incomes. In the NFL and NBA, cities with a high proportions of blacks

---

18. Ira Horowitz, "Sports Broadcasting," *Government and the Sports Business*, ed. Roger Noll (Washington D.C.: Brookings Institute, 1974), 275–325.

19. Benjamin A. Okner, "Taxation and Sports Enterprises," *Government and the Sports Business*, ed. Roger Noll (Washington D.C.: Brookings Institute, 1974), 159–185.

20. James Quirk, "An Economic Analysis of Team Movements in Professional Sports," *Law and Contemporary Problems* 38 (Winter/Spring 1973): 42–66.

21. Ibid., 66.

22. Frank P. Jozsa, Jr., "An Economic Analysis of Franchise Relocation and League Expansions in Professional Team Sports, 1950–1975" (Ph.D. diss., Georgia State University, 1977).

23. Ibid., 137–141.

attracted franchises. In short, the demand for cities was a demand derived by the demand the city might have for the sport.

The expansion model was less conclusive. Jozsa could not find one significant factor regarding the decision to expand a sports league. Once having decided to expand, however, the new teams sought the same attributes as their established counterparts. The only difference between expansion team location and established team relocation is that the former preferred locations with a track record of supporting a major league franchise in another sport.

While Jozsa's research studied the sports franchises as demanders of home sites, he did not treat the behavior of the suppliers of home sites. Jozsa admitted that the effect of public policy on relocation and league expansion would be an area for further research.[24]

Jerome Ellig, in an unpublished dissertation, employed new institutionalist models of industrial organization to explain a spectrum of league behavior, including league control of franchise location and relocation.[25] Ellig found that franchise location depended upon attendance and attendance-related revenues, broadcast revenues, and the potential for stadium subsidies.[26] Ellig used his model to project which cities could support teams without stadium subsidies.[27] In this way, Ellig studied the effect of stadium subsidies on team location, but the suppliers' (the cities') motivation for providing the subsidies remained ignored.

Benjamin Okner, writing in Noll's collection, explored the estimated magnitude of stadium subsidies.[28] Okner first attempted to develop a pricing model to determine the "proper price" for a city to charge for a sports facility. Okner reasoned that it is difficult to determine if the franchise is receiving a subsidy without knowing what the fair rental price would be. Any shortfall in the actual price from the fair market rental value would be considered a subsidy.

Okner argued, however, that the establishment of the fair market rental value is difficult to estimate using traditional economic models of public finance that are based upon markets in which the city is the sole provider of the good, serving a large number of patrons. These patrons possess the standard sloping demand functions for the publicly provided good so that when the price increases the quantity demanded for the product decreases.

Okner argued that the market for professional sports franchises differs from this conventional model in at least two ways. First, the city is not facing a large number of users for the facility; instead, there is only one team that owns

---

24. Ibid., 143.
25. Jerome R. Ellig, "Law, Economics, and Organized Baseball: Analysis of a Cooperative Venture," (Ph.D. diss., George Mason University, 1987).
26. Ibid., 229.
27. Ibid., 207–216.
28. Benjamin A. Okner, "Subsidies of Stadiums and Arenas," *Government and the Sports Business*, ed. Roger Noll (Washington D.C.: Brookings Institute, 1974), 325–349.

the rights to that geographic region and the city must cut the best deal it can with this consumer or risk not having any major tenant.

Second, the season in which the teams play is fixed. The number of games that a home team will play in a stadium is determined not by price, but by the league. In this sense, the team possesses a vertical demand curve for the facility at the number of home dates, at least for the short run, regardless of rent.[29]

Since the marginal cost of operating the stadium (the determinant of the supply curve for a competitive firm) is low and rises quickly once the stadium reaches capacity, Okner contended that there could be no equilibrium price for the stadium. That is, the supply curve may not intersect the team's vertical demand curve at any positive price.

Okner then settled on the profit maximizing (or loss minimizing) rule in which price exceeds the average variable costs related to producing the good. A subsidy is the amount by which the revenues received from the team do not cover the variable costs of hosting the franchise.

By estimating the average operating costs of a stadium to be between $8 million and $12 million during the 1970–71 season, Okner estimated the subsidy, if any, that the teams were receiving from the host cities. Using this estimate, Okner concluded that the total subsidy to all sports teams for the 1970–71 season was close to $23 million.[30]

Okner reviewed thirty indoor arenas and found only five that were able to cover all of their costs. The costs of the remaining twenty-five arenas exceeded the revenues by as much as $1 million every year.[31] Okner concluded that older indoor arenas with little or no debt service made profits, while new stadiums designed for outdoor sports were the biggest losers.[32]

These figures are curiously determined, however, because they included all costs, fixed and variable. This is contrary to the profit maximizing rule that only variable costs are relevant to short run decisions, such as the use of an existing stadium. The decision to sign a lease with a professional sports franchise will not alter fixed costs such as debt service, insurance, and routine maintenance.[33] Thus, it is incorrect to say older stadiums with little or no debt

---

29. There is some precedents for teams to play some of their "home games" in foreign facilities: The Utah Jazz have played some of their home games in Las Vegas; the Chicago White Sox played some of their home games in Milwaukee during the late 1960s; and the Green Bay Packers played in Milwaukee. These outings were designed to increase the exposure in nearby markets, not because the demand for arena dates was responsive to rental rates charged by their normal landlord.
30. Okner, "Subsidies of Stadiums and Arenas," 345.
31. Ibid., 346–347.
32. Ibid.
33. This, of course, assumes the facility is built. For a structure that has not been built, all costs are variable, and it would be preferable to account for all expenditures.

service generate lower subsidies than larger newer stadiums with higher fixed costs.

Arthur T. Johnson wrote two articles on the relationship between sports and the law. The first is a chronology of the nearly 300 bills related to professional sports that Congress considered between 1951 and 1978.[34] Johnson concluded that historically Congress has been swayed by the mystique of sports and has not passed legislation opposed by the leagues. Since 1960, however, Congress's view of professional sports has changed, and this change has, "on occasion," led to the enactment of legislation against league opposition.

Johnson's second article focused on Congress's relationship with sports on the issue of franchise relocation.[35] A chronological review of franchise relocations from the mid-1950s to 1982 is followed by a review of the legislation considered by Congress to end what Quirk termed "abuses." Johnson argued that long-term leases that foster an atmosphere of belonging for team owners is superior to legislative relief as a method to maintain franchise stability.

Cities, Johnson continued, must "resist threats to relocate. They must be prepared to negotiate hard, and in their public statements show a willingness to allow the team to leave if its price for remaining is too high. Their negotiation style must be the same as with any other business seeking public benefits. The message to the franchise must be that it is welcome to stay, but it is not crucial to the city's future."[36] Johnson advised city negotiators to keep the populace updated on the issues so that owners would find it difficult to raise their demands.[37]

Franchise relocation has several issues to be researched. First is the team's right to move and the impact such a move has upon local economies. This issue received much scholastic attention during the late 1970s and early 1980s.[38] Most objective scholars viewed restrictions on businesses' right to move as less than optimal.

The difference between a sports franchise relocation and a "normal business" relocation are not trivial. First, the team is highly visible and requires a large physical and financial commitment if a new stadium is being constructed. Second, losing the team is a serious psychological blow to a city, and gaining one is a psychological boost.

The second issue of franchise relocation is to determine the true gains to the local economy of hosting a sports franchise. Stadiums and teams do not hire

---

34. Arthur T. Johnson, "Congress and Professional Sports: 1951–1978," *ANNALS* of the American Academy 445 (September 1979): 102–115.
35. Arthur T. Johnson, "Municipal Administration and the Sports Franchise Relocation Issue," *Public Administration Review* 43, no. 6 (November/ December 1983): 519–528.
36. Ibid., 526.
37. Ibid., 527.
38. See, for example, Richard McKenzie, *Restrictions on Business Mobility* (Washington, D.C.: American Enterprise Institute, 1979).

large numbers directly. A city with one team as a tenant will use the stadium less than ninety days a year. Economic impact studies of stadiums are not in short supply, but many of these were written as a house organ for a team, or an institution with ties to the team or professional sports, and are far from objective.[39] The flurry of franchise moves by the Brooklyn Dodgers and the New York Giants in 1957 produced some interest in the economic impact of franchise relocations. One article that appeared in *American City*, a magazine for city planners, praised city fathers who spent money on a drawing card (such as a professional sports team) for keeping the city "vital," as opposed to those planners who allow the decline of the central business district.[40]

Where the *American City* article romanticized the economic impact of a stadium on the inner city economy, Rosentraub and Nunn looked at the economic impact of a stadium on suburban communities. Their conclusion of the paper was that the host suburb receives a spur to economic growth, but that the economy of an individual suburb is too small to capture all the economic growth.[41]

Shubnell, Petersen, and Harris reviewed several methods of financing stadiums.[42] The article, little more than a list of financing techniques, concluded with the advice "regardless of the form of the governmental commitment, the bondholders' legal entitlement to a specific source of dependable funds must be unconditional and irrevocable during the period over which any portion of the bonds remain outstanding."[43] The authors saw local governments as providing this dependable source of funds. More practically, Petersen used case studies to

---

39. For example, Maryland Department of Economic and Community Development, *The Economic Impact of Professional Sports on the Maryland Economy* (January 1985); William A. Schaffer, George D. Houser, and Robert A. Weinberg, *The Economic Impact of the Braves on Atlanta: 1966* (Atlanta GA: Industrial Management Center, February 1967); William A. Schaffer and Lawrence S. Davidson, *Economic Impact of the Falcons on Atlanta* (Atlanta, GA: The Atlanta Falcons, 1972), and a follow-up report in 1984; Robert E. Coughlin, Janet E. McKinnon, and Thomas A. Reiner, *The Economic Impacts of the Spectrum on the City of Philadelphia and the Metropolitan Region* (Philadelphia, PA: Regional Science Research Institute, May 1978).

40. Douglas S. Powell, "Is Big League Baseball Good Municipal Business?," *American City* (November 1957): 162.

41. Mark S. Rosentraub, Samuel Nunn, "Suburban City Investment in Professional Sports: Estimating the Fiscal Returns of the Dallas Cowboys and Texas Rangers to Investor Communities," *American Behavioral Scientist*, 21 no. 3 (February 1978): 393–413.

42. Lawrence D. Shubnell, John E. Petersen, and Collin B. Harris, "The Big Ticket: Financing a Professional Sports Facility," *Government Finance Review* 1, no. 2 (June 1985): 7–11.

43. Ibid., 11.

provide developers with background on how successful stadium, arena, and convention center projects were started.[44]

Private and Public Production of Sports Facilities

Economists since Adam Smith have realized the power of self-interest in motivating individuals to behave for the "social good." Economists only recently, however, have appreciated the critical role property rights, and the ability to exchange those rights, play in promoting the type of "efficient" self-interest described by Smith.

In 1960 Ronald Coase showed that clearly defined and exchangeable property rights would lead to the same level of pollution regardless of the original owner of the property rights.[45] Furthermore, since the ownership of the property right goes to the highest valued user, an argument can be made that the resulting pollution is "socially optimal." Despite this revolutionary article, as late as 1965 Armen Alchian could write:

Yet if we look at the "fields" of economics, as presented by the American Economic Association's classification of areas of interest or specialization, we find no mention of the word "property." Either we can infer that the profession is so obviously aware of the pervasiveness of the effects of various forms of property that property rights cannot sensibly be regarded as merely a subfield; or else we can infer that economists have forgotten about the possibility of subjective, rigorous, systematic, coherent analysis of the various forms of property rights. My conviction is that the latter inference is the more valid one.[46]

Alchian adds another dimension to the traditional argument that when property rights are clearly defined the decision maker becomes more aware of the costs and benefits of his or her actions. When rights are easily traded, they flow from low valued users to high valued users. Since productive resources are valued for the profits they generate, the individual who purchases a firm does so because he or she believes his or, her talent, combined with the firm's resources, will bring a higher return than it did to his or her predecessor. What will develop, according to Alchian, is a degree of specialization in knowledge regarding specific industries, such as automobile parts or sports management. Those who successfully identify mismanagement will be rewarded with increased wealth.

With public ownership, everyone who lives in the jurisdiction shares in the costs and benefits of management's behavior. The only way for a citizen to

44. David Petersen, *Convention Centers, Stadiums, and Arenas* (Washington, D.C.: Urban Land Institute, 1989).

45. Ronald H. Coase, "The Problem of Social Costs," *Journal of Law and Economics* 3 (October 1960): 1–45.

46. Armen A. Alchian, "Some Economics of Property Rights," *Il Politico* 30 (1965): 817-829. See also A. A. Alchian, "Corporate Management and Property Rights," in *Economic Forces at Work*, ed. Daniel K. Benjamin (Indianapolis, Indiana: Liberty Press, 1977), 227–257.

divest himself or herself unilaterally of a government-owned resource is to move out of the area served by that government agency—not a costless procedure.

Since government agencies rarely sell assets, it is not possible for better management to come about through a change in ownership. This leaves only a change from within as the way of improving the management of a public agency. Since many promotions come from existing personnel, it is likely that pressure to adopt new management techniques will not be as strong in the public sector as in the private sector. Citizens might identify and correct mismanagement, but the benefits of this act are shared by all citizens, and the investigators bear all the costs. Such a distribution of costs and potential benefits does not promote in-depth investigation of public management practices.

Testing the implications of this hypothesis, David Davies compared two Australian domestic air carriers.[47] One, Ansett, is privately owned, while the second, Trans-Australian, is owned publicly. Despite many similarities (most induced by regulation) in scheduling, equipment, staff, and even cabin design, Davies found that Ansett carried more than twice the amount of freight per employee. The number of passengers per worker averaged 20 percent more for Ansett than for Trans-Australian. In every year studied, Ansett earned higher revenues per employee than Trans-Australian despite the similarity of the wages in both firms.

George Borjas uncovered further evidence of non-market incentives in the provision of government goods and services.[48] Borjas found that the federal government paid minorities and women substantially less than what "similar" white males were earning. This trend was reversed, however, in agencies that had large minorities and women constituencies. From this Borjas concluded that a major incentive for public employees is the maximization of political support from constituents and not necessarily to produce at the lowest possible cost. In an article cited previously,[49] Arthur Johnson argued that providing the team owner(s) with an economic stake in the community, such as ownership in the sports facility, is one way of alleviating the relocation pressures facing many cities today.

THE ORGANIZATION OF THIS BOOK

Part I of this book, data on fifteen stadiums, reviews in chronological order the financial aspects of fifteen stadium projects. Each stadium's chapter has a

---

47. David Davies, "The Efficiency of Public versus Private Firms, the Case of Australia's Two Airlines," *Journal of Law and Economics* 14, 1 (April 1971): 149–165.
48. George J. Borjas, "The Politics of Employment Discrimination in the Federal Bureaucracy," *Journal of Law and Economics* 25, no. 2, (October 1982): 271–299.
49. Johnson, "Municipal Administration and Sports Relocation," 526.

history of that facility and the construction costs of the stadium. These facilities range from the private Dodger Stadium to the ward of Louisiana, the New Orleans Superdome. They were chosen because there is enough data for fourteen of these stadiums to determine if the stadium has returned a "profit" to the municipal investor in the same sense that a private investor would measure a profit. The fifteenth stadium, Milwaukee County Stadium, is included because it is the first example of a municipality using a stadium to lure a professional sports team to the city, although there is not enough data to conclude if the stadium is "profitable." If the facility did not make a "profit" then there is sufficient data to measure the amount of the short fall (subsidy) to date. This financial analysis makes up the third component of each stadium chapter.

Part II is devoted to analysis. Chapter seventeen summarizes the data in Part I and studies the data to determine the source of any subsidy, the size of the per capita subsidy, as well as the determinants and the beneficiaries of a subsidy. The chapter concludes with an attempt to project the future prospects for the fourteen stadiums for which profitability was estimated.

Chapter eighteen looks at the issue of external benefits that accrue to the city from a sports team. Recall, that most stadium investments are justified by the economic stimuli or other external benefits that allegedly are derived from the professional team playing in a city. Previous studies are reviewed, and a new one is offered in this chapter, as well as a warning against taking any of these projections too seriously.

Chapter nineteen tests the strength of private property incentives by comparing publicly and privately owned stadiums for differences in construction costs, amenities, days of use, and team loyalty.

Chapter twenty is a summary that reviews the findings in Part II, and offers directions for future research.

As mentioned in the preface, this study has its roots in the doctoral dissertation, *Home Field Advantage: Municipal Subsidies to Professional Sports Teams*.[50] While the current version has more complete and accurate financial data than the dissertation, it is also more compact in that it includes a history of only the stadiums for which enough financial data were available to estimate an accumulated net present value (ANPV). The doctoral dissertation, by contrast, has a historical discussion for all stadiums used in the NFL and Major League Baseball from 1953 through 1988. Those who are interested in getting a more complete historical view of stadium projects and the politics involved with stadium investments, are invited to look at the dissertation.

A NOTE ON METHODOLOGY

The standard financial tool used to determine the advisability of an investment is net present value (NPV). As any student in a basic financial management

---

50. Dean V. Baim, *Home Field Advantage: Municipal Subsidies to Professional Sports Teams* (Ann Arbor, MI: University Microfilm Inc., 1988).

class learns, the NPV procedure involves discounting future cash flows by a risk adjusted discount rate. This technique allows the investor to compare cash flows of different time periods so that the proposed investment can be compared with investments of similar risk.[51]

Traditional NPV calls for the investor to estimate the cash flows for the entire project. In this study, actual cash flows are discounted. However, in most cases the financial history of the stadium investment is a work in progress. That is, the cash flows for the fourteen stadiums reviewed are not finished because the stadiums are still in use. For that reason, the sum of the discounted cash flows have been named accumulated net present values (ANPV).

Use of the ANPV is similar to NPV—a project compares well with investments of similar risk if it has a positive ANPV. A stadium investment with a negative ANPV would be one that did not do as well as a similarly risky investment. While the ANPV does not present the total picture, because it does not attempt to estimate the future cash flows, in most cases these future cash flows are discounted so heavily that there is little significant difference between the ANPV and the eventual NPV.

The yield earned on Treasury bonds that would mature in each of the years in the cash flow was used as a measure of the risk-free return. The yield was computed as of January of the first year of the cash flows. The risk premium for the stadium project was estimated using a beta, the standard measure of market risk, computed from the correlation of stadium returns to market returns.[52] The stadium investment's beta was multiplied by an average market risk premium and added to the risk-free rate to determine the risk-adjusted discount rate.[53]

---

51. The formula for net present value is:

$$\sum_{t=0}^{T} \frac{C_t}{(1+k_t)^t}.$$

Where
   C_t is the expected cash flow in period t.
   k is the risk adjusted discount rate for period t.
52. Beta, β, is found by the formula:
   $$\beta = \frac{\text{Covariance of stadium investment return and market return}}{\text{Variance of market return}}$$

53. The risk adjusted discount rate in period t, k_t, is found by:
   $$k_t = r_f + \beta(R_m - r_f)$$
Where:
   r_f is the risk-free interest rate.
   R_m is the market rate of return.
   β is the measure of systematic risk computed as shown in footnote 52.

Part I
Financial Data

Chapter 2
Milwaukee County Stadium

HISTORY

The study of municipal stadium investment with the purpose of securing a major league franchise begins with Milwaukee, Wisconsin. As shown previously, major league sports franchises in 1953 played in facilities that were either privately owned or built by municipal authorities for some purpose other than hosting a major league sports franchise. Milwaukee was the first city to use a city-built facility to lure a team from one city to another. Many of the franchise moves, and the related municipal investments in stadiums to lure or keep franchises that followed, came as a direct or indirect consequence of the initial success the Braves found in Milwaukee.

The idea of a municipally financed stadium in Milwaukee was proposed as early as 1909 and progressed to the point of site selection, but it was not until 1950 that the proposal received final approval. Milwaukee became growth conscious after World War II,[1] and a major league baseball team was considered a way to maintain the city's economic base.

Milwaukee County Stadium was designed to replace Athletic Field, the home of the minor league Brewers. The announcement that the Braves would relocate to Milwaukee from Boston came during the construction of Milwaukee County Stadium, and the plans were revised bringing the structure up to major league standards.

Although the Boston Braves was one of the original National League franchises, the team's attendance was never as consistent as that of the crosstown Red Sox. When Braves Field was opened on 18 August 1915, the team set a single game major league attendance record of 40,000 fans. Three years later, the Braves drew only 84,938 fans for the entire war-shortened 1918 season. During

---

1. See, for example, City of Milwaukee, *Report of the Commission on the Economic Study of Milwaukee*, published in 1948.

their tenure in Boston, the Braves drew over one million fans in only two seasons (1947 and 1948). During the last three seasons the team played in Boston, the Braves lost more than $1 million. Distressed by this instability in attendance, the Braves displayed mercurial behavior of their own, announcing they would play their home games in Milwaukee less than a month before the season began.

Motivated by finances, the move by the Braves to Milwaukee proved to be a financial success. The Milwaukee Braves attracted 1,826,397 fans in their first season, more than six times the attendance for the team's last year in Boston. For the next four seasons, the Braves drew more that two million fans, setting major league records in attendance. Jerome Ellig concluded that the relocation of the Braves to Milwaukee was sufficiently lucrative to have been made without any subsidy from the city or county. It is hypothesized by some that the Braves' immediate success in Milwaukee led Horace Stoneham and Walter O'Malley to consider moving the Giants and Dodgers, respectively, to the West Coast.

The euphoria of the mid-1950s withered as the Braves' professional success waned. After only thirteen seasons in Milwaukee, the Braves announced they would be moving to Atlanta, Georgia [see Atlanta–Fulton County Stadium—1966–present: Atlanta Braves]. The decision by the Braves to leave Milwaukee triggered several law suits against officials and organizations in the Braves organization and Major League Baseball.

The Chicago White Sox used Milwaukee County Stadium for one home game with each American League opponent in 1968. The fan response was strong enough that the city hoped to receive a 1969 American League expansion franchise. The announcement that those franchises were awarded to Seattle, Washington and Kansas City, Missouri, meant that Milwaukee would get only two more games in the 1969 season, as the White Sox would add these two new teams to their Milwaukee "home" schedule.

The return of the White Sox in 1969 led to speculation that they might consider relocating to Milwaukee, but this speculation ended when the Seattle expansion franchise, the Pilots, failed to successfully navigate the first season in the Pacific Northwest. A Milwaukee syndicate purchased the Pilots in a Seattle bankruptcy court and announced their intention to move the team, renamed the Brewers, to Milwaukee.

Not unlike the move by the Braves, the announcement that the Brewers would be playing their 1970 home games in Milwaukee was made shortly before the season was to begin. The American League had printed schedules showing the Pilots' home games in Seattle. The trim on the Brewers' uniform was blue and gold, the same as the Pilots' colors, since the team could not get new uniforms before the season started.

The NFL Green Bay Packers use Milwaukee County Stadium for one or two games a season.

CONSTRUCTION COSTS

Construction costs for the stadium were predicted to be $4.5 million. The actual cost of construction was $5,768,365.[2] The overrun included $500,000 to upgrade the seats and lights to accommodate major league baseball. The majority of the construction funds came from bond issues in 1950 of $1.8 million and 1951 of $2 million. The remainder of the costs were financed from "unexpected" balances in other parts of the city budget.[3] The seating capacity of the stadium during the 1953 season was 35,911.

In 1954, at a cost of $1,412,547, the city expanded the stadium to increase its capacity to 44,091.[4] This began a trend of almost continuous improvement in the facility. As Table 2.1 shows, the only year between 1953 and 1976 in which there was no expenditure for capital improvement was 1962.

The original construction cost of the stadium is the equivalent of $15,179,908 in 1977 dollars. The last two columns of Table 2.1 compute the 1977 cost of each of the capital improvements made through 1976. These total $18,385,778. The total cost, in 1977 dollars, of the stadium construction and improvements through 1976 is $33,565,686. Given the stadium's capacity of 55,958, the stadium's inflation-adjusted-average-cost-per-seat is $600.

SUBSIDY ANALYSIS

Financial reporting for the stadium is uneven. Operating profits and losses are reported for every year from 1953 through 1985, but little data on the transfers to or from the general fund are available. Table 2.2 reviews the former.[5]

The lease with both the Braves and the Brewers explains some of the variation in profit levels for the stadium. In that lease, the teams were to pay $1.00 for any season that attendance fell below one million. If attendance exceeded one million the rent became an increasing percentage of the admissions revenues. Milwaukee officials prided themselves that their lease made them partners with an interest in the team's success.

---

2. Milwaukee County, *1953 Financial Report for the Year Ended December 31, 1953*, 16.
3. Ibid. 27, 33.
4. Milwaukee County, *1954 Financial Report for the Year Ended December 31, 1954*, 27.
5. For those years for which data are not available using the annual *Finanical Report*, the operating profit or loss is taken from an undated private letter from the Milwaukee County Comptroller's Office. These data have the same order of magnitude as the the county's financial statements, but they differ in that the comptroller's figures include fixed costs, such as depreciation, and are too aggregated to subtract out this component. The data that come from the comptroller's office are marked with an asterisk(*).

During the late 1950s, when the Braves were enjoying success and breaking National League attendance records, the stadium was operating in the black. When the Braves' fortunes turned sour on the field, and the gate, Milwaukee found out what it meant to be a partner in a business with declining popularity.

Between 1967 and 1969, when there was no or little professional baseball in Milwaukee, the operating loss was less than during the Braves' last year. This is consistent with the $1.00-a-year lease. The Braves, having announced their departure for Atlanta in 1965, drew less than one million fans, and paid only $1.00 in rent. The county, however, incurred the costs of operating the stadium for the baseball season. From 1967 through 1969, the city was able to reduce operating expenses and lost only $1.00 in annual rental.

Financial reporting for the Brewers' era at Milwaukee County Stadium is more carefully documented and closely parallels the earlier experience with the Braves. In the early 1970s, the Brewers were establishing themselves as a local franchise. When it moved to Milwaukee, the franchise had only its ill-fated maiden season in Seattle for tradition. The largest increase in income to Milwaukee was a 250 percent increase in parking concessions. By 1978, the Brewers began contributing money to, rather than drawing resources from, the general fund.

Figures in Table 2.3 in parenthesis show those years in which funds had to be taken from the general fund to help pay the stadium's expenses. Those years in which the figures are not in parenthesis are the amounts the stadium contributed to the general fund.[6]

The relationship between the team's professional and financial success and the stadium's profitability continues into municipal subsidies to the stadium. In those years when the Brewers performed well on the field and at the box office, the stadium did well and contributed to the general fund.

In addition to the fragmented data, there is a second reason why it is not possible to conclude whether Milwaukee County Stadium was a worthwhile investment for the county. Milwaukee does not compute property assessments on public properties. Therefore it is not possible to estimate the extent to which the city has lost property tax revenues due to public ownership of the facility. This point is critical in estimating the true size of the subsidy to the Braves, since it appears that the move to Milwaukee was one that would have been financially successful in the absence of a municipal subsidy.[7] Therefore, the property taxes that the stadium could have earned if the stadium had been privately owned is a relevant cost of municipal ownership.

---

6. Milwaukee County, Financial Report for years 1956, 1957, 1959, 1960, 1961, 1962, 1963, 1964, 1965, 1966, 1967, 1968, 1969, 1970, 1971, 1972, 1973, 1974, 1975, 1976, 1977, 1978, 1979, 1980, 1981, 1982, 1983, 1984, 1985. The stadium contributed $18,335 and $89,673 to the general fund in fiscal year 1956 and 1957, respectively. These are the only two years for which these computations are available during the Braves' tenure at Milwaukee County Stadium.

7. Jerome R. Ellig, "Law, Economics, and Organized Baseball: Analysis of a Cooperative Venture," (Ph.D. diss., George Mason University, 1987), 211.

While no computation regarding the advisability of the construction of Milwaukee County Stadium is possible, there is evidence to suggest that the stadium may have earned enough revenues to generate close to an accumulated net present value that, if negative, is close to positive. The accumulated net present values of the cash flows in Table 2.3 and for 1956 and 1957 discounted back to 1953 is negative $14,624. It must be stressed that this figure does not take into account the cash flows generated for fifteen of the first seventeen years. During some of these years, when the Braves were setting attendance records, it is possible that the stadium was contributing to the general fund. Not only might these cash flows be positive, they would have the greatest impact on the net accumulated values, coming as they did early in the stream of cash flows.

Table 2.1
Milwaukee County Stadium
Capital Improvements
(1953–1976)

Fiscal Year	Capital Improvement Expenditures	Construction Cost Index	Real Cost Capital Expenditures
1953	$1,184,077	38	$3,115,992
1954	$1,412,547	38	$3,717,229
1955	$189,989	39	$487,151
1956	$252,830	41	$616,659
1957	$171,406	42	$71,991
1958	N/A		
1959	$80,850	42	$192,500
1960	$252,628	42	$601,495
1961	$102,780	41	$250,683
1962	$0	42	$0
1963	$131,204	42	$312,390
1964	$123,750	422	$293,246
1965	$39,104	436	$89,688
1966	$6,063	454	$13,355
1967	$110,142	471	$233,847
1968	$11,145	496	$22,470
1969	$45,665	534	$85,515
1970	$25,077	568	$44,150
1971	$140	605	$231
1972	$180,208	641	$281,136
1973	$438,028	696	$629,351
1974	$1,472,900	818	$1,800,611
1975	$2,677,472	893	$2,998,289
1976	$2,335,687	924	$2,527,800

Table 2.2
Milwaukee County Stadium
Operating Profits (Losses)
(1956-1985)

Year	Net Profit (Loss)	Year	Net Profit (Loss)
1953*	$120,909	1970	($74,200)
1954*	$300,908	1971	($244,800)
1955*	$286,583	1972	($242,200)
1956	$271,165	1973	($34,800)
1957	$261,079	1974	($74,100)
1958*	$390,629	1975	($16,500)
1959	$337,500	1976	($432,700)
1960	$271,600	1977	$20,566
1961	$209,600	1978	$856,100
1962	$133,500	1979	$842,100
1963	($18,700)	1980	$527,900
1964	$30,100	1981	($527,400)
1965	($57,400)	1982	$1,260,533
1966	($197,300)	1983	$1,386,600
1967	($171,000)	1984	$81,300
1968	($162,200)	1985	($908,755)
1969	($164,000)		

Table 2.3
Milwaukee County Stadium
Direct Municipal Inflows (Subsidies)
(1971–1985)

Year	Direct Inflow (Subsidy)	Year	Direct Inflow (Subsidy)
1971	($244,903)	1979	$523,700
1972	($249,673)	1980	$43,900
1973	($34,940)	1981	($493,800)
1974	($74,027)	1982	$562,055
1975	($16,505)	1983	$700,600
1976	($255,469)	1984	($823,800)
1977	($22,078)	1985	($1,063,874)
1978	$861,100		

Chapter 3
Baltimore Memorial Stadium

HISTORY

Baltimore's Memorial Stadium began as Venable Park, a wooden stadium constructed in 1922 to house college football, track and field, and boxing events. The stadium never met the expectations of those who had proposed the construction. A 1933 article appearing in *The Baltimore Sun* referred to the facility as a "white elephant." A sidebar article gave a depression-flavored concept of the opportunity costs related to stadium operations, when it computed that the funds spent on building and maintaining the stadium could feed 17,655 babies for one year.[1]

In 1949 an evolutionary process began transforming Venable Stadium into a facility worthy of a minor league baseball franchise. The reconstruction had not been completed when it became necessary to improve the facility to major league standards. This metamorphis began when the NFL Dallas Texans folded after one season, only to surface as the Baltimore Colts before the 1953 season.

In 1954 the St. Louis Browns migrated to Baltimore and took the name of the last major league baseball team to play in Baltimore before that team moved to New York in 1903 to become the Yankees.

The Browns shared St. Louis with the Cardinals since 1902, the year the Browns moved to St. Louis from Milwaukee. Both teams played in Sportsman's Park, a facility owned by the Browns for thirty-four seasons. Although the Cardinals used the Browns-owned facility, the Cardinals were the more popular team in St. Louis, stemming mostly from the Cardinals' World Series victory in 1926. The Cardinals' popularity irritated the Browns, but they could not evict the Cardinals because the Browns needed the revenues they received from renting the stadium to the Cardinals.

---

1. "City's White Elephant Going on Short Rations," *The Baltimore Sun*, 24 August 1933.

Browns' owner Bill Veeck anticipated the Cardinals would move to Milwaukee leaving St. Louis to his team. The Braves' relocation to Milwaukee, combined with the purchase of the Cardinals by August Busch spelled the end of the Browns' tenure in St. Louis. In a move to improve the Browns' cash flow, Veeck sold Sportman's Park to the Cardinals for $800,000. The day after the sale was completed, the new owner modestly named the facility Busch Stadium.

Veeck wanted to move the team to Baltimore before the 1953 season. Veeck, who saw revenue sharing between teams as a way wealthier teams could help cash-strapped teams, such as the ones he could afford, alienated most of the powerful owners, and they viewed the crisis in St. Louis as a way of forcing Veeck from the game.[2] The proposal to move the Browns to Baltimore was defeated by the owners, in a 5–3 vote. After the 1953 season, in which the Browns attracted only 297,238 fans, Veeck secured one more vote, but the move was still blocked by a 4–4 tie. Two days after the tie vote, and after Veeck sold the team to a syndicate of Baltimore businessmen, the move by the Browns to Baltimore was approved unanimously.[3]

Beginning in the mid-1970s Baltimore came under pressure to provide a more modern facility. This led the city to make some improvements: replacing benches with theater-type seats in the upper deck, a 1978 renovation of all concession stands, and between 1979 and 1981, restrooms were added to relieve a perceived problem. The renovations were insufficient to satisfy the Colts, who moved in 1984 to the Indianapolis Hoosierdome, a facility partially financed with private funds in a loosely veiled attempt to attract a NFL franchise.

The departure of the Colts, combined with rumors that the Orioles were considering a move to Washington, D.C. or Phoenix, Arizona put pressure on the city to build a new stadium. The financial burden to retain the Orioles was too much for Baltimore, and it turned to the State of Maryland to fund a downtown stadium. The plan proved to be controversial with the debate reminiscent of the 1933 article in *The Baltimore Sun*.

The new, state financed, baseball only stadium, Oriole Park at Camdem Yards, opened on 6 April 1992. The University of Maryland football team continues to use Memorial Stadium as a home field, and it will be the interim home of an NFL franchise if one locates in Baltimore.

Memorial Stadium is located in the proximity of Johns Hopkins University. As if the economy in the stadium/Hopkins corridor was supported by two pillars, the standard of living in this neighborhood is superior to the standard of living in neighborhoods immediately surrounding the stadium/Hopkins corridor. With the departure of the Orioles to their new downtown facility, the neighborhood between Johns Hopkins and Memorial Stadium will serve as a laboratory on the impact a professional sports franchise has on a local economy.

---

2.   James Edward Miller, *The Baseball Business* (Chapel Hill: University of North Carolina Press, 1990), Chapter 1.

3.   Ibid.; also James Quirk, "An Economic Analysis of Team Movements in Professional Sports," *Law and Contemporary Problems* 38 (Winter/Spring 1973), 50.

CONSTRUCTION COSTS

The original 1922 construction costs are not available. This does not create a serious loss in construction cost analysis since the original construction predates the construction cost index, making it impossible to estimate the Inflation-Adjusted-Cost-Per-Seat for Memorial Stadium. The 1949–54 and 1979–81 renovations are estimated to have cost $6 million and $10 million, respectively.

SUBSIDY ANALYSIS

Table 3.1 displays the operating profits for Memorial Stadium during the Orioles' era.[4] The data stop at 1982, because this is the last year the stadium was treated as an enterprise fund.

It is difficult to discern a trend in the operating profits earned by Memorial Stadium. The stadium earned an operating profit nineteen of the twenty-nine years shown, but a pattern does not surface immediately. Observation of the strike years does little to clarify the picture. During the baseball strike year of 1977, the operating loss increased from the previous year, but this trend is not repeated in 1981, a year in which the baseball strike was longer. Likewise, the NFL strike year of 1974 was one in which the stadium operated at a loss following a profitable year. The NFL 1982 strike year, however, was the most profitable year in the survey.

Reference to the Orioles' attendance records can explain some of the changes. The stadium's first operating loss occurred in 1966, the same year the Orioles drew over 1.2 million fans, a club record at that time. The following year the Orioles drew less than 900,000 fans and operating profits rose by almost $300,000 from 1966. The losses in 1971 and 1972 also came in years when the Orioles drew well.[5] In 1973, attendance fell and operating profits rose. In each of the seasons between 1975 and 1980, when the stadium consistently ran up large operating losses, the Orioles' attendance exceeded 1 million. The most severe loss was incurred in 1979, a season in which the Orioles set a club attendance record. Only one of the eleven years in which the stadium incurred a loss saw the Orioles draw less than one million fans. The year in which that occurred, 1974, was one in which a player strike shortened the NFL season.

---

4. Data for Table 3.1 come from the City of Baltimore, Finance Director, *Annual Financial Report for Fiscal Year Ended* for the years 1954, 1955, 1956, 1957, 1958, 1959, 1960, 1961, 1962, 1963, 1964, 1965, 1966, 1967, 1968, 1969, 1970, 1971, 1972, 1973, 1974, 1975, 1976, 1977, 1978, 1979, 1980, 1981, 1982.
5. The 1972 attendance was 899,950 during a season in which nearly one-fourth of the season was lost due to a player strike. The attendance per game would have created an annual attendance close to 1.2 million fans for a full season.

Unfortunately, the NFL does not itemize attendance figures by team so similar inferences regarding the Colts' lease is not possible. Comparison of operating profits before and after the Colts' departure might be instructive in this endeavor, but it is not possible since the city ceased reporting operating profits after 1982.

Table 3.2 shows the direct and indirect municipal costs of Memorial Stadium.[6] The costs are made net of depreciation, and data on the direct outlay in 1972 were not available.

In that historical property tax evaluation of the property upon which Municipal Stadium is built is not available, the property values are computed by taking the 1987 assessed valuation of $9,961,800,[7] and deflating (for prior years) or inflating (for subsequent years) at a rate of 10 percent a year.

Table 3.3 computes the property tax cost differently, in that it assumes the land would remain undeveloped. This is probably an unrealistic assumption, but it gives a lower boundary to the costs to Baltimore of owning the stadium in comparison with the figures in Table 3.2, which serves as the upper boundary.

Both Table 3.2 and Table 3.3 omit the direct municipal outlays as reported in the city's 1985 financial statements. That year the city took a $15,787,000 write-off on the stadium as a final step of closing out the stadium's enterprise fund.

Baltimore experienced two seemingly different approaches to the stadium as a source of municipal revenues. For more than fifteen years, the city received little tax revenue from stadium operations outside of a 2.5 percent payroll tax on the relatively small stadium payroll.

A new era began in 1970 when the city took a more aggressive stance in levying taxes on stadium related-commerce. A parking tax and license fee were imposed from 1970 to 1980, and a tax on admissions was also enacted. Table 3.4 exhibits the change in revenues experienced during these various schemes.

The stadium's payroll for 1954 and between 1967 and 1972 was not available. Given the relative magnitude of the payroll tax revenue, this omission does not jeopardize the conclusions that will be drawn from these data. This understatement of municipal tax revenues generated by Memorial Stadium is balanced somewhat by the realization that many stadium employees would be employees for another employer in Baltimore and thus would be paying payroll taxes at that location. To the extent that this is not true, the payroll tax revenues in Table 3.4 overstate the stadium municipal tax revenues, but again, the order of magnitude is not significant.

---

6. City of Baltimore, Finance Director, *Annual Financial Report for Fiscal Year Ended* for 1954, 1955, 1956, 1957, 1958, 1959, 1960, 1961, 1962, 1963, 1964, 1965, 1966, 1967, 1968, 1969, 1970, 1971, 1972, 1973, 1974, 1975, 1976, 1977, 1978, 1979, 1980, 1981, 1982, 1983, 1984, 1985. Private conversation with Doug Brown, Department of Finance, City of Baltimore, 26 June 1987.
7. Private conversation with Doug Brown, Department of Finance, City of Baltimore, 26 June 1987.

The second column of Table 3.5 combines the last columns of Table 3.2 (Direct and Indirect City Outlays) and Table 3.4 (Municipal Tax Revenues from Stadium) to arrive at the city's net gain or loss from the stadium for each of the years from 1954 to 1985. The third column computes the discount rate for each year, while column four discounts the profit or loss back to 1954, using the discount rate and the standard property tax assumption. The sum of these figures is at the foot of the column and represents the accumulated net present value.

Since the implementation of the admission tax and parking license fee, the stadium has shown signs of profitability. In five of the last six years of the survey, the revenues from admission taxes and parking licenses have more than offset the direct and indirect municipal costs.

The accumulated net present value (ANPV) of the stadium investment is negative using the standard property tax assumptions. The magnitude of the loss is relatively small, less than $3 million. If the trend of profitability continued through the last years of Municipal Stadium's life, the $3 million will improve slightly. It is unlikely that the net present value of the stadium will be positive, using the standard property tax assumption, unless it were sold in the near future. The last years of the cash flows, even when positive, are discounted heavily. However, it is not difficult to assume that the city received $3 million in direct or indirect benefits in the form of increased hotel, restaurant revenues and increased economic activity supporting the surrounding neighborhood in the stadium's thirty-eight years of hosting major league sports.

Using the assumption that the stadium land would not have been developed, the ANPV becomes positive. These computations are in Table 3.6.

Memorial Stadium would appear to be a well-advised investment.

Table 3.1
Baltimore Memorial Stadium
Operating Profits
(1954–1982)

Year	Operating Profit	Year	Operating Profit
1954	($10,768)	1969	$179,572
1955	$20,016	1970	$109,089
1956	22,659	1971	($100,667)
1957	$52,928	1972	($188,484)
1958	$25,587	1973	$63,000
1959	$112,477	1974	($2,300)
1960	$243,884	1975	($217,300)
1961	$227,212	1976	($709,900)
1962	$139,021	1977	($801,295)
1963	$164,693	1978	($619,300)
1964	$183,180	1979	($829,712)
1965	$91,425	1980	($131,798)
1966	($11,026)	1981	$163,900
1967	$282,081	1982	$707,000
1968	$111,341		

	Table 3.2				
	Baltimore Memorial Stadium				
	Direct and Indirect Outlays				
	(1954–1985)				
Year	Direct Municipal Outlay	Property Tax Rate	Property Tax Valuation	Foregone Property Taxes	Direct & Indirect City Outlays
1954	($46,768)	0.0282	$2,202,927	($62,123)	($108,890)
1955	($14,484)	0.0282	$2,420,799	($68,267)	($82,751)
1956	($10,311)	0.0313	$2,420,799	($75,771)	($86,082)
1957	$21,428	0.0288	$2,660,219	($76,614)	($55,186)
1958	($197,424)	0.0298	$2,660,219	($79,275)	($276,698)
1959	($182,835)	0.0334	$2,923,317	($97,639)	($280,473)
1960	($41,663)	0.036	$2,923,317	($105,239)	($146,903)
1961	($332,531)	0.036	$3,212,436	($115,648)	($448,179)
1962	($215,309)	0.0391	$3,212,436	($125,606)	($340,915)
1963	($211,346)	0.0395	$3,530,150	($139,441)	($350,787)
1964	($184,576)	0.0414	$3,530,150	($146,148)	($330,725)
1965	($246,311)	0.0445	$3,879,285	($172,628)	($418,939)
1966	($33,276)	0.0219	$3,879,285	($84,956)	($118,233)
1967	($75,434)	0.0473	$4,262,951	($201,638)	($277,071)
1968	($201,034)	0.0442	$4,262,951	($188,422)	($389,457)
1969	($127,897)	0.0474	$4,684,562	($222,048)	($349,945)
1970	($193,317)	0.0494	$4,684,562	($231,417)	($424,734)
1971	($403,073)	0.0534	$5,147,870	($274,896)	($677,969)
1972		0.0565	$5,147,870	($290,855)	($290,855)
1973	($251,467)	0.0586	$5,657,000	($331,500)	($582,967)
1974	($226,800)	0.0583	$5,657,000	($329,803)	($556,603)
1975	($322,900)	0.0609	$6,216,483	($378,584)	($701,484)
1976	($885,100)	0.0602	$6,216,483	($374,232)	($1,259,332)
1977	($741,845)	0.0588	$6,831,300	($401,680)	($1,143,525)
1978	($720,600)	0.0599	$6,831,300	($409,195)	($1,129,795)
1979	($904,576)	0.0597	$7,506,924	($448,163)	($1,352,739)
1980	($143,338)	0.0595	$7,506,924	($446,662)	($590,000)
1981	($296,500)	0.0593	$8,249,367	($489,187)	($785,687)
1982	($257,000)	0.0597	$8,249,367	($492,487)	($749,487)
1983	($1,151,000)	0.0596	$9,065,238	($540,288)	($1,691,288)
1984	($565,000)	0.0599	$9,065,238	($543,008)	($1,108,008)
1985		0.06	$9,961,800	(597,708)	($597,708)

Table 3.3
Baltimore Memorial Stadium
Direct and Indirect Outlays
Using Alternative Property Tax Assumption
(1954–1985)

Year	Direct & Indirect City Outlays	Year	Direct & Indirect City Outlays
1954	($52,980)	1971	($430,563)
1955	($21,311)	1972	($29,085)
1956	($17,888)	1973	($284,617)
1957	$13,767	1974	($259,780)
1958	($205,351)	1975	($360,758)
1959	($192,599)	1976	($922,523)
1960	($52,187)	1977	($782,013)
1961	($344,096)	1978	($761,519)
1962	($227,869)	1979	($949,392)
1963	($225,290)	1980	($188,004)
1964	($199,191)	1981	($345,419)
1965	($263,573)	1982	($306,249)
1966	($41,772)	1983	($1,205,029)
1967	($95,597)	1984	($619,301)
1968	($219,877)	1985	($59,771)
1969	($150,102)		
1970	($216,459)		

		City Payroll Tax Rate	Payroll Tax Revenues	Parking Tax & License	Admissions Tax	Municipal Tax Rev. From Stad
Year	Stadium Payroll					
1954		0.025	$0			$0
1955	$77,000	0.025	$1,925			$1,925
1956	$95,000	0.025	$2,375			$2,375
1957	$156,060	0.025	$3,902			$3,902
1958	$173,740	0.025	$4,344			$4,344
1959	$162,220	0.025	$4,056			$4,056
1960	$162,220	0.025	$4,056			$4,056
1961	$175,592	0.025	$4,390			$4,390
1962	$180,500	0.025	$4,513			$4,513
1963	$188,594	0.025	$4,715			$4,715
1964	$197,024	0.025	$4,926			$4,926
1965	$210,334	0.025	$5,258			$5,258
1966	$136,236	0.025	$3,406			$3,406
1967		0.025	$0			$0
1968		0.025	$0			$0
1969		0.025	$0			$0
1970		0.025	$0	$37,490	$300,551	$338,041
1971		0.025	$0	$54,855	$510,307	$565,162
1972		0.025	$0	$53,077	$735,795	$788,872
1973	$360,151	0.025	$9,004	$51,546	$518,382	$578,932
1974	$403,500	0.025	$10,088	$52,689	$527,284	$590,061
1975	$414,963	0.025	$10,374	$40,179	$603,000	$665,777
1976	$543,081	0.025	$13,577	$47,286	$756,000	$806,553
1977	$564,356	0.025	$14,109	$48,756	$785,000	$845,863
1978	$580,358	0.025	$14,509	$40,353	$803,000	$865,865
1979	$567,716	0.025	$14,193	$42,793	$816,000	$870,862
1980	$698,731	0.025	$17,468	$28,724	$689,000	$745,986
1981	$708,317	0.025	$17,708		$1,000,000	$1,046,192
1982	$778,000	0.025	$19,450		$1,140,000	$1,157,708
1983	$734,000	0.025	$18,350		$1,195,000	$1,214,450
1984	$784,000	0.025	$19,600		$2,149,000	$2,167,350
1985			$0		$1,182,000	$1,201,600

Table 3.4
Baltimore Memorial Stadium
Tax Revenues
(1954–1985)

Table 3.5
Baltimore Memorial Stadium
Accumulated Net Present Value of Stadium Investment
(1954–1985)

Year	Total Profit (Subsidy)	Risk Adjusted Discount Spot Rate	PV of π (Subsidy)
1954	($108,890)	1.00298	($108,890)
1955	($80,826)	1.0144	($79,678)
1956	($83,707)	1.0175	($80,852)
1957	($51,285)	1.0193	($48,426)
1958	($272,355)	1.0194	($252,207)
1959	($276,418)	1.0219	($248,041)
1960	($142,847)	1.0244	($123,610)
1961	($443,789)	1.0259	($371,058)
1962	($336,402)	1.0271	($271,617)
1963	($346,072)	1.0271	($272,052)
1964	($325,799)	1.0271	($249,358)
1965	($413,680)	1.0271	($308,265)
1966	($114,827)	1.0271	($83,309)
1967	($277,071)	1.0271	($195,716)
1968	($389,457)	1.0283	($263,501)
1969	($349,945)	1.0283	($230,252)
1970	($86,693)	1.0283	($55,471)
1971	($112,807)	1.0283	($70,194)
1972	$498,017	1.0283	$301,361
1973	($4,035)	1.0289	($2,349)
1974	$33,457	1.0295	$18,705
1975	($35,707)	1.0301	($19,155)
1976	($452,779)	1.0307	($232,796)
1977	($297,662)	1.0307	($148,485)
1978	($263,930)	1.0307	($127,736)
1979	($481,877)	1.0307	($226,271)
1980	$155,986	1.0307	$71,063
1981	$260,505	1.0307	$115,145
1982	$408,221	1.0307	$175,062
1983	($476,838)	1.0307	($198,397)
1984	$1,059,342	1.0307	$427,630
1985	$603,892	1.0307	$236,515
Accumulated Net Present Value			($2,922,206)

Table 3.6
Baltimore Memorial Stadium
Accumulated Net Present Value of Stadium Investment
Using Alternative Property Tax Assumptions
(1954–1985)

Year	Total Profit (Subsidy)	PV of π or (Subsidy
1954	($52,980)	($52,980)
1955	($19,386)	($19,111)
1956	($15,513)	($14,984)
1957	$17,669	$16,683
1958	($201,007)	($186,138)
1959	($188,543)	($169,188)
1960	($48,131)	($41,650)
1961	($339,706)	($284,032)
1962	($223,356)	($180,342)
1963	($220,575)	($173,398)
1964	($194,235)	($148,686)
1965	($258,315)	($192,491)
1966	($38,366)	($27,835)
1967	($95,597)	($67,527)
1968	($219,877)	($148,765)
1969	($150,102)	($98,762)
1970	$121,582	$77,795
1971	$134,599	$83,754
1972	$759,787	$459,764
1973	$294,315	$171,286
1974	$330,281	$184,653
1975	$305,019	$163,628
1976	($115,970)	($59,626)
1977	$63,850	$31,851
1978	$104,346	$50,486
1979	($78,530)	($36,875)
1980	$557,982	$254,203
1981	$700,773	$309,747
1982	$851,409	$365,141
1983	$9,421	$3,920
1984	$1,548,049	$624,908
1985	$1,141,829	$447,199
Accumulated Net Present Value		$1,342,626

Chapter 4
Buffalo War Memorial Stadium

HISTORY

The year 1960 was a memorable year in professional football. In that year one franchise relocated (the Chicago Cardinals moved to St. Louis, Missouri), another was founded (the Dallas Cowboys) and a league was formed (the American Football League [AFL]). The last event had an imprint on the financial statements in two cities in this survey, Buffalo, New York and Denver, Colorado.

Buffalo's War Memorial Stadium was a PWA project, built in 1937 to stimulate the depression economy of Buffalo. The stadium was used to host civic events and sports at the college and subcollege levels, but the facility was not built to host major league sports.

With the announcement in 1960 that Buffalo would be one of the recipients of a franchise in the newly formed American Football League (AFL), the City of Buffalo spent $750,000 to renovate the one-deck facility to major league standards. In 1964, the city yielded to the Bills' threats to leave the city if a second deck was not added to the stadium. The addition increased the capacity by 5,000 seats. Although the city could only secure a five-year lease with the Bills (with ten one-year extensions solely at the Bills' option), the city financed the 1964 addition to the stadium with bonds that matured in fifteen years.

The Bills continued to be unhappy in Buffalo, although not with the Buffalo metropolitan area. In 1971, the Bills signed a twenty-five–year lease with Erie County to play football in Orchard Park, a suburb of Buffalo. The agreement called for the county, which includes the City of Buffalo, to build and maintain the new stadium at county expense. The new stadium was completed in time for the Bills' 1973 season, some six years before the bonds used to finance the second deck expropriated by the Bills matured.

CONSTRUCTION COSTS

As a PWA project, the War Memorial Stadium was built with few municipal funds. Although federal funds were used, there appears to be no reliable record as to how much the stadium cost to construct.

As already mentioned, the 1960 renovation and improvements to the depression-era facility cost $750,000.[1] The addition of the second deck in 1964 cost $1.5 million.[2]

SUBSIDY ANALYSIS

Even if the original construction costs could be determined, they would not be a relevant component of a subsidy to the Bills, since the stadium was not intended to house a professional sports team when it was built. Similarly, the foregone property taxes are not included as a subsidy to the Bills.

Because the city aggregated the stadium's accounts with those of the Memorial Auditorium, it is not possible to determine if the Bills reimbursed the city for its operating expenses by comparing the operating profits during the years prior to 1960 with the operating profits during the Bills' tenure. This practice was reinstated after 1985. Table 4.1 shows the operating profits for War Memorial Stadium for the years 1960 to 1985.[3]

A review of Table 4.1 leads to the conclusion that the Bills did not pay fully for the operating costs of a typical football season. The stadium turned an operating profit in only five of the thirteen years the Bills used the stadium. These five seasons coincided with seasons in which the Bills were successful. The operating loss fell by a factor of two-thirds when the Bills left for the suburbs. The implication is clear: The Bills did not pay the full costs of their tenure at War Memorial Stadium.

When the observer recalls that the data in Table 4.1 do not include the debt service on the 1960 refurbishment or the 1964 expansion, it is easy to conclude that the Bills drained the Buffalo city treasury more than they contributed. Table 4.2 reports the municipal outlay for the stadium from 1960-1985.[4] These data include the expenditures for debt service as well as any operating losses.

Table 4.2 has several unmistakable periods. During the first five seasons, the Bills' drain on the Buffalo treasury was relatively modest, averaging $77,245, with the losses during 1963 and 1964 adding almost $20,000 to this average.

---

1. City of Buffalo, Department of Audit and Control, *Comptroller's Report, 1960*, 97, 100.
2. House Select Committee on Professional Sports, *Inquiry into Professional Sports, Part I*, 96th Cong., 2d sess., 1976.
3. City of Buffalo, Department of Audit and Control, *Annual Report of the Fiscal Year ended* 1960, 1961, 1962, 1963, 1964, 1965, 1966, 1967, 1968, 1969, 1970, 1971, 1972, 1973, 1974, 1975, 1976, 1977, 1978, 1979, 1980, 1981, 1982, 1983, 1984, 1985.
4. Ibid.

The stadium's municipal burden took a quantum leap with the debt service related to the 1964 expansion. The average annual loss is $328,044 between 1965, the first year of the debt service, and 1973, the year the Bills departed.

The period 1973 to 1979 is the interval when the city was still servicing the 1964 expansion debt but did not have the Bills as tenants. During this six-year period, the average loss fell to $205,120, further evidence the Bills failed to contribute enough to cover their operating costs.

During the final six years of Table 4.2, the 1964 expansion bonds had been paid, and when the Bills were only a memory, the average loss fell to $63,117. The loss for this last period is of the same magnitude as the losses incurred during the first period, even without any allowance for inflation.

There are no significant tax revenues to offset the losses in Table 4.2. Buffalo had neither a municipal income, payroll, stadium use, or ticket tax during the period.[5] The amounts in Table 4.2 are the city's net cash flows attributable to War Memorial Stadium from 1960 to 1985.

The $63,117 in average net annual municipal expenditures after the 1964 expansion debt had been retired indicates that not all of the amounts shown in Table 4.2 are due to the Bills' presence at War Memorial Stadium. This is used as a baseline cost estimate. The difference between this baseline amount, adjusted for inflation, and the municipal outlays in Table 4.2 is an estimate of the subsidy the Bills received. Table 4.3 relates the results of these calculations. The last column, how much more actual expenditures exceeded the inflation adjusted baseline, represents the subsidy to the Bills. For the two years (1960 and 1962) that the total expenditures did not exceed the inflation-adjusted baseline, the Bills did not receive a subsidy.

The last column of Table 4.3 discounts the subsidy calculations in Table 4.2. The subsidy to the Bills, for their stay and for improvements added at the Bills' request, amounts to $836,021.

---

5. Private conversation with Charles Leon of the City of Buffalo Budget Office, 25 November 1987.

Table 4.1
Buffalo War Memorial Stadium
Operating Profits (Losses)
(1960–1985)

Year	Operating Profit	Year	Operating Profit
1960	($41,646)	1973	($276,682)
1961	($30,665)	1974	($53,482)
1962	$30,122	1975	($22,441)
1963	$14,699	1976	($43,926)
1964	$11,675	1977	($42,425)
1965	$5,389	1978	($41,651)
1966	$13,069	1979	($41,092)
1967	($18,606)	1980	($39,991)
1968	($50,922)	1981	($27,708)
1969	($67,936)	1982	($51,878)
1970	($56,568)	1983	($48,171)
1971	($138,414)	1984	($64,202)
1972	($151,875)	1985	($69,202)

Table 4.2
Buffalo War Memorial Stadium
Municipal Outlays
(1960–1985)

Year	Municipal Outlay	Year	Municipal Outlay
1960	($41,647)	1973	($355,672)
1961	($71,534)	1974	($268,185)
1962	($59,022)	1975	($232,185)
1963	($106,519)	1976	($197,791)
1964	($107,504)	1977	($195,959)
1965	($271,821)	1978	($176,676)
1966	($238,387)	1979	($159,924)
1967	($278,324)	1980	($62,009)
1968	($315,991)	1981	($48,775)
1969	($327,537)	1982	($71,817)
1970	($317,324)	1983	($62,697)
1971	($441,092)	1984	($64,202)
1972	($406,246)	1985	($69,202)

Year	Baseline Outlays	Total Outlays	Deviations (Above) or Below Baseline	Present Value of Deviations
		Table 4.3		
		Buffalo War Memorial Stadium		
		Estimate of Bills' (Subsidy) over "Baseline"		
		(1960–1979)		
1960	$20,309	$13,401	$6,909	$6,909
1961	$20,309	$23,018	($2,708)	($2,583)
1962	$20,374	$19,052	$1,322	$1,199
1963	$20,309	$34,275	($13,966)	($12,071)
1964	$20,396	$34,739	($14,343)	($11,823)
1965	$20,743	$89,331	($68,589)	($53,767)
1966	$21,415	$80,881	($59,467)	($44,783)
1967	$21,675	$95,578	($73,904)	($53,157)
1968	$22,282	$111,552	($89,270)	($61,350)
1969	$23,105	$119,902	($96,797)	($63,640)
1970	$23,907	$120,195	($96,288)	($60,481)
1971	$24,644	$172,226	($147,582)	($88,581)
1972	$25,403	$163,503	($138,100)	($79,221)
1973	$27,722	$156,217	($128,495)	($70,463)
1974	$31,970	$135,842	($103,872)	($54,534)
1975	$35,417	$130,285	($94,869)	($47,635)
1976	$36,977	$115,876	($78,899)	($37,896)
1977	$39,383	$122,272	($82,889)	($38,090)
1978	$42,461	$118,856	($76,395)	($33,594)
1979	$47,186	$119,559	($72,373)	($30,461)
		Accumulated Net Present Value		($836,021)

Chapter 5
Denver Mile High Stadium

HISTORY

Mile High Stadium in Denver, Colorado did not become a municipally owned facility until the late 1960s. Built in 1948 to house the minor league baseball Bears, Bear Stadium was built economically, with the playing field converted from a garbage dump and a hill serving as the foundation for the bleachers.[1] The owners of the Bears received an AFL franchise, and they made modifications to make the stadium a multipurpose facility and to increase the capacity to 33,000. At this point, the stadium's name was changed to Mile High Stadium.

The success of the Denver Broncos during their first seven seasons created interest in a new sports facility. A referendum to construct a municipally owned facility near the airport was defeated in 1966. The following year, a group called the "Doers" purchased Mile High Stadium and donated it to the City and County of Denver.[2] In 1968, the new owners expanded the stadium to seat 50,000 by building three decks over the original grandstand site.

The voters approved financing in 1974 to raise the capacity to 75,000 and modernize the stadium. The major feature of the expansion completed in 1977 was the installation of a movable section of seats in place of the original grandstand. At the time, the three-tiered, 450-foot, nine million-pound movable grandstand was the largest undertaking of its kind. The stadium is now part of a sports complex, which includes McNicols Arena, used by the NBA Denver Nuggets.

1. Denver, Colorado, *Denver's Mile High Stadium is "On the Move" in Colorado* (Denver, 1980) 1.
2. In Denver, the city and county are the same entity.

CONSTRUCTION COSTS

Since the initial construction costs of the stadium and the 1960 renovation were done by the Denver Bears franchise, the costs are not a matter of public record. The purchase of the stadium by the "Doers" and the subsequent donation to the city meant the city was able to acquire the facility without the use of municipal funds. The 1968 addition and the 1977 expansion and modernization cost the city $10 million and $75 million, respectively.[3]

SUBSIDY ANALYSIS

Direct municipal outlays for the stadium are reported in the city's financial statements. They are reported in Table 5.1 and show that the stadium received a subsidy in only six years of the twenty-one included in the survey, a net cash gain was realized by the city in four of the years, and no cash inflows or outflows for the remainder of the years.[4] The data for 1976 and 1978 are not reported because the data were not in good form.

Since Mile High Stadium was originally privately owned and was donated to the city and county so that it could better serve the Broncos, the construction and the acquisition cost is not part of the subsidy to the Broncos. The foregone property taxes on the stadium, after the municipal acquisition, are an appropriate cost of the stadium's civic ownership.

The total valuation of Mile High Stadium in 1987 was $52,312,800.[5] In Denver, the property tax is assessed on 29 percent of the total value, meaning that Mile High Stadium represents a property tax base of $15,089,309. Reliable historical and subsequent valuations of the stadium were not available, so the current valuation was depreciated and appreciated at an annual rate of 6 percent to get the figures shown in Table 5.1.[6]

Several trends are worth noting. Mile High Stadium did not receive a direct municipal outlay any time during the 1980s. The foregone property taxes, however, are so great that they exceed the income generated in every year in the survey, leaving the stadium with an implicit cash outflow. Because the implicit

---

3. Private conversation with Pat Galvin of Mile High Stadium management, February 1985.
4. City and County of Denver, Auditor's Office, *Auditor's Annual Report for the City and County of Denver* for years 1968, 1969, 1970, 1971, 1972, 1973, 1974, 1975, 1976, 1977, 1978, 1979, 1980, 1981, 1982, 1983, 1984, 1985, 1986, 1987, 1988, 1989.
5. Private conversation with Linda Wendt of the commercial property division of the Denver Assessor's Office on 3 June 1987.
6. City and County of Denver, Auditor's Office, *Auditor's Annual Report for the City and County of Denver* for the years 1968, 1969, 1970, 1971, 1972, 1973, 1974, 1975, 1976, 1977, 1978, 1979, 1980, 1981, 1982, 1983, 1984, 1985, 1986, 1987, 1988, 1989. Private conversation with Mike Flaherty of Mile High Stadium, 23 June 1987.

cost of the foregone property taxes has been increasing due to increases in the estimated property value of the stadium, the total subsidy has been growing in recent years. This, in spite of the fact that the stadium explicitly has been self-sufficient.

Tax receipts generated by Mile High Stadium come from two sources. The first, an employee tax of $4 per employee every month does not generate significant revenues because stadium staff is relatively small.[7] Even if the Bronco's payroll is included in the tax computation, the sum would total less than $5,000 a year and not contribute much to the revenues shown in Table 5.2.

The major source of tax revenues comes from a 10 percent tax imposed upon admissions to three city-owned facilities, including Mile High Stadium. Through 1984, any excess revenues generated from the admissions tax were turned over to the Budget Management Office and included in the general fund. After 1984, any surplus generated by a facility was allocated to a fund for the other participating facilities.[8]

Specific admissions tax revenues were not available from either stadium or Denver officials. It was learned that the stadium's admissions tax revenues exceeded the costs of operating the stadium and the debt service, for the years 1983, 1984, and 1985, the only years for which data were available. This means that the stadium subsidized the general fund in the first two years and the operation of the other two facilities in 1985.

In order to estimate the size of the admissions tax revenues, it was necessary to make several assumptions. It was assumed that the stadium was sold out for eight football games each season. From 1968 to 1976 it was assumed the capacity was 50,000, while the capacity in the later years was 75,000 per game. The price of the tickets was assumed to be $5 in 1968 and increased at a rate of 9 percent per year. Under this assumption a 1985 ticket to a Bronco game would cost $21.64 and gives results that match closely the size of the surplus in 1983 to 1985.

Table 5.2 summarizes the estimated tax revenues from admissions to Mile High Stadium. The third column combines the tax revenues with the direct and indirect municipal outlays from Table 5.1 to get the net subsidy or receipts. The last column in Table 5.2 discounts the figure in the third column back to 1968.

The results of Table 5.2 indicate the City and County of Denver have subsidized the Broncos equal to a one time 1968 subsidy of about $2,000,000.

Two issues should be addressed regarding this estimate. First, the subsidy is relatively small because there were no municipal expenditures for acquisition of the facility.

Second, since the prime source of the municipal subsidy comes from the foregone property taxes, the size of the subsidy is very sensitive to the assumptions made in determining the historical property values. For example, if property values were depreciated at 10 percent from the 1987 figure instead of the

---

7.   The stadium's staff is six full-time employees from April to September and fifteen the remainder of the year. Information derived from private conversation with Mike Flaherty, 23 June 1987.

8.   Private conversation with Mike Flaherty, 23 June 1987.

6 percent utilized in these calculations, the property value of the stadium declines sufficiently so that the foregone property taxes are so small that the net accumulate value becomes a positive $133,523.

Table 5.1
Denver Mile High Stadium
Direct and Indirect Outlays
(1968–1989)

Year	Direct Municipal Revenue (Outlay)	Property Tax Rate	Property Tax Valuation	Foregone Property Taxes	Direct & Indirect Outlays
1968	$0	0.07164	$4,987,213	($357,284)	($357,284)
1969	$296,064	0.07374	$5,286,446	($389,823)	($93,759)
1970	($251,705)	0.07419	$5,603,632	($415,733)	($667,438)
1971	($59,417)	0.0808	$5,939,850	($479,940)	($539,357)
1972	$403,195	0.08409	$6,296,241	($529,451)	($126,256)
1973	($132,445)	0.080211	$6,674,016	($535,329)	($667,774)
1974	($311,714)	0.073301	$7,074,457	($518,565)	($830,279)
1975	$573,674	0.079336	$7,498,924	($594,935)	($21,261)
1976	n/a	0.080813	$7,948,860	($642,371)	($642,371)
1977	($586,800)	0.080753	$8,425,791	($680,408)	($1,267,208)
1978	n/a	0.082409	$8,931,339	($736,023)	($736,023)
1979	$858	0.082287	$9,467,219	($779,029)	($778,171)
1980	($2,609,000)	0.081336	$10,035,252	($816,227)	($3,425,227)
1981	$0	0.084076	$10,637,367	($894,347)	($894,347)
1982	$0	0.084661	$11,275,609	($954,604)	($954,604)
1983	$0	0.089261	$11,952,146	($1,066,861)	($1,066,861)
1984	$0	0.089879	$12,669,275	($1,138,702)	($1,138,702)
1985	$0	0.094579	$13,429,431	($1,270,142)	($1,270,142)
1986	$0	0.096019	$14,235,197	($1,366,849)	($1,366,849)
1987	$0	0.049745	$15,089,309	($750,618)	($750,618)
1988	$0	0.058947	$15,994,668	($942,838)	($942,838)
1989	$0	0.067375	$16,954,348	($1,142,299)	($1,142,299)

Table 5.2
Denver Mile High Stadium
Accumulated Net Present Value of Stadium Investment
(1968–1989)

Year	Municipal Tax Rev. From Stadium	Total Profit (Subsidy)	Net Accumulated Value
1968	$200,000	($157,284)	($157,284)
1969	$218,000	$124,241	$117,098
1970	$237,620	($429,818)	($380,309)
1971	$259,006	($280,351)	($233,138)
1972	$282,316	$156,060	$121,766
1973	$307,725	($360,050)	($264,155)
1974	$335,420	($494,859)	($340,100)
1975	$365,608	$344,347	$222,465
1976	$398,513	($243,859)	($148,124)
1977	$651,568	($615,640)	($351,656)
1978	$710,209	($25,814)	($13,868)
1979	$755,200	($22,971)	($11,610)
1980	$628,100	($2,797,127)	($1,330,156)
1981	$919,741	$25,394	$11,468
1982	$1,002,518	$47,914	$20,581
1983	$1,092,745	$25,884	$10,592
1984	$1,191,092	$52,390	$20,456
1985	$1,298,290	$28,148	$10,504
1986	$1,415,136	$48,287	$17,248
1987	$1,542,498	$791,881	$249,824
1988	$1,681,323	$738,486	$222,581
1989	$1,832,642	$690,343	$195,187

Accumulated Net Present Value... ($2,010,631)

Chapter 6

Dodger Stadium

HISTORY

When the Dodgers vacated Brooklyn after a bitter row with New York's city fathers, it ended a more-than-a-century-long relationship between Brooklyn and professional baseball. The first enclosed ball park, Union Grounds, was constructed in Brooklyn in 1862 and made Brooklyn a favored site for many ball games, even if they did not include New York teams. In 1890, three major league franchises called Brooklyn home.

Ironically, the original grandeur of the Dodgers' old home, Ebbet's Field, planted the seeds of the Dodgers' relocation to Los Angeles, California. To pay for cost overruns in the construction of Ebbet's Field in 1913, Charles Ebbet gave half ownership of the team to the construction company. This action led to an ownership that was divided four ways by the 1940s. Half of the team was owned by a syndicate made up of Walter O'Malley, Branch Rickey, and John Smith. O'Malley served as team legal counsel, Rickey was the team president, and Smith, who was president of the Phizer Chemical Company, served as a silent partner.

Friction between O'Malley and Rickey soon became apparent. Rickey, a long-time baseball executive, liked to use his influence in baseball to implement his traditional values, as long as those values did not interfere excessively with the team's performance or profits. Rickey left the St. Louis Cardinals in part because of his opposition to a brewery's sponsorship of Cardinals' broadcasts. Rickey's role in breaking baseball's color barrier is further evidence of his use of baseball to pursue his social agenda.

O'Malley had no baseball experience prior to his position with the Dodgers. To O'Malley, baseball was entertainment, and he clashed with Rickey on the team's expenditures for farm teams and their spring training facility in Vero Beach. By 1950, the split became disruptive, and Rickey sold his portion of the team to O'Malley.

With his control of the team solidified, O'Malley could concentrate on operating the team and increasing its attendance. O'Malley felt that the aged Ebbet's Field was limiting attendance. The 1953 World Series supported O'Malley's position. In the three games played at Yankee Stadium, attendance totaled 198,520, yielding receipts of $1,141,098.10, while three games at Ebbet's Field drew almost 90,000 fewer fans and grossed more than $500,000 less.[1]

O'Malley felt that the East Coast weather adversely affected attendance, and he requested Buckminster Fuller, then a faculty member at Princeton University, to study the feasibility of his geodesic dome to cover a ball park in Brooklyn. In spring 1956, almost a decade before the Astrodome opened in Houston, Texas, a graduate student at Princeton concluded, at a master's thesis defense, that such a project would be feasible. A member of the thesis committee was O'Malley.[2]

All this planning came to nothing when O'Malley was not able to get the land he wanted on the corner of Atlantic and Flatbush avenues "for a reasonable price." O'Malley believed the city had the authority to use its right of eminent domain to condemn the land through Title I of the Federal Housing Act of 1949. The law was written to alleviate urban blight by providing local agencies funds to buy land for public housing projects or to sell to a private developer whose construction would conform to a larger "public purpose." O'Malley wanted the city to use Title I to buy land for a stadium and sell it to the Dodgers.

O'Malley's protagonist was Robert Moses, the city's master builder for several decades and administrator of Title I authority. On 10 August 1955, O'Malley sent Moses a letter requesting that the city use its Title I powers to condemn certain sites at the corner of Flatbush and Atlantic avenues. O'Malley waited only five days to get Moses' response: "I can only repeat what we have told you verbally and in writing, namely, that a new ball field for the Dodgers cannot be dressed up as a Title I project." Moses continued, "If you need only three and a half acres of land, if it is indeed distressed property, if you have a million dollars in the bank, if you have railroad easements, if you really want to stay in Brooklyn, why don't you buy the property at a private sale?"[3]

The Dodgers did appear to be poor candidates for municipal largess. As the chart below illustrates, the team had been profitable and had attendance of more than one million fans for the years 1952 to 1956.[4] Those years with asterisks include attendance and revenues from World Series games.

1. Neil J. Sullivan, *The Dodgers Move West* (New York: Oxford University Press, 1987), 70.
2. "A Geodesic Dome for Brooklyn Dodgers," *Progressive Architecture* 36 (November 1955): 95.
3. Sullivan, *Dodgers Move West*, 48 and 56.
4. Ibid., 69.

Year	Attendance	Net Income
1952*	1,088,704	$446,102
1953*	1,163,419	$290,006
1954	1,020,531	$209,979
1955*	1,033,589	$427,195
1956*	1,213,562	$487,462

O'Malley wanted to buy the property in one parcel from the city to avoid the possibility of an individual owner "extorting" a higher price from the Dodgers when the buyer and the purpose of the land purchase were made public. O'Malley's concerns were not without foundation. The source of the Ebbet's Field cost overruns was the higher price Ebbet paid for land when it became public Ebbet was the buyer.[5]

In Robert Moses, O'Malley found an immovable object. Moses had planned a housing project for the Flatbush-Atlantic site. Over the years of awarding construction contracts, Moses had acquired a political power base that he used to thwart plans to build a private stadium on the location or to do it through a proposed government sports authority.

O'Malley, however, was not about to give up without a fight. The day after Moses responded to his written request, O'Malley announced that the Dodgers would play seven of their 1956 home games in Jersey City, New Jersey. The not-so-subtle threat did little to thaw Moses' attitude toward O'Malley. In January 1957, citing that Ebbet's Field was sold and could be used for no more than three more seasons, O'Malley gave the city six months to do something to keep the Dodgers in Brooklyn.

To fortify his remarks, the Dodgers raised the ante in February 1957 by trading their minor league franchise in Fort Worth to the Cubs for the Cubs' minor league team and ball park, Wrigley Field, in Los Angeles. The announcement that the Dodgers had acquired a minor league team in the Los Angeles region generated a reaction in New York. Nelson Rockefeller, two years from his run for governor of New York, offered to buy land and build the stadium under certain conditions. Neither O'Malley nor New York found the conditions agreeable. New York City's Corporate Counsel ruled that the disputed land could qualify for Title I treatment if the New York Board of Estimate would declare the land as substandard and unsanitary.[6] At the next meeting of the Board of Estimate, however, Moses used his political strength to defeat the proposal.

In contrast to New York, Los Angeles aggressively courted the Dodgers. O'Malley described the Los Angeles representatives as "The first group of people that came up and showed that they had a little old-fashion American initiative and what not were the people from Los Angeles, and they showed that they had political unanimity out there, the Republicans and the Democrats, and the publishers of the papers, and they said, 'We are for you, and when you tell us

5.   Peter Golenbaock, *Bums* (New York: Putnam, 1984), 19.
6.   Sullivan, *Dodgers Move West*, 134.

you don't want us to build you a ball park, that is most refreshing and amazing."[7]

Ironically Los Angeles used Title I, the measure that Moses refused to invoke in Brooklyn, to make land available for the Dodgers in Los Angeles. In 1951, the Los Angeles City Council, with support from Mayor Fletcher Bowron, unanimously approved a program giving eleven sites, including Chavez Ravine, to the National Housing Authority (NHA).

The Chavez Ravine project was to be the jewel of the program, but with the Red scare of the early 1950s federal housing projects fell into disfavor.[8] In 1953, Norris Poulson defeated Bowron using an antihousing platform. Under an agreement Poulson negotiated with the NHA, projects that were under construction would be completed, but projects not started would be canceled. These parcels would be sold to private contractors who would develop the area for the ubiquitous "public purpose." Thus, the very act used to thwart the Dodgers' plans in Brooklyn was used to accommodate the Dodgers in Los Angeles.

It is not clear what O'Malley wanted from Los Angeles. Kenneth Hahn, a city council member who made one of the initial contacts with O'Malley, recalls O'Malley's rejection of the offer of a municipal stadium.[9] Poulson remembers that in their first meeting, O'Malley wanted the city to build the stadium.[10] The mayor argued that a municipal stadium would not be feasible and suggested that the franchise purchase Chavez Ravine for a modest sum and build their own stadium. When this was proposed Poulson remembers O'Malley "hit the ceiling." According to Poulson, O'Malley responded, "I already have one ball park there, what am I going to do with two?"[11] This response planted the seed for the final deal that called for the Dodgers to trade Wrigley Field for the land in Chavez Ravine. Once the idea of a land swap was agreed upon, the issue became "how much land?" Harold McClellan, the city's negotiator, recollects that O'Malley originally wanted 600 acres in Chavez Ravine, instead of the 200 acres they ultimately received.[12] Far from the unanimity O'Malley said he saw in Los Angeles, many questioned if a home for a major league baseball team would serve the "public purpose." Another concern was whether the city was receiving full value for Chavez Ravine.

The difference between the behavior of the executives in New York and Los Angeles could not have been greater. New York's mayor Wagner delegated all authority he had to Moses, while Poulson aggressively lobbied for the deal he negotiated with the Dodgers. As the 1 October National League deadline for the

7. Ibid., 127.
8. Thomas Hines, "Housing, Baseball, and Creeping Socialism: The Battle of Chavez Ravine, Los Angeles, 1949–1959," *Journal of Urban History* 8, no. 2 (February 1982): 123–143.
9. Sullivan, *Dodgers Move West*, 96.
10. Norris Poulson, *Memoirs*, Department of Special Collections, Research Library, University of California, Los Angeles, 200.
11. Ibid., 201.
12. Sullivan, *Dodgers Move West*, 100.

Dodgers to announce their move neared, Poulson chided opponents of the deal as retarding progress. When the 30 September city council debate stretched beyond midnight, Poulson wired O'Malley to assure him that Poulson had the necessary ten votes to pass the resolution, even though there was no such accord.[13]

The debate did not end with the Dodgers' announcement to relocate. Less than two months after the Dodgers disclosed they would move to California, a petition challenging the validity of the contract had gained enough signatures to place the issue on the June 1958 ballot as a referendum. The referendum process, instituted during the California progressive movement, caught O'Malley, son of a New York City public official, off guard. O'Malley candidly admitted later, "I was completely unaware of the thing they call a referendum because they never had that in New York. Very few places have it. They have initiatives and referendums out there. Very peculiar. No boss."[14]

The referendum, entitled Proposition B, asked voters to vote "yes" if they favored the arrangement with the Dodgers and "no" if they wanted to see the deal renegotiated. The outspoken critic of the proposition was John Smith, the owner of the San Diego Padres, a Pacific Coast League franchise. Smith correctly viewed the Dodgers' arrival to Los Angeles as an economic threat to his team.

Polls at the start of the campaign showed the proposition received the support of 70 percent of the voters. As the vote neared, however, it appeared the issue would be defeated. At this point Warren Giles, National League president, entered the campaign, claiming that a-no-vote would prompt him to recommend relocating the franchise to another city. The June 1958 vote supported the land swap but only narrowly. Of the 666,577 votes cast, the "yes" votes out numbered the "no" votes by 24,293.

The Dodgers' trials did not end with the passage of Proposition B. A taxpayer suit claiming that a privately owned baseball stadium did not meet the "larger public purpose" qualifications for the land at Chavez Ravine followed.[15] The complaint was upheld in Los Angeles Superior Court, but this decision was overturned in the California Supreme Court.

CONSTRUCTION COSTS

Dodger Stadium marked the close of an era. It is the last stadium built with private funds that did not receive a property tax abatement. This does not mean, however, that the stadium was built without some minimal financial assistance from local governments.

Critics argue that the city, by receiving the downtown Wrigley Field, did not receive full value for the 200 acres of land. More concretely, the City of Los Angeles spent $2 million on grading, and Los Angeles County Public Works

---

13. Ibid., 132.
14. Ibid., 138.
15. Ibid., 162.

spent $2.7 million to build twenty-seven lanes of roads leading to the stadium site.[16]

The Dodgers spent approximately $18 million to build the stadium.[17] In that these were private funds, they are not included here as part of a civic subsidy.

SUBSIDY ANALYSIS

While the magnitude of the municipal financial commitment is small compared to those made by other cities, the civic involvement in Dodger Stadium was (and still is) a controversial arrangement. The Dodgers are reported to be the most financially successful franchise in professional sports. Since it is sometimes alleged that the Dodgers achieved their success, in part, because they were the recipients of a "give away," it is instructive to see the results of the limited investment Los Angeles made in the Dodgers.

Since the stadium is privately operated, operating expenses and revenues are not relevant to our study. Municipal agencies, on the other hand, receive tax revenues of several types from the operation of the facility. By far, the largest source of municipal revenues comes in the form of property taxes on the privately owned stadium. Table 6.1 lists the property tax revenues the Dodgers have paid on the land and improvements. Table 6.1 also shows that the Dodgers pay a business tax to Los Angeles City and, since 1990, a parking occupancy tax.[18] The negative entry of $4.7 million in 1958 represents the infrastructure expenditures made by the city and county of Los Angeles.

The data in Table 6.1 represent cash inflows the city and county would have foregone if the property was used as a federal housing project, as originally planned. The pact that brought the Dodgers to Los Angeles has an accumulated net presented value of almost $8 million through 1991 and grows every year. Financially, the deal between the Dodgers and Los Angeles seems to have benefited both parties.

---

16. "Job Site Casting," *Engineering News Record* 168 (5 April 1962): 32.
17. Private correspondence from Robert V. Graziano, vice president of finance for the Los Angeles Dodgers, dated 23 October 1992.
18. Data for Table 6.1 came from private correspondence with Robert V. Graziano, vice president of finance for the Los Angeles Dodgers, 23 October 1992.

Table 6.1
Los Angeles Dodger Stadium
Net Municipal (Outlays) or Receipts
(1958–1991)

Year	Direct & Indirect City Subsidy	Property Taxes	Los Angeles City Business Tax	Parking Occupancy Tax	Net Gain (Loss)	PV of π or (Subsidy)
1958	($4,224,144)	nil	nil	n/a	($4,224,144)	($4,224,144)
1959	$0	nil	nil	n/a	$0	$0
1960	$0	nil	nil	n/a	$0	$0
1961	$0	$146,580	nil	n/a	$146,580	$134,063
1962	$0	$444,935	nil	n/a	$444,935	$394,629
1963	$0	$705,195	$509	n/a	$705,704	$606,682
1964	$0	$748,045	$11,699	n/a	$759,744	$629,643
1965	$0	$755,350	$11,005	n/a	$766,355	$612,948
1966	$0	$755,530	$12,915	n/a	$768,445	$592,446
1967	$0	$756,835	$23,518	n/a	$780,353	$579,224
1968	$0	$664,385	$18,113	n/a	$682,498	$487,139
1969	$0	$711,360	$17,326	n/a	$728,686	$499,641
1970	$0	$795,900	$18,600	n/a	$814,500	$537,774
1971	$0	$846,315	$29,160	n/a	$875,475	$556,279
1972	$0	$829,755	$35,004	n/a	$864,759	$528,485
1973	$0	$831,890	$32,286	n/a	$864,176	$507,665
1974	$0	$913,315	$35,146	n/a	$948,461	$535,280
1975	$0	$926,050	$43,001	n/a	$969,051	$528,559
1976	$0	$897,316	$41,700	n/a	$939,016	$495,095
1977	$0	$1,083,672	$46,148	n/a	$1,129,820	$575,940
1978	$0	$378,042	$59,426	n/a	$437,468	$215,651
1979	$0	$395,355	$73,070	n/a	$468,425	$223,340
1980	$0	$402,919	$67,764	n/a	$470,683	$217,099
1981	$0	$402,163	$80,110	n/a	$482,273	$215,234
1982	$0	$408,483	$90,244	n/a	$498,727	$215,404
1983	$0	$496,822	$111,948	n/a	$608,770	$254,508
1984	$0	$519,100	$146,450	n/a	$665,550	$267,361
1985	$0	$531,052	$124,710	n/a	$655,762	$253,026
1986	$0	$540,984	$114,237	n/a	$655,221	$242,740
1987	$0	$553,159	$119,681	n/a	$672,840	$239,239
1988	$0	$560,873	$114,133	n/a	$675,006	$230,265
1989	$0	$575,687	$133,884	n/a	$709,571	$232,140
1990	$0	$503,010	$150,434	$91,000	$744,444	$233,481
1991	$0	$556,498	$164,747	$528,903	$1,250,148	$375,734

Accumulated Net Present Value..............$7,992,568

Chapter 7
Robert F. Kennedy Stadium

HISTORY

When the District of Columbia Stadium opened in 1962, it ended a five-year soap opera that involved Calvin Griffith, owner of the original Washington Senators baseball franchise; American League owners; the owner of the Washington Redskins, George Marshall; and, literally, several acts of Congress.

Griffith threatened to move the team as early as 1957. The talk of relocation was taken so seriously that a minority owner introduced four resolutions at the team's 1958 stockholders' meetings, calling for Griffith to renounce any relocation plans because the speculation was hurting attendance.[1] The resolutions were defeated, and in July 1958, Griffith approached the American League owners to request permission to move. The request came at a time when Congress was considering a bill to extend a blanket antitrust exemption to all major league sports, including baseball. Given this setting, the American League owners were not in the mood to risk the ire of Congress, and they denied Griffith's application.[2] The league owners went so far as to suggest that Griffith sell the team.[3]

During all of this, plans went forward for a new stadium to be constructed with federal funds. The enabling legislation called for a $6 million stadium, including the cost of the land. When the bids were received in 1958, the cost was estimated to be between $7.5 and $8.6 million, without the purchase of the

---

1. "Murphy's Resolution Defeated and Annual Meeting Is Tranquil," *Washington Post*, 1 February 1958.
2. "League Tells Griffith to Stay in D. C.," *Washington Post*, 8 July 1958.
3. "Minneapolis No Sure Gold Mine as Big League Town," *Washington Post*, 24 August 1958.

land.[4] To keep the cost of the stadium close to the original proposed cost, Congress passed legislation that allowed the National Armory Board, the owner and operator of the stadium, to lease for $100 a year, rather than buy, the land from the Interior Department, the owner of the stadium site.[5]

The first proposal called for construction to begin only after there was agreement from two major league tenants, the Senators and the Redskins. This condition was revised in light of Griffith's indifference to the stadium. An agreement by the Redskins and the expectation of other events at the stadium was considered enough to make the project solvent. Marshall agreed to tentative terms of a lease, calling for him to pay 10 percent of his after-tax revenues to use the new stadium. Marshall would keep the souvenir revenues, and the Armory Board would retain the income from food and parking.

All seemed well. Morris Cafritz, a member of the special stadium advisory stadium board said, "With the Redskins, we're optimistic about the entire project. The stadium will pay for itself and be a great help to the community at large."[6] Marshall said he thought the stadium would be so successful that he would like to operate the facility.[7]

Since Congress authorized only $6 million in bonds for the construction of the stadium, additional action was necessary to make up the difference of up to $2.4 million before construction could begin. The legislation that passed to do this obligated the District of Columbia to pay any shortfall between the stadium's income and the interest payments due on the bonds.[8] Stadium advisory board chairman Edward F. Carr declared there was little risk of the District of Columbia having to make good on this issue.[9] In July 1958, President Dwight D. Eisenhower signed the bill removing the $6 million cap on the Armory Board's expenditures.

All of this did little to impress Griffith, who refused to take his earlier rebuke by the American League owners for an answer and continued to negotiate with officials in Minneapolis. On 29 August 1958, Griffith received a lease from Minneapolis that promised the Senators a newly expanded stadium, low rent, and a guaranteed attendance of one million paid admissions for the first three years.[10] Griffith gave such strong assurances that he would move to

---

4. "Armory Board Reveals Stadium Plan for D. C.," *Washington Post*, 23 April 1958.
5. "Stadium Land Leased to Armory Board," *Washington Post*, 13 December 1958.
6. Ibid.
7. "George Marshall Sure of Stadium Success," *Washington Post*, 18 July 1958.
8. "Armory Board Reveals Stadium Plan for D. C." *Washington Post*, 23 April 1958.
9. Ibid.
10. "Griffith Delay Stuns Officials," *Washington Post*, 9 September 1958.

Minneapolis that the city's Board of Estimate approved a $9 million bond issue to expand the city's stadium in preparation for the move.[11]

Griffith again overestimated his persuasive powers among his American League peers. When the American League owners, once more facing pressure from Congress and two law suits from minority Senator stockholders, forced Griffith to announce that he would remain in Washington unless there were "serious stadium problems or other economic difficulties of a serious nature," Minneapolis withdrew the lease and the bond approval.[12]

It is interesting that Griffith should bring up the stadium and economic issues. The Senators enjoyed twenty-five consecutive seasons with a profit. While this was in part because there was no mortgage on their stadium and the Senators held little, if any, debt, it was a claim no other franchise in Major League Baseball could make. Griffith continued to show indifference to a new stadium, saying he was not eager to move into the proposed District of Columbia Stadium since this would mean he would have to pay rent and share concessions.

Apparently Griffith's search for a new city involved his stereotypical view of blacks which led him to believe that his team would not prosper in Washington with its largely black population. In a 1 October 1978 speech to the Lions' Club of Waseca, Minnesota, Griffith explained that the small black population in Minneapolis was the attraction for him: "I'll tell you why we moved the team to Minnesota: It's when I found out you only had 15,000 blacks here. Black people don't go to ball games, but they'll fill up a rasslin' ring and put up such a chant, it'll scare you to death . . . you've got good hard working white people here."[13] Further evidence showed that economics was not a cause of the Senators' move to Minneapolis. The Senators moved to Minneapolis to become the Twins following the 1960 season. In 1960, the Senators drew more fans than they had in eleven years.

The early enthusiasm that George Marshall felt toward the stadium project cooled when the Armory Board attempted to change the terms of the original lease agreement in early 1959. The Armory Board now wanted Marshall to pay the same rent he was paying Griffith to use Griffith Stadium: 15 percent of the live gate below $400,000 a year and 10 percent of ticket sales over $400,000. Griffith also kept all concession revenues. The chairman of the stadium advisory board, George Shea, reasoned, "I don't think we can justify a lesser payment for the Redskins in a new stadium." Marshall looked at the new terms as a reneging of the original agreement but offered the compromise of 15 percent of the first $200,000 in live gate. The Armory Board rejected this compromise. The friction created such bad feelings between Marshall and the Armory Board that the Redskins did not play in the new stadium for five years after it was completed. Thus, by the fall of 1960, a stadium that was not to be started

11. "Minneapolis Board OK's Plan," *Washington Post*, 3 September 1958.
12. "Griffith Will Not Seek Shift," *Washington Post*, 8 September 1958.
13. Mike Downey, "He Was Wrong, He Knows It, and He Should Admit It," *Los Angeles Times*, 8 April 1987.

without commitments from two major league tenants was half built and had no major league tenant.

This was not an issue for long. No franchise received as quick a reincarnation as the Washington Senators. Facing an angry Congress for allowing the Senators to move to Minneapolis, the American League announced its first expansion beginning with the 1961 season. Washington, D. C., found itself the recipient of one of the franchises. The new stadium had a year before completion, so the new Washington Senators played its first season in the stadium that the old franchise had abandoned.

The franchise's lease in District of Columbia Stadium was for ten years—a stormy decade. The second Senators fared no better professionally than their predecessors and performed worse financially. By 1969, Robert Short purchased the team. Short tolerated the existing lease, although the team was not always able to make the lease payments. The lease called for the Senators to pay the greater of $65,000 a year or 7 percent of ticket revenues, 13 percent of all food concessions, and all parking revenues generated at Senators' games. When the lease was up for renewal, Short asked for better terms.

Short proposed that the Senators use the stadium rent free for the first million patrons every year and that the Armory Board keep all receipts after one million fans. In addition, Short wanted the Senators to receive all revenues from the sale of concession items during baseball games and receive all parking and advertising revenues generated during the Senators' games. Short also asked that the back rent be forgiven.[14]

The Armory Board responded that they were forbidden by law to enter into a contract that might cause them to lose money. The board saw that possibility with Short's offer. They countered instead by offering Short the stadium rent free for the first million fans if Short would assume the operating expenses for which the board was responsible under the old lease. The Senators would keep the revenues from food and beverage concessions at baseball games and a prorated amount of advertising revenues. The Armory Board would not surrender the parking revenues generated at the baseball games, nor would the Armory Board forgive the back rent, although they offered to hold a three-year interest bearing note for the back rent.

When Short and the board could not come to an agreement on terms, the Senators left Washington for Arlington, Texas, and became the Texas Rangers. This prompted a congressional investigation into the operation of the stadium. During those hearings, Short complained not only about the Armory Board's difficult attitude but the location of the facility. Short claimed the stadium was

14. U.S. Senate Committee on the District of Columbia, *Future Use and Financing of RFK Stadium*, 92nd Cong., 1st sess., 1971, 27. All references to the negotiations between Short and the Armory Board are from this source, which continues on to page 28.

located in an area perceived as dangerous by fans. During the 1968 Washington riots, the Senators played several "night" games during the day.[15]

Bill Veeck, who offered to buy the Senators from Short before they moved, disagreed with Short's perception of the stadium's surroundings.[16] But Veeck went on to say that he felt the design of the stadium was one reason baseball found it difficult to survive in Washington. Veeck saw the design of the parking lots, where patrons would park their cars near the surrounding neighborhood and walk through a parklike area, as backwards.[17] Veeck also commented that the concession stands were poorly planned and were not optimally located. Veeck recalled that the concession stands were omitted in the architect's drawings and were added later as an afterthought.[18]

Feelings were running so strongly against the Armory Board that a bill was introduced that transferred control of the stadium to the secretary of the interior.[19] The bill was defeated, but the Armory Board lost more supporters in the mid 1970s when it failed to secure a contract with the San Diego Padres, who were looking for a new home before Ray Kroc's purchase of the team. Many considered that a National League franchise, which would bring different teams and players to the nation's capital than the American League Orioles did in neighboring Baltimore, might be the answer to the failing popularity of baseball in Washington.

The relocation of the Padres never occurred because the differences between the Armory Board and the team proved too big for compromise. The team wanted to pay 10 cents for every ticket up to 1,000,000, while the Armory Board wanted a minimum rent of $1,200 per game. The Armory Board suggested the team keep 15 percent of all food concession revenues, while the Padres wanted to retain all such revenues. The Padres wanted up to $142,000 a season in parking revenues, but the Armory Board was not willing share any of these revenues. Both sides wanted 100 percent of the advertising revenues, and neither side wanted responsibility of utility bills.

The bungled negotiations brought another fire storm of protest on Capitol Hill. Robert Sigholtz, manager of the Armory Board, received strong criticism for the Board's risk aversion. Several congressmen suggested that the Board would have to be more flexible to attract a team, given the city's record of indifference towards baseball. Congressman Bernice Sisk, of California, was most vocal:

If we here aren't willing to take risk, then we are not going to get somebody else to. This is the very point I am making. I would hope that you wouldn't in every case assume the worst possible situation. If in fact they can only pull 500,000 or

15. Lowell Reidenbaugh, *Take Me Out to the Ball Park* (St. Louis: The Sporting News, 1983), 286.
16. Senate Committee on the District of Columbia, *Future Use and Financing of RFK Stadium*, 122.
17. Ibid., 116.
18. Ibid.
19. Ibid., 11–15.

750,000 [in annual attendance], then nobody wants a team here and I don't think we should have one.[20]

The prospects for a baseball franchise in RFK Stadium, as it was called after the 1968 assassination of the New York Senator, have not improved. The city made it to the "short list" of candidates for the 1993 National League expansion team, but that proposal called for building a new facility. Even with this incentive, Washington lost out to Denver and Miami.

The days of RFK Stadium as the home of the Redskins may also be numbered. In July 1992, the Redskins announced an agreement with the State of Virginia to build a new stadium in northern Virginia. While that proposal was defeated by popular opposition to the plan, Redskins owner Jack Kent Cooke in late 1993 announced he will be constructing a stadium in Maryland if he can secure property tax concessions from the local authorities.

CONSTRUCTION COSTS

As reported above, the original construction cost estimate for District of Columbia Stadium was $6 million. In July 1958, the estimate increased to $7.5 to $8.6 million. By 1959, the estimate of construction costs had risen to $10 million, prompting Congress to agree to contribute $2.9 million for parking lots and related facilities.[21]

In spite of this aid, the Armory Board still found it necessary to sell $19.8 million in bonds for the new stadium.[22] The stadium eventually cost $18,756,946.37 to build.[23] Adding the $2.9 million Congress spent for parking, the figure is approximately $21.7 million, more than three times the original estimate and more than twice as much as the estimate just four years before.

Twelve years after the stadium opened, the Redskins received permission to build 1,605 seats in the stadium at a cost of $1.5 million.[24] This is not included in the public costs of construction even though the Armory Board used its funds to pay for the expansion. The Redskins agreed to pay the Armory Board for the cost and 8 percent interest on the loan of the funds.

---

20. House Select Committee on Professional Sports, *Inquiry into Professional Sports, Part I*, 96th Cong., 2d sess., 1976, 550.
21. "GAO Insists on Open Bidding for Stadium," *Washington Post*, 20 August 1959.
22. Senate Committee on the District of Columbia, *Future Use and Financing of RFK Stadium*, 1.
23. District of Columbia Armory Board, *Final Construction Report on District of Columbia Stadium* (Washington D.C., June 1963) 5.
24. House Committee on Professional Sports, *Inquiry into Professional Sports*, 537–538.

SUBSIDY ANALYSIS

RFK Stadium went through four distinct financial periods. In the first period (fiscal years 1962 to 1967), the stadium was used by the Senators. During the next period (1968 to 1972) the Senators and the Redskins cohabited the stadium. In the third period (1973 to 1979), the Senators had departed, leaving the Redskins as the major tenant, but construction bonds were still being serviced. In the final period (after 1979), the Redskins remained as the sole major tenant but without the debt burden. The District of Columbia and the federal government paid off the $19.8 million in principal and unpaid interest in equal shares.[25]

The District of Columbia National Armory Board has been most co-operative in this survey by providing all financial reports they had available. This permits a detailed review of the financial operation of RFK Stadium except for fiscal years 1965 to 1967. For these years financial records could not be found.

Table 7.1 shows the operating profits (losses) in the first period for which data were available.[26] The operating gains earned by the Armory Board were dwarfed by the debt service on the stadium, and the total losses averaged $472,719.28. The interest income line item refers to income the Armory Board received by investing bond revenues that exceeded the construction costs. The implication of Table 7.1 is that the Senators paid the cost they imposed upon the Armory Board for hosting the baseball games, but the stadium did not earn enough in rent to pay off the bond's debt service.

Table 7.2 reviews the income statements of RFK Stadium during the second financial period, when both the Redskins and the Senators occupied the stadium. The average operating profit during this period was $392,332.30, compared with the average profit during the first period which was $280,349.02. While there are not enough data points to determine conclusively if there is a statistical difference between these two periods, it seems safe to conclude that the Redskins contributed more than their costs to the Armory Board. The financial reports of 1970 to 1972 also belie the allegations that the Senators paid only the minimum rent of $65,000 a year.

The financial reports for the third period, the one in which the Redskins were the only tenant, but debt service was still due, is reviewed in Table 7.3. The first year, 1973, was a good, but misleading omen for future years. The operating profit for that year was the highest up to that time. When this is

25. District of Columbia Armory Board, *Annual Reports for the District of Columbia National Armory Board and the Robert F. Kennedy Stadium for the Fiscal Year Ending December 31, 1980*, footnote 2 to the financial statements.
26. *Annual Reports for the District of Columbia National Armory Board and the Robert F. Kennedy Stadium for the Fiscal Years* 1962, 1964, 1968, 1969, 1970, 1971, 1972, 1973, 1974, 1975, 1976, 1977, 1978, 1979, 1980, 1981, 1982, 1983, 1984, 1985, 1986, 1987, 1988, 1989, 1990.

combined with unusually high interest income, the stadium incurred the lowest loss for any year up to that point.

In the long-run, the stadium missed the Senators' contributions. While the average operating profit was $145,244.27 during the third period, three of the seven years showed an operating loss. The average operating profit for this period compares unfavorably with the period in which the Senators were tenants.

The argument that the Senators "paid their way" can be tested using the statistical test of the difference between two means[27]:

$$z = \frac{\mu_a - \mu_b}{\sqrt{\dfrac{s_a^2}{n_a} + \dfrac{s_b^2}{n_b}}}$$

Where:

•μ_a and μ_b represent the means of the period with the Senators ($344,339.47) and the period after the Senators left ($145,244.27), respectively.

•s_a and s_b represent the standard deviations of the two periods, $153,324.04 and $262,951, respectively.

•n_a and n_b represent the number of data points for each period, seven each.

The calculations give a z value of 2.19. The chance of this difference in the two means occurring randomly is less than 2 in 100. From this, it can be surmised that the Senators covered their operating costs while they used the stadium. The conclusion is stronger when one realizes the profits for the latter period (the one in which the Senators were not tenants) are enlarged by inflation.

There is virtually no statistical difference between the total losses of the two periods. This is understandable given that the facility's fixed costs made up more than 50 percent of the facility's costs.

Financial records for the fourth period, the years after the construction bonds were paid off, are summarized in Table 7.4. During this period, the stadium experienced a period of unprecedented financial success. The stadium operated with an average operating profit of $598,454. If the stadium operated this successfully during the previous two periods, the Armory Board would have been able to pay most of the debt service on the construction bonds. In 1983, the stadium's operating profit was so large it would have exceeded annual interest payments by more than $900,000. In 1984, the debt service would have been satisfied with over $400,000 to spare. It seems that when the Armory Board no longer had the subsidy of the federal government and the District of Columbia to pay the interest on the bonds, it began to operate the stadium with a more vigilant eye toward the bottom line.

---

27. Robert L. Brite, *Business Statistics* (Menlo Park, CA., Addison Wesley, 1980), 232.

This conclusion is challenged by an operating loss in 1982 of $219,952.65, the largest in the history of the stadium. This loss can be explained by the 1982 NFL players' strike, which took up almost half of the season. Rent, food, and parking concession revenues were less than half of what the previous year's income was from those items. The result of the strike was a decline in overall income that exceeded $900,000. Operating costs fell as well in 1982, but by only $400,000, meaning the operating profit in 1982 was almost $500,000 less in 1982 than in 1981. The comparison of the strike year, 1982, with the surrounding years is evidence that the Redskins play an important role in the financial health of RFK Stadium.

The construction cost of RFK Stadium on the Armory Board location did not cost the District of Columbia any foregone property taxes because the Interior Department previously owned the land: therefore, it did not generate property tax for the District.

Table 7.5 summarizes the total profit and loss data from Table 7.1 through Table 7.4. The estimate of the stadium's accumulated net present values is an understatement. The missing years 1963 and 1965 to 1967 was a period when the stadium was experiencing losses of around $400,000 to $500,000. These losses in turn would be discounted very little since it was at the beginning of the cash flows, creating a large impact on accumulated net present values.

Table 7.1
Robert F. Kennedy Stadium
Revenues and Expenses
(1962–1968)

	1962	1964	1968
Net Operating Income	$478,352.34	$637,322.64	$1,010,962.49
Operating Expenses	$303,452.69	$433,347.66	$548,790.06
Operating Profit (Loss)	$174,899.65	$203,974.98	$462,172.43
Interest Charges	$641,429.44	$871,579.25	$837,913.51
Interest Income	$77,256.45	$2,675.87	$11,784.97
Net Income Expense	$564,172.99	$868,903.38	$826,128.54
Total Profit (Loss)	($389,273.34)	($664,928.40)	($363,956.11)

Table 7.2
Robert F. Kennedy Stadium
Revenues and Expenses
(1969–1972)

	1969	1970	1971	1972
Operating Income	$1,023,891.46	$1,215,949.13	$1,299,849.26	$964,778.73
Operating Expenses	$602,962.56	$686,132.12	$856,385.71	$789,703.99
Operating Profits (Losses)	$420,928.90	$529,817.01	$443,508.55	$175,074.74
Interest Expenses	$838,425.87	$838,033.94	$845,022.39	$848,023.78
Interest Income	$14,108.51	$21,205.83	$18,950.96	$27,437.07
Net Interest Expenses	$824,317.36	$816,828.11	$826,071.43	$820,586.71
Total Profit (Losses)	($403,388.46)	($287,011.10)	($382,562.88)	($645,511.97)

Table 7.3
Robert F. Kennedy Stadium
Revenues and Expenses
(1973–1979)

	1973	1974	1975	1976
Operating Income	$1,633,245	$1,267,773	$1,348,230	$1,667,748
Operating Expenses	$1,025,423	$1,394,968	$1,237,784	$1,292,638
Operating Profit	$607,821	($127,195)	$110,446	$375,109
Interest Expenses	$850,986	$856,727	$855,989	$854,417
Interest Income	$41,577	$73,139	$78,431	$68,723
Net Interest Expenses	$809,409	$783,588	$777,557	$785,694
Total Profit (Loss)	($201,588)	($910,783)	($667,111)	($410,585)

	1977	1978	1979
Operating Income	$2,317,752	$2,104,739	$2,131,936
Operating Expenses	$2,180,847	$2,120,282	$2,202,769
Operating Profit	$136,905	($15,543)	($70,833)
Interest Expenses	$1,077,728	$873,696	$9,571
Interest Income	$89,457	$52,838	$39,740
Net Interest Expenses	$988,271	$820,858	($30,169)
Total Profit (Loss)	($851,366)	($836,401)	($40,644)

Table 7.4
Robert F. Kennedy Stadium
Revenues and Expenses
(1980-1990)

Year	Operating Revenues	Operating Expenses	Total Profit (Losses)
1980	$2,640,714	$2,666,734	($26,020)
1981	$2,631,692	$2,338,903	$292,789
1982	$1,723,992	$1,943,944	($219,952)
1983	$4,777,256	$2,992,548	$1,784,708
1984	$4,627,606	$3,361,167	$1,266,439
1985	$3,334,292	$2,841,534	$492,758
1986	$4,595,559	$3,447,865	$1,147,694
1987	$4,389,638	$3,375,344	$1,014,294
1988	$5,075,345	$5,063,395	$11,950
1989	$6,235,753	$5,942,085	$575,437
1990	$5,292,645	$5,354,208	$293,668

Table 7.5
Robert F. Kennedy Stadium
Present Value of Cash Flows
(1962–1990)

Year	Operating Profit	Net Interest Expense	Net Profit or (Subsidy)	PV of Profit or (Subsidy)
1962	$174,900	($564,173)	($389,273)	($389,273)
1963	data not available			
1964	$203,975	($868,903)	($664,928)	($616,184)
1965	data not available			
1966	data not available			
1967	data not available			
1968	$462,172	($826,129)	($363,956)	($282,062)
1969	$420,929	($824,317)	($403,388)	($298,615)
1970	$529,817	($816,828)	($287,011)	($203,156)
1971	$443,509	($826,071)	($382,563)	($258,807)
1972	$175,075	($820,587)	($645,512)	($417,178)
1973	$607,821	($809,409)	($201,588)	($124,401)
1974	($127,195)	($783,588)	($910,783)	($536,439)
1975	$110,446	($777,557)	($667,111)	($376,713)
1976	$375,109	($785,694)	($410,585)	($222,359)
1977	$136,905	($988,271)	($851,366)	($442,325)
1978	($15,543)	($820,858)	($836,401)	($417,009)
1979	($70,833)	($19,830,169)	($19,901,002)	($9,524,566)
1980	($26,020)	$11,047	($14,973)	($6,886)
1981	$292,769	$37,879	$330,648	$145,529
1982	($219,953)	$93,384	($126,569)	($53,311)
1983	$1,784,708	$136,771	$1,921,479	$774,468
1984	$1,266,439	$258,354	$1,524,793	$588,059
1985	$492,758	$251,991	$744,749	$274,807
1986	$1,147,694	$250,183	$1,397,877	$492,793
1987	$1,014,294	$270,390	$1,284,684	$432,599
1988	$11,950	$366,812	$378,762	$121,805
1989	$575,437	$467,776	$1,043,213	$320,332
1990	$293,668	$517,950	$811,618	$238,554

Accumulated Net Present Value ..... ($10,780,339)

Chapter 8
Anaheim Stadium

HISTORY

Anaheim Stadium is a clear example of a municipal facility constructed to help a city "make it to the big leagues." In the spring of 1963, Anaheim mayor Rex Coons led a group of about 100 civic leaders to Washington, D.C., to lobby for Anaheim's consideration for Standard Metropolitan Statistical Area (SMSA) status. Coons recalls:

Up to that time, all the statistical information for Orange County was lumped in with Los Angeles and Long Beach. We had the population, the industry, the educational facilities, everything you needed to qualify. I noticed that almost all the other SMSA areas had a professional sports team.

We were awarded the SMSA standing, and on the way back from Washington, it occurred to me that the Angels weren't happy at Dodger Stadium. I figured, "What the hell, we'll pitch for 'em."[1]

The Angels indeed were unhappy at Dodger Stadium. Angel owner Gene Autry was quoted as saying, "There wasn't anything I wouldn't do for Walter O'Malley, and there wasn't anything he wouldn't do for me. And that's how it was while I was at Dodger Stadium, we wouldn't do anything for each other."

The feelings between the two franchises began during the Angels' formative years. The Dodgers, still playing in the Los Angeles Coliseum, refused to surrender their exclusive rights to play Major League Baseball in that facility. This forced the Angels to play in Wrigley Field, the minor league park that the Dodgers traded to the city for the land on which Dodger Stadium was being built.

---

1. John Weyler, "20th Anniversary...The Big A," *Los Angeles Times*, 19 April 1986.

The Angels and Dodgers shared Dodger Stadium after it was completed, but the friction between the two franchises continued. The Angels chafed under the terms of the lease allowing them to use the stadium, and the Dodgers were upset that the Angels referred to Dodger Stadium as Chavez Ravine, bringing back memories of the bitter struggle the Dodgers braved while evicting squatters before the stadium's construction.

The disagreements were petty enough to spill over into window washing and toilet paper expenses. The lease agreement between the Angels and the Dodgers called for the Angels to pay for half of the toilet paper expenses, although three times as many fans attended Dodger games. The Angels also resented sharing the window washing costs since they were housed in a windowless basement.[2]

When Coons approached Autry, the Angels had just failed to negotiate a relocation to Long Beach, partly because the Angels refused to call themselves the Long Beach Angels. The name was not a major issue with Coons: "Podunk Angels would have been fine. All the stories would've been datelined Anaheim."[3]

Coons's pitch was a hit. In 1964, the Angels agreed to move to Anaheim if a major league facility could be ready by opening day 1966. Autry remembered that he was "excited about moving to Anaheim because we thought that Orange County and Riverside County would keep growing by leaps and bounds. But we were worried about racing the clock . . . because we'd burned our bridges behind us [at Dodger Stadium]."[4]

The plan was to have the facility constructed jointly by Orange County and the City of Anaheim. Autry's concern must have turned to terror when two weeks after the agreement with Autry, the Orange County Board of Supervisors decided to withdraw from the project. When the county backed out, the city decided to go it alone.

The dilemma that Walter O'Malley wanted to avoid by getting Robert Moses to secure the Brooklyn site for a new Dodger Stadium arose in Anaheim. An owner of 50 acres of the proposed 144-acre site demanded $35,000 an acre for his land.[5] He had been offered a total of $25,000 for the land, but when the announcement was made that the stadium would be built, the owner said his offers rose to $35,000 an acre.

The two-year deadline forced compromises from all parties. Anaheim bought the land based upon a letter from the Angels, and Del Webb's construction company began preliminary design and engineering work without a contract.[6] Much has been made of Webb's company beginning work on the project before a formal contract had been signed, but Bill Veeck suggested that the contract for

---

2. Lowell Reidenbaugh, *Take Me Out to the Ball Park* (St. Louis: The Sporting News, 1983), 8.
3. Ibid.
4. Ibid.
5. "Grower Demands Fair Price for Stadium Site," *Los Angeles Times*, 3 April 1964.
6. Weyler, "20th Anniversary."

Anaheim Stadium was the price Autry paid to receive Webb's support when the expansion franchises were awarded.[7]

Anaheim also believed it would be able to attract a professional football team also. The team named most often was the San Diego Chargers. Coons hints that authoritative contacts from the city had been "warmly received" by the owner of the Chargers, Baron Hilton.[8] The city manager at the time, Keith Murdoch, recalls:

The Chargers were almost a given. When we were building the stadium, Hilton had his general manager and some assistants came [sic] over and designed the Charger offices for the floor above the Angels. Then the people got concerned and built a stadium, and he stayed. But prior to that he often referred to Anaheim Stadium as his stadium.[9]

The Chargers did not move to Anaheim because they received a new stadium in San Diego [see Jack Murphy Stadium]. Anaheim Stadium's management has earned a reputation for keeping the facility busy.[10] The pursuit of a professional football team is evidence of this trait. Almost fifteen years after the Chargers declined to move to Anaheim, the Los Angeles Rams announced they would begin to play their home games in Anaheim beginning with the 1980 season.[11]

The coming of the Rams started a new era for the stadium. The stadium's original design had an open outfield, but this was enclosed in 1979 to oblige larger NFL crowds. Other improvements included a better sound and lighting system and luxury boxes.

Part of the contract that lured the Rams to Orange County will be unfulfilled. The Rams and Orange County planned to build a $200 million office complex on part of the parking lot surrounding the stadium. The Angels, who receive parking revenues earned during Angel games, felt strongly enough that the proposed office complex would reduce their earnings that they filed a $100 million law suit to halt the project.[12] While the Angels received no monetary compensation, they were able to block the building of the office complex.

The future of Anaheim Stadium became more uncertain in 1993. In that year, Angels owner Gene Autry expressed a willingness to sell the team, with no guarantee that the franchise would remain in Southern California. The Rams, after a series of disappointing seasons, have started to see a drop in their

---

7. Bill Veeck and Ed Linn, *Veeck as in Wreck* (New York: G. P. Putnam's Sons, 1962), 369.
8. "Angel Prospects Grow," *Los Angeles Times*, 7 April 1964.
9. Weyler, "20th Anniversary."
10. See, for example, Senate Committee on the District of Columbia, *Future Use and Financing of RFK Stadium*, 92nd Cong., 1st sess., 1971, 65–66.
11. Preston Cox, Gary W. Finger, Ronald L. Promboin, and James S. Vas Dias, *Financial Evaluation of Los Angeles Rams Football Company and the City of Anaheim Lease Agreements* (Sacramento, CA: SRI International, 1978), 1.
12. Weyler, "20th Anniversary."

attendance. Rumors have started that the Rams are considering a move to Baltimore, following that city's unsuccessful bid for an expansion NFL franchise in 1993.

CONSTRUCTION COSTS

The original construction cost of the stadium was $16 million for the structure and $4 million for the land.[13] The original configuration had a capacity of 43,250, although this was exceeded on special occasions such as the 1967 All-Star game.

The 1979 expansion cost $31 million ($29 million for the construction and $2 million for a new scoreboard).[14]

SUBSIDY ANALYSIS

Table 8.1 supports the argument that Anaheim Stadium is one of the most successful facilities of its kind. The aggressive nature of the stadium operations has earned the stadium an operating profit in every full year of its existence.[15] The primary tenants clearly are paying the operating expenses they impose upon the stadium managers.

The second column of Table 8.2 shows the municipal income generated by the stadium or, when the number is in parenthesis, the stadium subsidy received from the general fund.[16] The early transfers were predominantly from the general fund. After 1977, just before the Rams' arrival, the direction of the funds reversed. After 1988, the stadium was made self-sufficient, with no funds going to or from the general fund.[17]

---

13. *Anaheim Stadium*, a souvenir booklet published by the Anaheim Stadium management.
14. Ibid.
15. Anaheim California, Finance Director, *Financial Report, City of Anaheim* for fiscal years 1967–1990. Operating profits were not available for fiscal years 1983 and 1984.
16. Ibid., for fiscal years 1967–1991.
17. The stadium fund shows funds entering from the general fund for years after 1988. These funds are for the purchase of land for a sports arena. Since the stadium is to be self-sufficient, the stadium fund now reflects the city's cost of the sports arena now being built. The city has agreed to purchase the land for this project and for eight years to contribute up to $2.5 million a year if the private manager is not able to find a professional sports franchise to play in the arena. If the manager can get one sports franchise for the arena, the subsidy is reduced to $1.5 million annually for eight years. If two sports franchise locate in the Anaheim Sports Arena, the subsidy goes to zero. Private conversation with Ken Stone, Budget Manager for City of

Foregone property taxes are considered costs of the stadium project. The $4 million price for the land is used for 1967 and compounded every year until 1978 by 10 percent. In 1979, the rate changed due to Proposition 13, while the base changed by the $31 million expansion.

The last column of Table 8.2 shows that even with foregone property taxes, the stadium made a net profit five of the last eight years that the stadium was not self-sufficient. The recession years of the early 1980s were the only years during this later period when the facility did not earn a profit after accounting for foregone property taxes. The expansion to accommodate the Rams was a financially sound move for the city.

The last column of Table 8.2 is reproduced as the second column in Table 8.3. Possessory property tax revenues that the city received from the Angels from 1971 to 1974 are added to the second column to get the net profit or loss in the fourth column. The last column in Table 8.3 is the present value of the profit or loss. The present values are summed to get the accumulated net present value of negative $4,268,715.

The negative ANPV indicates that the rents, reimbursements, and taxes received by Anaheim through 1990 have not yielded a rate of return equal to what could have been earned over this period in a similarly risky investment. Given the current agreement that calls for the city to receive no more net profits from the stadium, the stadium subsidy will not get smaller even if the stadium continues to be profitable in the future.

Anaheim, 15 September 1992. One professional sports team, the NHL expansion Mighty Ducks, began play in the fall 1993. The Ducks' lease calls for the sports arena now to be called "the Pond in Anaheim."

Table 8.1 Anaheim Stadium Operating Profits (1967–1990)			
Year	Operating Profit	Year	Operating Profit
1967	$551,444	1979	$1,315,000
1968	$682,909	1980	$979,000
1969	$586,551	1981	$3,147,000
1970	$511,079	1982	$2,623,000
1971	$414,221	1983	not available
1972	$314,076	1984	not available
1973	$324,838	1985	$3,375,000
1974	$469,390	1986	$4,306,000
1975	$176,056	1987	$3,029,000
1976	$441,022	1988	$2,553,000
1977	$494,629	1989	$3,610,000
1978	$529,000	1990	$4,546,000

Table 8.2 Anaheim Stadium Direct and Indirect Municipal Outlays (1967–1991)					
Year	Direct Municipal π or (Subsidy)	Property Tax Rate	Property Tax Valuation	Foregone Property Taxes	Direct and Indirect π or (Subsidy)
1967	($764,076)	0.011	$4,000,000	($44,000)	($808,076)
1968	($544,185)	0.011	$4,400,000	($46,200)	($590,385)
1969	($800,636)	0.011	$4,840,000	($50,820)	($851,456)
1970	($349,259)	0.011	$5,324,000	($55,902)	($405,161)
1971	($691,782)	0.011	$5,856,400	($61,492)	($753,274)
1972	($42,618)	0.011	$6,442,040	($67,641)	($110,259)
1973	($1,075,950)	0.011	$7,086,244	($74,406)	($1,150,356)
1974	($1,298,330)	0.011	$7,794,868	($85,744)	($1,384,074)
1975	$20,054	0.010	$8,574,355	($87,458)	($67,404)
1976	($752,729)	0.010	$9,431,791	($92,903)	($845,632)
1977	($16,834)	0.010	$10,374,970	($102,484)	($119,318)
1978	$1,636,000	0.013	$11,412,467	($142,656)	$1,493,344
1979	$194,000	0.013	$42,412,467	($530,156)	($336,156)
1980	$921,000	0.013	$42,412,467	($530,156)	$390,844
1981	$59,000	0.013	$42,412,467	($530,156)	($471,156)
1982	$15,000	0.013	$42,412,467	($530,156)	($515,156)
1983	$184,000	0.013	$42,412,467	($530,156)	($346,156)
1984	$1,144,000	0.013	$42,412,467	($530,156)	$613,844
1985	$1,031,000	0.013	$42,412,467	($530,156)	$500,844
1986	$874,000	0.013	$42,412,467	($530,156)	$343,844
1987	$1,528,000	0.013	$42,412,467	($530,156)	$997,844
1988	$841,000	0.013	$42,412,467	($530,156)	$310,844
1989	$0	0.013	$42,412,467	($530,156)	($530,156)
1990	$0	0.013	$42,412,467	($530,156)	($530,156)
1991	$0	0.013	$42,412,467	($530,156)	($530,156)

Table 8.3
Anaheim Stadium
Profit and Losses and Present Values
(1967–1991)

Year	Direct and Indirect Profit or (Subsidy)	Possessory Property Tax Revenues	Net Profit or (Loss)	Present Value Profit (Loss)
1967	($808,076)		($808,076)	($808,076)
1968	($590,385)		($590,385)	($560,191)
1969	($851,456)		($851,456)	($766,590)
1970	($405,161)		($405,161)	($345,532)
1971	($753,274)	$218,564	($534,710)	($432,774)
1972	($110,259)	$214,457	$104,198	$79,990
1973	($1,150,356)	$145,052	($1,005,304)	($732,418)
1974	($1,384,074)	$145,819	($1,238,255)	($856,891)
1975	($67,404)		($67,404)	($44,322)
1976	($845,632)		($845,632)	($528,566)
1977	($119,318)		($119,318)	($70,921)
1978	$1,493,344		$1,493,344	$844,385
1979	($336,156)		($336,156)	($180,884)
1980	$390,844		$390,844	$199,973
1981	($471,156)		($471,156)	($229,867)
1982	($515,156)		($515,156)	($239,798)
1983	($346,156)		($346,156)	($153,589)
1984	$613,844		$613,844	$260,132
1985	$500,844		$500,844	$203,179
1986	$343,844		$343,844	$132,669
1987	$997,844		$997,844	$355,218
1988	$310,844		$310,844	$105,296
1989	($530,156)		($530,156)	($171,278)
1990	($530,156)		($530,156)	($165,936)
1991	($530,156)		($530,156)	($161,924)

Accumulated Net Present Value...... ($4,268,715)

Chapter 9
Atlanta–Fulton County Stadium

HISTORY

Thirteen years after Milwaukee lured the Boston Braves to the Midwest, the team was enticed to Atlanta, Georgia by the same incentive that brought the team to Wisconsin. Atlanta promised a new publicly owned stadium in a city not exposed to Major League Baseball.

Like many cities, Atlanta had made plans to build a stadium in the 1930s as a public works project. In Atlanta, however, no building took place.[1] The stadium idea was reborn in 1960 when the Georgia General Assembly created the City of Atlanta and Fulton County Recreation Authority. The authority was empowered to "acquire and operate an athletic stadium and coliseum."[2] The stadium project was part of an urban renewal project. The stadium eliminated some forty-seven acres of what one local publication called "urban blight."[3]

The city and county agreed to pay any inability of the authority to meet the debt service up to a ceiling amount, which increased with each new bond issue.[4] By 1981, the agreement called for the city to pay any debt service that exceeded revenues up to $1,350,000 annually for the stadium and $1,315,000 annually for

1. "Atlanta Pitches for the Big Leagues," *Atlanta Magazine* 3 (November 1963): 55.
2. City of Atlanta, Department of Finance, *Annual Financial Report for Fiscal Year Ending December 31, 1975*, 64.
3. Ibid.
4. There have been bond issues in 1975 and 1977 to increase the capacity of the stadium or otherwise make improvements. In addition, another series of bonds was issued in 1970 to underwrite the construction of the arena next to the stadium.

the arena.[5] In turn, Fulton County agreed to reimburse the city for one-third of the city's debt service subsidy.[6] In addition, the city could allocate up to 50 percent of a tax for park improvement to pay for debt service on the stadium's bonds.[7] In return, the City of Atlanta and Fulton County will receive title to the stadium when the bonds have matured and been paid.

During the pre-construction period, however, there was little talk of subsidies. A popular magazine reported that authority members visited several stadiums to "capitalize on those points which worked well and to find solutions for some problems which had not been satisfactorily solved."[8] Among the sites visited was San Francisco's Candlestick Park, "the most problemsome [sic] new stadium in the major leagues."[9] Candlestick was used as proof that an Atlanta sports facility could be self-supporting.

There is, naturally, considerable discussion on the subject of economic feasibility, and on this thought, Atlanta takes courage from a recent report out of San Francisco. When Candlestick Park was built four years ago at a cost of $10,500,000, it was conceded that payment would require thirty-five years. Instead, after three years of operation, during which the San Francisco Giants have been the most productive tenants, reliable financial authorities have concluded that Candlestick, in spite of its many controversial aspects will be paid for fifteen years ahead of schedule.[10]

In spite of improvements made in 1975, 1977, and 1986, the two tenants have been unhappy with the facility. The Atlanta Falcons began play in a new, state-financed facility, the Georgia Dome, in 1992. Atlanta–Fulton County Stadium remains the home of the Braves after a ceiling was placed on the rent the Braves will pay Atlanta for use of the stadium, but they are expressing the desire for a new facility.

CONSTRUCTION COSTS

The 1965 construction costs were $18.5 million, representing a relatively small increase over the $18 million estimated when the authority issued its bonds. Two reasons account for the $500,000 over run. First, the finished stadium was larger than designed. Plans called for a stadium with a capacity of

---

5. City of Atlanta, Finance Department, *Annual Finance Report for Fiscal Year Ended December 31, 1981*, 13.
6. Ibid.
7. City of Atlanta, City Controller, *City Finances Report of the City Controller for the Year Ending December 31, 1967*, 16.
8. "Atlanta Pitches for the Big Leages," 56.
9. Ibid.
10. Ibid.

45,000 for baseball and 55,000 for football.[11]   The completed stadium holds 51,567 and 57,133, for baseball and football, respectively.[12]

The stadium could have been built for $18 million even with this change in design if it had not been for the speed with which the stadium was completed. Atlanta had hoped to have a Major League Baseball franchise on opening day 1965 and offered the prime contractor a $700,000 premium if he could complete the stadium in twelve months. The circular frame of the stadium was designed to reduce construction time. Each of the eighty angular bends used in the frame of the stadium was identical.[13] The contractor earned the premium, but legal complications kept the Braves in Milwaukee.[14]

In 1975 the authority spent $1.5 million to install new movable seats for the Falcons. The 1977 improvements cost $44,110,924. In 1986, authority began spending the proceeds of $14,000,000 in bonds sold for capital improvements to the stadium.

SUBSIDY ANALYSIS

The direct municpal subsidies to Atlanta–Fulton County Stadium are estimated in Table 9.1.[15]   After 1983, the stadium's financial records are comingled with those of the city-owned arena and the zoo. Post-1984 subsidies come from financial statement footnotes that reflect write-offs taken by the city for past losses incurred by the stadium not reported in previous financial statements. The city pays two-thirds of the municipal deficit shown in the second column of Table 9.1 and Fulton County pays the remaining one-third.

By reviewing Table 9.1, it is clear that the optimism present during construction was poorly founded. The teams that play in the stadium do not pay the full costs of the stadium. Review of Table 9.1 shows that the subsidies went down in 1972 and 1981, years when the Major League Baseball players went on strike. Although the decline in 1972 may reflect a general trend toward lower subsidies, the data for the 1981 season are quite damning. The 1981 subsidy was approximately one-third of that in 1980, even though fewer games were played and fewer fans attended the games that were played in 1981.[16]

---

11. Ibid.
12. "State of the Stadium," *Atlanta Magazine* 4 (March 1965): 53.
13. "Build Now Roof It Later," *Engineering News Record* 171 (11 November 1963): 57.
14. "State of the Stadium," 53.
15. City of Atlanta, Department of Finance, *Annual Financial Report* for fiscal year listed; Private conversations with Rick Anderson, Atlanta City Finance Department, 4 June and 22 June 1987; Private conversation with Michael Bell, chief financial officer of the City of Atlanta, 13 August 1992.
16. For details on the reduced attendance and an estimated $10 million loss by cities who host Major League Baseball, see Robert C. Berry, William B.

Nineteen eighty-one was also a recession year that hurt many entertainment-oriented businesses. Yet, despite this decline in ticket and concession revenues, the proximate cause of the decline in the subsidy in 1981 was due to a sharper decline in operating costs brought on by the lower attendance.

The evidence for the Falcons is more ambiguous than for the Braves. While it is true the subsidy declined in 1974, this reflects the downward trend mentioned above. The outlays were larger during the NFL strike year of 1982 than in either 1981 or 1983, but that was the year immediately following the artificially low subsidy brought on by the baseball strike in 1981, and the $304,000 outlay in 1982 is compatible with the declining trend. The unprecedented subsidy in 1987 may be more a reflection of the higher debt service following the expansion in 1986 and a change in reporting than a sign that the NFL strike of that year caused subsidies to increase. With no post-1987 data available, it is not possible to compare the 1987 figures with a developing trend following the new bond issue. In short, the evidence supporting the inference that the Falcons receive an operational subsidy from Atlanta is weaker than the evidence supporting the arguement that the Braves receive a subsidy. More light should be shed on this issue after reviewing post-1992 financial reports which will reflect the stadium's costs and revenues after the Falcons move to their new home facility in Atlanta.

Property tax valuations for years before 1986 were based upon the assessed valuation in 1986.[17] The property tax base in 1985 was $14,191,870 for the structure and $207,030 for the land. This amount reflects an 18 percent increase in valuation in 1985 and was increased 9 percent every odd year before 1984. In 1992, the stadium and land represented a total tax base of $16,073,400.[18] Using this information, it is possible to estimate the foregone property taxes. The third, fourth, and fifth columns of Table 9.1 show these calculations.[19]

The only verifiable tax revenues derived by Atlanta Stadium to offset these costs are property taxes assessed against the Braves' team property at the stadium. The market value of this property was $2,139,050 in 1985, for a tax base of $855,620 in 1985.[20] Using the same assumptions as were used in calculating the foregone property taxes in Table 9.1, the amount of Braves' property taxes over this period is estimated in column 4 of Table 9.2.

Gould, IV, and Paul D. Staudohar, *Labor Relations in Professional Sports* (Dover, MA: Auburn House, 1986), 75–76.

17. Private conversation with Charles Hogan, Fulton County Assessor's Office, 29 May 1987.
18. Private 24 July 1992 correspondence with Fulton County Assessor's Office.
19. Property tax rates are from City of Atlanta, Department of Finance,*Annual Financial Report for* 1966, 1967, 1968, 1969, 1970, 1971, 1972, 1973, 1974, 1975, 1976, 1977, 1978, 1979, 1980, 1981, 1982, 1983, 1984, 1985, 1986, 1987.
20. Private conversation with Charles Hogan, 29 May 1987. The property tax base is 40 percent of market value.

Adding these tax revenues to the direct and indirect outlays from Table 9.1, repeated as the second column of Table 9.2, the net subsidy for each of the years is calculated. As Table 9.2 shows, the property tax contribution by the Braves is trivial compared to the subsidies made each year. The result is that the annual net subsidy to the two teams ranges from a low of $420,480 to a high of $3,801,074. The stadium generated a net cash outflow in each of the years shown.

Discounting these annual losses shows that the Braves and the Falcons have received a subsidy through 1988 that would have amounted to a one-time grant of approximately $16.5 million in 1966.

These estimates were made using the assumption that a private party would have built the stadium. Given the negative net present values sum to more than $16.5 million, this is not appropriate. Since the value of the stadium structure is more than 98.56 percent of the total assessed valuation, reducing the foregone property tax receipts by 98.56 percent would estimate the subsidy, assuming the land would have remained in its "blighted" condition. Table 9.3 adjusts the estimates in Tables 9.1 and 9.2 by diminishing the foregone property taxes by the amount of the stadium structure. The direct outlays are assumed to be constant, as is the tax revenue earned from the Braves' property tax payments. Using these more generous assumptions, the first twenty-two years of operation of Atlanta–Fulton County Stadium appears to represent a subsidy of $10 million in 1966 to the two major tenants.

The trend of the annual subsidies now appears to be getting larger and will probably not get smaller in the future for two reasons. First, there is no evidence from these data that the 1986 expansion generated enough revenues to recover the added debt service incurred to finance them. Second, the city agreed in 1990 to limit their share of the gate from Braves' games.[21] Given that the Braves do not reimburse the operating costs, much less the fixed costs, this new agreement, along with the Falcons vacating the stadium, will probably mean the future subsidies of Atlanta–Fulton County Stadium will increase.

A factor that will mitigate the size of the subsidies after 1992 is that the city took advantage of the drop in interest rates during the early 1990s and refinanced the debt. The city projects it will save approximately $250,000 a year in interest because of the refinancing.[22]

Even this $250,000 a year in savings, however, will do little to change the magnitude of the losses Atlanta incurred in the last several years of the survey. On the basis of these direct cash flows, an argument can be made that the investment in Atlanta–Fulton County stadium was not a wise venture.

---

21. Private conversation with Michael Bell, chief financial officer for the City of Atlanta on 13 August 1992.
22. Ibid.

Table 9.1
Atlanta–Fulton County Stadium
Direct and Indirect Municipal Subsidy
(1966–1985)

Year	Direct Municipal Subsidy	Property Tax Rate	Property Tax Valuation	Foregone Property Taxes	Direct and Indirect Subsidy
1966	($987,453)	0.03200	$5,618,350	($179,787)	($1,167,240)
1967	($236,157)	0.03200	$6,124,002	($195,968)	($432,125)
1968	($900,057)	0.03600	$6,124,002	($220,464)	($1,120,521)
1969	($896,991)	0.04150	$6,675,162	($277,019)	($1,174,010)
1970	($937,653)	0.04475	$6,675,162	($298,714)	($1,236,367)
1971	($929,520)	0.05303	$7,275,927	($385,842)	($1,315,362)
1972	($601,707)	0.06255	$7,275,927	($455,109)	($1,056,816)
1973	($690,453)	0.05630	$7,930,760	($446,502)	($1,136,955)
1974	($518,178)	0.05600	$7,930,760	($444,123)	($962,301)
1975	($464,201)	0.06284	$8,644,529	($543,222)	($1,007,423)
1976	($953,140)	0.05934	$8,644,529	($512,966)	($1,466,106)
1977	($712,362)	0.05984	$9,422,536	($563,845)	($1,276,207)
1978	($787,342)	0.05984	$9,422,536	($563,845)	($1,351,187)
1979	($622,964)	0.05830	$10,270,564	($598,774)	($1,221,738)
1980	($514,000)	0.05790	$10,270,564	($594,666)	($1,108,666)
1981	($173,000)	0.05710	$11,194,915	($639,230)	($812,230)
1982	($304,000)	0.06165	$11,194,915	($690,167)	($994,167)
1983	($62,000)	0.06168	$12,202,458	($752,648)	($814,648)
1984	($509,000)	0.05310	$12,202,458	($647,951)	($1,156,951)
1985	($84,000)	0.04732	$14,398,900	($681,356)	($765,356)
1986	($1,578,000)	0.04927	$14,398,900	($709,434)	($2,287,434)
1987	($3,097,000)	0.04995	$14,957,067	($747,105)	($3,844,105)

Year	Direct and Indirect Subsidy	Braves' Property Tax Base	Braves' Property Tax	Net Profit (Subsidy)	Present Value of Profit or (Loss)
		Table 9.2			
		Atlanta–Fulton County Stadium			
		Present Value of Stadium Investment Cash Flows			
		(1966–1987)			
1966	($1,167,240)	$333,857	$10,683	($1,156,557)	($1,167,240)
1967	($432,125)	$363,904	$11,645	($420,480)	($411,078)
1968	($1,120,521)	$363,904	$13,101	($1,107,421)	($1,012,870)
1969	($1,174,010)	$396,655	$16,461	($1,157,549)	($1,007,232)
1970	($1,236,367)	$396,655	$17,750	($1,218,616)	($1,008,298)
1971	($1,315,362)	$432,354	$22,928	($1,292,435)	($1,026,704)
1972	($1,056,816)	$432,354	$27,044	($1,029,772)	($782,333)
1973	($1,136,955)	$471,266	$26,532	($1,110,423)	($802,112)
1974	($962,301)	$471,266	$26,391	($935,910)	($647,860)
1975	($1,007,423)	$513,680	$32,280	($975,144)	($647,172)
1976	($1,466,106)	$513,680	$30,482	($1,435,625)	($899,205)
1977	($1,276,207)	$559,911	$33,505	($1,242,701)	($747,737)
1978	($1,351,187)	$559,911	$33,505	($1,317,681)	($756,704)
1979	($1,221,738)	$610,303	$35,581	($1,186,157)	($654,365)
1980	($1,108,666)	$610,303	$35,337	($1,073,329)	($568,988)
1981	($812,230)	$665,231	$37,985	($774,245)	($399,165)
1982	($994,167)	$665,231	$41,011	($953,155)	($468,115)
1983	($814,648)	$725,102	$44,724	($769,923)	($367,733)
1984	($1,156,951)	$725,102	$38,503	($1,118,448)	($500,952)
1985	($765,356)	$790,361	$37,400	($727,956)	($316,911)
1986	($2,287,434)	$790,361	$38,941	($2,248,493)	($904,207)
1987	($3,844,105)	$861,493	$43,032	($3,801,074)	($1,450,643)

Accumulated Net Present Values .... ($16,547,623)

Table 9.3
Atlanta–Fulton County Stadium
Present Values of Stadium Cash Flows with Alternative Property Valuation
(1966–1987)

Year	Property Tax (Alternative Assumption)	Direct & Ind (Subsidy) Alt Assumption	Net (Subsidy) & Profit	PV Using Alt Assumption
1966	($2,589)	($990,042)	($979,359)	($979,359)
1967	($2,822)	($238,979)	($227,334)	($216,261)
1968	($3,175)	($903,232)	($890,131)	($804,614)
1969	($3,989)	($900,980)	($884,519)	($758,865)
1970	($4,301)	($941,954)	($924,204)	($753,719)
1971	($5,556)	($935,076)	($912,148)	($711,976)
1972	($6,554)	($608,261)	($581,217)	($430,259)
1973	($6,430)	($696,883)	($670,350)	($472,926)
1974	($6,395)	($524,573)	($498,182)	($335,397)
1975	($7,822)	($472,023)	($439,744)	($282,493)
1976	($7,387)	($960,527)	($930,045)	($570,423)
1977	($8,119)	($720,481)	($686,976)	($402,503)
1978	($8,119)	($795,461)	($761,956)	($426,718)
1979	($8,622)	($631,586)	($596,006)	($319,222)
1980	($8,563)	($522,563)	($487,227)	($250,054)
1981	($9,205)	($182,205)	($144,220)	($70,876)
1982	($9,938)	($313,938)	($272,927)	($128,511)
1983	($10,838)	($72,838)	($28,114)	($12,691)
1984	($9,330)	($9,330)	($479,828)	($207,762)
1985	($9,812)	($9,812)	($56,412)	($23,358)
1986	($10,216)	($10,216)	($1,549,275)	($612,418)
1987	($11,289)	($11,289)	($3,064,727)	($1,156,531)

Accumulated Net Present Value.....($9,926,936)

Chapter 10
Oakland–Alameda County Coliseum Complex

HISTORY

For the first three seasons of their existence, the Oakland Raiders were far from the proud team of silver and black that dominated opponents and headlines during the late 1960s through the mid-1980s. Professionally, the trend was in the wrong direction: the team won six games in 1960, its maiden season, two in 1961, and only one game in 1962. In the first three seasons, the Raiders played in three different facilities. Like their record, the Raiders' home stadiums showed a continual decline. They played their first home games in Keezar Stadium, then moved to Candlestick Park, both in San Francisco, before finally settling at Frank Youell Field.[1]

Described as a makeshift municipal facility built "a few blocks from downtown,"[2] Youell Field, did little to make the few Raider fans who attended forget the team's difficulties. Rumors began that the team would move to either Portland, New Orleans, Cincinnati, or San Antonio.[3]

The 1963 season saw the beginning of the Al Davis era. When Davis, now the managing partner of the team, became the Raiders' head coach in 1963, the team immediately turned its fortunes around, winning ten games that season. The increased fan interest was evidenced by the classified ads in the Bay Area papers by San Francisco 49'er fans offering to trade their tickets for seats at the Raider games.

With the Raiders' increased popularity, there was more concern about the franchise leaving for other cities, and calls were made for the construction of a new stadium. The results were the Oakland–Alameda Coliseum Complex, a

---

1. Edwin Shrake, "Thunder Out of Oakland," *Sports Illustrated*, 23, no 20, 4 November 1965, 86.
2. Ibid.
3. Walter Bingham, "I Don't Need Money, I Need Points," *Sports Illustrated*, 19, no. 19, 4 November 1963, 27-28.

project that includes an outdoor stadium, an indoor arena, and an exhibit hall. The arena is used by the Golden State Warriors of the NBA, and the many hockey franchises that have passed through Oakland. The three facilities share common amenities such as parking lots. As the name implies, the City of Oakland and Alameda County jointly own the facility. The facilities were built and are operated by a non-profit organization called Oakland–Alameda County Coliseum, Inc. (OACCI).

In 1968 the Athletics (the A's) moved from Kansas City into the Coliseum. According to Bill Veeck, the reason the Athletics received permission for the move from Philadelphia to Kansas City in 1955 was because Del Webb wanted to get the contract to renovate Blues' Field in Kansas City. The new owner of the A's, Arnold Johnson, owned the minor league park, and as an incentive to get Johnson to move his team to the Midwest, Kansas City offered to buy the stadium for $500,000 and construct an upper deck. Veeck wrote that Webb sought this promised renovation when he sided with Johnson to move west, even though the market might not be sufficient to support a Major League Baseball franchise: "Even while they [the owners] were voting Johnson in, everyone felt that Kansas City would have difficulty supporting a major-league operation after the original enthusiasm wore off. According to my information, the Athletics will definitely be on the wing again within two years."[4]

Veeck's projections, written in 1962, were moderately accurate. When the A's moved to Kansas City, their attendance went from 300,000 in Philadelphia to almost 1,400,000 during the first season in Kansas City, a mark the A's were never able to match again while in Kansas City. By the mid-1960s attendance had fallen to around 600,000 per season.

Charles O. Finley bought the team from Johnson's estate in 1960. Finley wanted to move the team at the end of the 1964 season, when the lease between the A's and Kansas City expired. Several well-publicized spats had arisen between Finley and Kansas City civic authorities. The American League owners, who were reluctant to offend Missouri's powerful senators, pressured Finley to sign an extension of the lease or risk losing his franchise. Major League Baseball granted Finley permission to move to Oakland after the 1967 season.

When the Rams announced they would vacate the Los Angeles Coliseum for Anaheim following the 1979 season, the Los Angeles Coliseum Commission (LACC) began looking for new tenants. They, like any owner of a vacant stadium, had two options: get an existing franchise to relocate or hope for an expansion franchise. The LACC favored the former option, because it was not known when the NFL would expand, nor if Los Angeles would receive a franchise when the league expanded.[5] The search focused on three AFL franchises; the Baltimore Colts, the Miami Dolphins, and the Oakland Raiders.

---

4. Bill Veeck and Ed Linn, *Veeck as in Wreck* (New York: G. P. Putnam's Sons, 1962), 268.
5. This has proven to be prudent. The NFL announced their first two team expansion in late 1993 since the Rams left Los Angeles.

The Colts and the LACC could not come to terms, and generally it was thought that the Colts were using the threat of a move to Los Angeles as leverage to extract better terms for a lease in Baltimore. Joe Robbi, owner of the Dolphins, soon began building his own facility north of Miami. In the Raiders, the LACC found a willing franchise, despite the rabid support for the team in the Bay Area.

When the Raiders requested permission to move to Los Angeles, it was denied on the grounds that Oakland had given the Raiders adequate support. This led the LACC and the Raiders to file a celebrated anti-trust suit against the NFL. When the Raiders and the LACC won in 1981, the team was free to move to Southern California.

The suit also awarded the plaintiffs treble damages which were divided among the LACC and the Raiders. These funds proved to be the grounds upon which the lease between the LACC and the Raiders was contested. The Raiders were to install luxury boxes at their expense, and the LACC was to use their proceeds from the suit to modernize the oldest stadium in the NFL.

The construction of the boxes proved to be contentious. Since the Raiders would be constructing the boxes with their own funds, they would control the boxes. This irritated the Coliseum's existing tenants, including the University of California, Los Angeles (UCLA), which had used the Coliseum for its home football games. UCLA, claiming it had not been consulted on the matter and saying it would not allow Davis to control the luxury boxes for UCLA games, moved to Pasadena's Rose Bowl. The 1984 Olympic Organizing Committee also expressed some concern that Davis would control the luxury boxes for the Olympic events scheduled at the Coliseum. This later problem was resolved by a compromise that called for Davis not to begin construction until after the Olympics.

When construction finally began in early winter 1987, there was no concurrent modernization, and the Raiders halted construction on their luxury boxes. This led Davis to announce that the lease with the LACC was void, and Davis began shopping his franchise to other cities.

Davis signed an agreement with Irwindale for the team to move to the Los Angeles suburb after a new facility was built. The arrangement served to (1) enrich the franchise by some $10 million that Irwindale paid to the Raiders, much as a franchise would pay a signing bonus to a rookie; and (2) cause Irwindale to come under severe scrutiny by state and local officials, who questioned how such a small city could arrange such a lucrative offer. The deal fell through, although Davis kept the $10 million.

Davis shopped elsewhere. There was speculation that Davis might move his team to his home town of New York City, after the Jets left Shea Stadium for the Meadowlands, but Sacramento and the Raiders' ancestral home of Oakland became the finalists.

The Sacramento offer featured a new stadium, which would be built by a private developer who hoped that the presence of a major league tenant would increase the property values of the surrounding land he owned. The city offered to pay a $50 million franchise fee, but Davis played Sacramento against

Oakland. The Sacramento city fathers lost their patience, putting a deadline on the offer. Davis allowed the deadline to pass.

This left Oakland and Los Angeles. Los Angeles regained interest in working with the Raiders, but only after Oakland offered Davis a deal that was too good to pass up. The Oakland proposal included a $54.9 million franchise fee to be paid over a nine-year period and a guaranteed sell out for fifteen years.[6]

The Oakland bid proved too much for many of Oakland's citizens, who quickly gathered signatures to put the deal on the ballot. At first, Oakland mayor Lionel Wilson claimed the issue was not subject to a referendum, but quickly backed down when public pressure against the deal mounted. Wilson later voided the deal after public sentiment ran strongly against the lease. Wilson lost his bid for re-election in the June 1990 primary because of dissatisfaction with the Raider deal.

Oakland quickly attempted to arrange another lease, but before then Los Angeles made amends with Davis by leasing the Coliseum to a private contractor who then concluded negotiations for the Raiders to stay in Los Angeles.

In January 1994, the Los Angeles earthquake reportedly created enough damage that it was questionable that the Raiders would be able to use the Coliseum for the 1994 season. The Oakland–Alameda Coliseum Commission quickly offered itself up as a substitute location. An offer that the Raiders, at the time of this writing (February 1994) have not accepted, due mainly to assurances by the Los Angeles Coliseum Commission that they will be able to repair the Los Angeles Coliseum by the 1994 season.

CONSTRUCTION COSTS

The three structures in the Coliseum Complex cost a total $30 million to complete.[7] Records of the construction cost of each facility were not kept. Even if estimates were available for each building, in some cases, it is not possible to allocate costs of jointly used fixtures such as parking lots and box offices. The Coliseum Complex has received approximately $17.75 million in improvements and renovations between 1980 and 1990.[8]

---

6.   Private correspondence with Wilson Riles, Jr., Oakland city council member, dated 19 June 1990.
7.   *The NFL's Official Encyclopedic History of Professional Football* (New York: Macmillan, 1977), 460
8.   Private correspondence, from Ray Ward, executive vice president, Oakland–County Coliseum Complex, 27 January 1987. Information for later years comes from private correspondence from Bob Quintella, executive vice president, 29 April 1992. Data for Table 10.1 came from a financial summary called "Oakland–Alameda County Coliseum, Capsuled Summary of First 25 Years of Coliseum Operation," sent by Bob Quintella, executive

SUBSIDY ANALYSIS

The Oakland–Alameda County Coliseum, Inc. (OACCI), which built the stadium also operates the facility. Like the construction cost data, the cost and revenue data are aggregated for the entire complex. Therefore, it is not possible to observe directly how the teams that occupy the stadium portion contribute (or contributed, in the case of the Raiders) financially to the complex. Table 10.1 gives the operating revenues and expenses for the first twenty-five years of the complex. The city and county each contribute $750,000 annually, for a total of $1.5 million, for the operation of the Coliseum Complex. This is designed to pay the annual debt service of $1,250,000.[9]

To offset the foregone property taxes due to public ownership of the land occupied by the complex, the OACCI pays the city and county a "possessory interest tax." The size of the payment shown in Table 10.1 is based upon the value of the contract the OACCI has to use the property.[10] This possessory interest tax is the only source of tax revenues from the stadium, as neither the city nor the county impose any tax on ticket sales.[11]

The net operating revenues after taxes are used first to build a reserve fund equal to the largest year's expenses.[12] Any funds left after the contingency fund has been funded to the level of last year's expenses are paid to the city and county. These funds are listed under "Distribution to City and County" in Table 10.1. In the nine years that the distribution exceeded $1.5 million, the city and county recovered their annual payment and received a "profit" from the stadium investment.

Eight of the nine profitable years occurred consecutively between 1978 and 1985. It appears that the city and county were starting to gain directly from their investment in the complex. The city and the county have not received any funds in the last six years of the survey. This is due to a number of reasons.

In 1986 the A's renegotiated their lease and received a guarantee of at least $1.5 million in concession revenues,[13] which reduced net operating revenue after taxes by $1.5 million. Combined with increasing expenses, this meant enlarging the reserve fund.

In 1989 and 1990, the Coliseum also incurred "developmental expenses" of $789,182 and $4,067,212, respectively.[14] These costs were related to the attempt to secure the Raiders or another NFL franchise and to a proposal to build

---

vice president Oakland–Alameda County Coliseum Complex, 29 April 1992.
9. Ibid.
10. Ibid.
11. Ibid.
12. Ibid. The reserve fund has never been utilized.
13. Private conversation with Charlie Adams, chief financial officer, Oakland–Alameda County Coliseum, 27 July 1992.
14. "Capsuled Summary of First 25 Years of Coliseum Operation."

a new indoor arena.[15] Since these were not "operating expenses" they are not included in Table 10.1.

Because of the nature of the Coliseum Complex, one cannot assume that positive net operating revenues indicate the A's and the Raiders reimbursed the Coliseum management fully for the operating expenses that were incurred on the teams' behalf. A cross subsidy may exist between other events (of which there are at least twice as many as there are baseball and football games) and the A's and Raiders.

A review of strike years does little to shed light on the subject of operational subsidies. The 1972 baseball strike year would have an impact on fiscal year 1972. While the net operating revenues were higher in 1972 than 1971, this seems to be reflecting a trend of larger net operating revenues.

The impact of the longer 1981 baseball strike is more difficult to assess. The strike, which began on 12 June and ended on 9 August, straddles fiscal years 1981 and 1982. The net operating revenues in both of these years show an increase, but again this is part of a trend toward larger net operating revenues.

If the loss of the A's games due to strikes does not seem to affect the net operating revenues, then it can be assumed the team is paying its share of operating expenses. This more than likely changed in 1986 with the more lucrative concession contract that the A's negotiated. Not only did the new lease coincide with an almost 94 percent drop in net operating revenues, but it marked the first year in fifteen that the city and county received no funds from the Coliseum. The city and county have received no funds from the Coliseum since the new lease terms have taken affect.

The Coliseum has missed the Raiders. The absence of Raider games is first reflected in fiscal year 1983 data. Nineteen eighty-three begins the first year of a trend of declining net operating revenues, despite the number of events increasing to 300 from 277.[16] The trend of declining net operating revenues would last for four years, the longest such period in the survey.

The second column in Table 10.2 duplicates the last column of Table 10.1, the distribution to the city and the county. The third column is the $1.5 million outlay the city and county make annually, while the fourth column subtracts column three from column two to get the municipal cash flow.[17] Finally, the last column represents the present value of the cash flows and adds them to get the ANPV of the cash flows.

The ANPV of the Coliseum Complex is a negative $10,534,636. This indicates that while the Coliseum Complex is, on whole, able to cover its operating expenses, it is not able to earn enough in revenues to cover the fixed costs of debt service. Recall the $10,534,636 is not a subsidy to the A's and Raiders, since the complex includes two other facilities and hosts more events

---

15. Private conversation with Charlie Adams, chief financial officer, Oakland–Alameda County Coliseum, 27 July 1992.
16. "Capsuled Summary of First 25 Years of Coliseum Operation."
17. No allowance is made for foregone property taxes, since these are reimbursed by the possessory interest tax revenues.

not related to baseball and football than baseball and football games. It should be noted, however, that the negative ANPV was approximately negative $7 million and getting less negative every year until the A's received their new lease terms.

The Sports Stadium as a Municipal Investment

					Table 10.1		
		Oakland–Alameda Coliseum Complex					
		Operating Revenues, Expenses, and Taxes					
		(1967–1991)					

Fisc. Year	Operating Revenue	Operating Expenses Before Taxes	Net Operating Revenue Before Taxes	Possessory Interest Taxes	Net Operating Revenue After Taxes	Distribut'n to City and County
1967	$1,326,448	$946,958	$379,490	$0	$379,490	$0
1968	$1,689,055	$1,262,019	$427,036	$186,991	$240,045	$0
1969	$1,733,095	$1,405,240	$327,855	$113,091	$214,764	$0
1970	$1,840,717	$1,360,795	$479,922	$85,543	$394,379	$0
1971	$2,249,073	$1,526,048	$723,025	$192,594	$530,431	$107,572
1972	$2,321,010	$1,540,965	$780,045	$172,498	$607,547	$402,070
1973	$2,400,039	$1,548,193	$851,846	$187,917	$663,929	$759,336
1974	$2,815,027	$1,672,402	$1,142,625	$218,105	$924,520	$795,620
1975	$3,413,221	$1,744,819	$1,668,402	$259,680	$1,408,722	$1,294,730
1976	$4,245,408	$1,951,938	$2,293,470	$336,020	$1,957,450	$1,673,990
1977	$3,930,248	$2,099,337	$1,830,911	$479,969	$1,350,492	$1,059,596
1978	$4,342,947	$2,201,319	$2,141,628	$113,414	$2,028,214	$2,028,212
1979	$3,889,574	$2,241,235	$1,648,339	$93,260	$1,555,079	$1,555,080
1980	$4,461,391	$2,297,578	$2,163,813	$93,633	$2,070,180	$2,070,180
1981	$5,016,867	$2,616,870	$2,398,997	$85,821	$2,313,176	$2,188,790
1982	$5,439,495	$2,950,432	$2,489,063	$94,954	$2,394,109	$2,052,414
1983	$5,369,848	$3,182,505	$2,187,343	$97,014	$2,090,329	$1,773,349
1984	$5,145,482	$3,332,528	$1,812,954	$98,052	$1,714,902	$1,563,842
1985	$5,335,776	$3,534,595	$1,801,181	$98,543	$1,702,638	$1,500,080
1986	$4,255,227	$4,153,195	$102,032	$98,581	$3,451	$0
1987	$5,330,898	$5,049,413	$281,485	$99,706	$181,779	$0
1988	$8,443,493	$6,319,142	$2,124,351	$101,263	$2,023,088	$0
1989	$10,523,992	$7,194,924	$3,329,068	$102,227	$3,226,841	$0
1990	$10,417,428	$7,865,562	$2,551,866	$103,966	$2,447,900	$0
1991	$10,253,542	$8,836,906	$1,416,636	$104,870	$1,311,766	$0

Table 10.2
Oakland–Alameda Coliseum Complex
Present Values of Cash Flows from Stadium Investment
(1967–1991)

Year	Distribution to City and County	City and County Contribution	Municipal Profit (Loss)	Present Value of π or (Loss)
1967	$0	$1,500,000	($1,500,000)	($1,500,000)
1968	$0	$1,500,000	($1,500,000)	($1,423,285)
1969	$0	$1,500,000	($1,500,000)	($1,350,493)
1970	$0	$1,500,000	($1,500,000)	($1,279,238)
1971	$107,572	$1,500,000	($1,392,428)	($1,126,979)
1972	$402,070	$1,500,000	($1,097,930)	($842,856)
1973	$759,336	$1,500,000	($740,664)	($539,614)
1974	$795,620	$1,500,000	($704,380)	($487,442)
1975	$1,294,730	$1,500,000	($205,270)	($134,977)
1976	$1,673,990	$1,500,000	$173,990	$108,753
1977	$1,059,596	$1,500,000	($440,404)	($261,769)
1978	$2,028,212	$1,500,000	$528,212	$298,668
1979	$1,555,080	$1,500,000	$55,080	$29,638
1980	$2,070,180	$1,500,000	$570,180	$291,729
1981	$2,188,790	$1,500,000	$688,790	$336,047
1982	$2,052,414	$1,500,000	$552,414	$257,141
1983	$1,773,349	$1,500,000	$273,349	$121,284
1984	$1,563,842	$1,500,000	$63,842	$27,055
1985	$1,500,080	$1,500,000	$80	$32
1986	$0	$1,500,000	($1,500,000)	($578,762)
1987	$0	$1,500,000	($1,500,000)	($549,422)
1988	$0	$1,500,000	($1,500,000)	($521,470)
1989	$0	$1,500,000	($1,500,000)	($494,846)
1990	$0	$1,500,000	($1,500,000)	($469,492)
1991	$0	$1,500,000	($1,500,000)	($444,338)

Accumulated Net Present Value .... ($10,534,636)

Chapter 11

Jack Murphy Stadium

HISTORY

Jack Murphy Stadium, or San Diego Stadium as it was officially called before 1980, was born as an effort to retain the San Diego Chargers. The AFL franchise had been coaxed from Los Angeles after one season to play their home games in Balboa Stadium. Located in Balboa Park, Balboa Stadium was a city-owned facility for which no other information is available.

As mentioned in chapter 8, in 1964 the Chargers' owner, Baron Hilton, was being courted by authorities in Anaheim to occupy their new stadium, which was scheduled for completion in 1966. Hilton made several trips to Anaheim and often referred to Anaheim Stadium as "his."

In May 1965, the San Diego City Council authorized a new stadium to keep the Chargers in San Diego. Unlike its contemporaries, there was little controversy as to whether the city should build the stadium. The stadium referendum received the support of 72 percent of the voters, even after the supporters explicitly stated the stadium was unlikely to recover its construction costs.[1]

The referendum permitted the San Diego Stadium Authority to be established jointly by the City and County of San Diego (the city and the county are separate entities in San Diego). The city leases the facility for semi-annual rental payments equal to the debt service. The city, in turn, subleases the stadium to the Chargers and Padres.

San Diego began hosting a Major League Baseball franchise when the National League expanded in 1969. Few San Diegans appreciated the event. The Padres, taking the name of the San Diego team in the Pacific Coast League, inherited the apathy that the city's residents felt for its predecessor. Only

---

1. Lowell Reidenbaugh, *Take Me Out to the Ball Park* (St. Louis: The Sporting News, 1983), 247.

512,970 fans attended the first season's games, and the team never drew more than 700,000 fans in any of the first four seasons. In 1971, San Diego was the only National League franchise to draw fewer than one million patrons.

Such figures do not make for a happy franchise. After the second Washington Senators moved to Texas, it was widely thought the Padres would move to Washington. The inability of the Padres' owners and the Armory Board to reach an agreement is described more fully in chapter 7. The purchase of the team by Ray Kroc has anchored the franchise in San Diego since the mid-1970s.

In 1983, the Stadium Authority removed the single deck of outfield bleachers and replaced them with additional seats, raising the capacity to 66,000.

CONSTRUCTION COSTS

The cost of the stadium's original construction was $28 million, just $500,000 over the approved budget. The 1983 expansion cost approximately $11 million.

SUBSIDY ANALYSIS

The city's expenditures on the stadium are outlined in the city's annual budget, which shows the actual expenditures and revenues for the previously completed fiscal year. Also included in the budget is the debt service for the previous fiscal year. Table 11.1 shows the operating profits from Jack Murphy Stadium.

The evidence in Table 11.1 suggests that the city is covering adequately the operating costs of the stadium. Through 1974, San Diego Management Company, a private firm, managed the stadium. The facility earned an average profit of $215,000 from 1969-1974. After 1974, the stadium has been managed by the city. Although the city has experienced several years when the surplus was low, these years were early in the self-managed period; the data for the later years suggest that the city managers moved down the learning curve well. The stadium averaged an operating surplus of $1,157,284 after 1974.

The evidence indicates that the teams pay rent approximating the cost they impose upon stadium management. Neither the baseball strike, which would be reflected in the data for fiscal year 1982, nor the football strikes in fiscal year 1983 and 1988 had much impact on the operating surplus or deficit.

This operating surplus offsets the city's semi-annual "lease" payments to the San Diego Stadium Authority, which equals the debt service payments on the structure. Any short fall of payments is made up by revenues on several land leases, including one for the San Diego Sports Arena.

The semi-annual payments sum to an annual payment of $1,506,250 for fiscal years 1970 through 1984. In fiscal year 1968 and 1969, the lease payments amounted to $617,263 and $1,381,250, respectively. The 1983 expansion was financed with bonds that raised the annual debt service to $2,567,050 starting with fiscal year 1985. In addition to the debt service costs, the stadium incurs fixed costs in the form of $15,000 annual lease payments to the San Diego Water Utilities Department. The Water Utilities Department owns land on which a portion of the stadium grounds is located.[2]

Table 11.2 surveys the direct municipal outlays for the stadium, the difference between the debt service, the $15,000 lease payments to the water district, and operating profits in Table 11.1. It should be noted that the data in Table 11.2 do not correspond to the amounts the city reports as transferred from the land leases. This is because the city transfers funds from the stadium fund to a "Capital Outlay Fund." The Capital Outlay Fund serves as a funding source for general capital improvements. Hence, the city uses the stadium fund to finance capital expenditures in the city.

It is unlikely that the stadium costs the city any significant foregone property tax revenues. The property used by the stadium was an undeveloped river wash, with some of the property owned by a municipal entity, the San Diego Water Utilities Department. Although the stadium is owned by the property-tax–exempt Stadium Authority, property taxes are charged on private property at the stadium. These possessory interests had a valuation of $25,086,359 in 1986 and $24,939,222 in 1987.[3] Given the property tax rate of 1.04855 percent,[4] these property taxes averaged $371,565. These revenues are discounted by 6 percent a year for years before 1986 and compounded at a 6 percent rate after 1987. The result of these computations are shown in Table 11.3. The last column in Table 11.3 computes the accumulated net present value of the stadium investment.

Like so many of the stadiums observed, the San Diego Stadium is a short-run success. Given that the stadium is constructed, the city is earning enough money from the operation of the stadium to cover the costs of leasing the facility to the Chargers and Padres. The construction of the stadium, however, resulted in a one-time reduction in wealth to the city equal to approximately $9 million over the first twenty-three years.

Even though the 1983 expansion added more than $1 million in annual lease payments, it has had little short-run net impact on the stadium's cash flows. After six fiscal years, the ANPV increased from approximately $8.75 million. By 1990, the stadium was earning revenues sufficiently high enough to cover the added debt service. If this trend continues, the ANPV will fall below the 1984 amount.

While the stadium is not likely to earn a positive accumulated net present value over its life because the current profitable years are discounted so heavily, if the trend in Tables 11.1 through 11.3 continues, the size of the lump sum subsidy should decline. In three of the last five years surveyed, the stadium was able to earn revenues that exceeded the variable and debt service costs. Furthermore, in 2001 and 2003 the original construction bonds and expansion

2. San Diego, California, City Manager's Office, *Annual Budget 1971*, 335.
3. Private correspondence with James A. Janette, assessor division chief with County of San Diego, 29 July 1987.
4. Ibid.

bonds will mature, respectively. In the absence of new capital improvements to the stadium, all the operating revenues will be considered net receipts by 2003.

Table 11.1
Jack Murphy Stadium
Operating Profit
(1968–1990)

Year	Operating Profit	Year	Operating Profit
1968	$155,200	1980	$544,300
1969	$230,500	1981	$1,059,100
1970	$289,200	1982	$1,148,100
1971	$283,500	1983	$1,130,000
1972	$246,500	1984	$1,636,600
1973	$193,100	1985	$1,696,932
1974	$106,000	1986	$2,217,661
1975	$60,700	1987	$1,643,107
1976	$258,900	1988	$1,635,045
1977	$10,700	1989	$2,217,661
1978	$329,400	1990	$2,702,559
1979	$215,800		

Table 11.2
Jack Murphy Stadium
Municipal Outlays
(1968–1990)

Year	Municipal Outlays	Year	Municipal Outlays
1968	($477,063)	1980	($976,950)
1969	($1,165,750)	1981	($462,150)
1970	($1,232,050)	1982	($373,150)
1971	($1,237,750)	1983	($391,250)
1972	($1,274,750)	1984	$115,350
1973	($1,328,150)	1985	($885,118)
1974	($1,415,250)	1986	($354,417)
1975	($1,460,550)	1987	($938,943)
1976	($1,262,350)	1988	($947,005)
1977	($1,510,550)	1989	($364,389)
1978	($1,191,850)	1990	$120,509
1979	($1,305,450)		

Table 11.3
Jack Murphy Stadium
Present Value of Cash Flows from Stadium Investment
(1968-1990)

Year	Municipal Tax Rev. From Stadium	Total Revenues (Subsidy)	Present Value of Receipt or (Subsidy)
1968	$121,993	($355,070)	($355,070)
1969	$129,780	($1,035,970)	($967,925)
1970	$138,064	($1,093,986)	($946,066)
1971	$146,877	($1,090,873)	($878,457)
1972	$156,252	($1,118,498)	($840,129)
1973	$166,225	($1,161,925)	($812,312)
1974	$176,835	($1,238,415)	($797,445)
1975	$188,123	($1,272,427)	($752,869)
1976	$200,131	($1,062,219)	($579,630)
1977	$212,905	($1,297,645)	($655,524)
1978	$226,494	($965,356)	($448,508)
1979	$240,952	($1,064,498)	($451,127)
1980	$256,331	($720,619)	($272,819)
1981	$272,693	($189,457)	($62,824)
1982	$290,099	($83,051)	($24,202)
1983	$308,616	($82,634)	($21,493)
1984	$328,315	$443,665	$102,384
1985	$350,299	($534,819)	($123,420)
1986	$372,658	$18,241	$4,209
1987	$370,472	($568,471)	($131,185)
1988	$392,700	($554,305)	($127,916)
1989	$416,262	$51,873	$11,971
1990	$441,238	$561,747	$129,634

Accumulated Net Present Value...... ($9,000,723)

Chapter 12
Cincinnati Riverfront Stadium

HISTORY

There was little controversy in Cincinnati that Crosley Field was due to be replaced. Crosley Field opened in 1912, replacing the wooden Redland Field that had burned in 1911. The neighborhood surrounding Crosley was deteriorating as quickly as the stadium, and it was hypothesized that the stadium and the neighborhood were a contributing reason to why the Reds were doing so poorly at the gate. The Reds were sufficiently unhappy with their lot that New York officials targeted them as one of the National League franchises that might fill the void created when the Dodgers and Giants moved from New York to the West. By the late 1960s, the propriety of municipalities providing sports facilities was rarely debated, so there was little protest over Cincinnati contributing to building a new stadium for the Reds.

Location of the new stadium provided the only debate regarding the stadium. One faction argued that the new stadium should be located near the suburbs, while another faction argued that the stadium should be a vehicle to regenerate the downtown business district. In all, twenty-two sites were investigated as potential sites for the new facility.[1]

The debate was settled in 1968 when Hamilton County voters approved a referendum that called for bonds to be issued to finance a stadium on the "decaying riverfront" in downtown Cincinnati.[2] The renewal project was not trivial. Involved was the removal of cobblestone streets and warehouse buildings and the relocation of sewer, water, electrical lines, and railroad tracks owned by the Pennsylvania railroads as well as the Louisville and Nashville railroads. The project also called for flood protection.

---

1. Julian Schienseson, "Public Works Features of Cincinnati's Riverfront Stadium," *Public Works* 102 (May 1971): 82.
2. Ibid.

Despite these difficulties, the present location was selected in hopes of revitalizing downtown businesses. To facilitate this goal, two bridges, one for pedestrians and another for vehicular traffic were constructed over an interstate highway that separated the downtown district from the stadium site.

The proposal approved by the Hamilton County voters called for the stadium to be built by Hamilton County and leased back to the city with the expectation that the lease payments would be large enough to cover the debt service.

The Reds' fans appreciated the facility, lending credence to the argument that the fifty-eight-year-old Crosley Field was hurting attendance to Reds' games. Only 567,937 fans attended the first thirty-four games in the 1970 season played in Crosley Field, while 1,235,631 fans attended the final forty-three 1970 home games played at Riverfront.[3]

Both the Reds and the NFL Bengals use Riverfront. The multiple-use nature of the stadium requires a separate bank of lights and motor-driven movable stands. This allows 54,700 fans to see a baseball game and 59,754 to attend a football game.

The relationship between the Reds and the Bengals sometimes shows signs of strain. In 1986, friction developed between the major tenants of the stadium when the Reds wanted to install a television scoreboard that the Bengals claimed would obstruct the view of some of their fans' seats. Over the last several years, the Bengals have attempted to convince civic leaders to build a new football-only stadium.

In December 1993, following a threat to leave Cincinnati if they did not get a new stadium, the Bengals received lease concessions that called for the city to build from between 60–90 luxury boxes, a stadium club, and the team will be permitted to increase ticket prices by $4. The Bengals are guaranteed increased revenues from these enhancements starting at $2.75 million in 1994 and increasing to $4 million in 1996. If there is any short fall, the city agrees to pay the difference. In return, the Bengals agree to remain in Riverfront Stadium until the year 2,000, unless the city decides not to continue paying the guaranteed increased revenues beginning in 1996. Between 1993 and 2000, proposals for a new stadium will be considered, and if a new stadium is not being constructed by 2000, the Bengals can terminate the lease which is scheduled to run until 2010.[4]

CONSTRUCTION COSTS

The construction costs of Riverfront Stadium to Hamilton County taxpayers was $38.7 million.[5] One of the advantages of the downtown site was that the stadium would qualify for federal urban renewal funds. Four million dollars in

---

3. Ibid., 81.
4. "Bengals Will Stay the Home Team," *The Cincinnati Inquirer*, 9 December 1993.
5. Ibid., 83.

federal funds were used to relocate the sewer and railroad lines. Another $8 million in federal funds were used to finance traffic control, waterway and roadway improvements, the construction of the pedestrian bridge.[6] This means that Hamilton County had approximately $5 million in unspent funds from the proceeds of the bonds sold to construct the stadium. These monies were invested in interest-bearing securities that made the first debt service payment.

SUBSIDY ANALYSIS

Constructing a time series for the revenues and expenditures related to Riverfront Stadium is complicated by the fact that Cincinnati changed its reporting format twice after 1970. With each change came a different aggregation of costs and revenues. Given this problem, Table 12.1 is the best effort at making a time series of the operating profits.[7]

The stadium operating profit was computed by subtracting the expenses incurred for personal and contractual services, material and supplies, maintenance and repair, insurance, taxes, and utilities from the total operating revenues. Calculated in this way, Table 12.1 indicates that the stadium earned an operating profit in all but two of its twenty years since it began operation. In one of those years, 1984, expenditures for maintenance and repairs was about $1 million more than usual, indicating that some renovation expenditures was undertaken in that year. If this amount was spread over the previous fifteen years, it would involve an annuity of approximately $31,474 at 10 percent interest. If the accounting conventions had allowed the Riverfront management to set a sinking fund aside for unusual expenses, the stadium operations would have earned a profit in all but one of the first twenty years of operation.

The only other operating loss, in 1981, can be directly attributable to the fifty-day baseball strike of that year. The income statement for 1981 showed that the city earned an operating profit of $304,200, but this was subsequently reduced when a settlement of a dispute on the Reds' rent during the strike-shortened season resulted in a 1982 write-off of $798,043 for "lease renegotiation."[8]

The financial evidence of 1981 shows that the Reds cover the variable costs they impose upon the stadium management. This is corroborated by a significant decline in operating profits in all years when the Reds drew poorly.

One year, 1974, has operating profits significantly below average that did not coincide with below-average Reds' attendance. That was the year of a forty-two–

---

6.   Ibid.
7.   City of Cincinnati, Department of Finance, *Financial Report for the Year Ended December 31* for 1969, 1970, 1971, 1972, 1973, 1974, 1975, 1976, 1977, 1978, 1979, 1980, 1981, 1982, 1983, 1984, 1985, 1986, 1987, 1988, 1989.
8.   City of Cincinnati, Department of Finance, *Financial Report for the Year Ended December 31, 1982*, 86.

day NFL strike. A decline in operating profits is also observable in 1982, a year that saw a fifty-seven–day NFL strike, indicating that the Bengals pay enough rent and expenses to reimburse the city for the operating costs they impose upon the stadium management.

Any direct municipal expenditures on Riverfront Stadium would be to pay for the fixed costs not covered in the leases with the Reds and Bengals. The last column of Table 12.1 details these direct outlays.

The third column includes the amount the city contributes to make the lease payment to Hamilton County. In those years when the revenues from stadium operations were low, the city had to make larger expenditures to make the lease payments than in years when there were larger revenues from stadium operations.

Table 12.2 shows the foregone property taxes incurred due to public ownership of Riverfront Stadium (assuming the stadium would have been constructed by a private party). As part of its lease agreement with Hamilton County, the city reimburses the county for a portion of the foregone property taxes. The fifth column of Table 12.2 shows the property taxes that have been paid to the county by the city. Although these tax payments to the county do not appear in the financial reports for the years 1969 to 1972, early experience shows the outstanding foregone property taxes to be about one-third of those calculated in the third column. Extending these assumptions to 1969 through 1972 yields the estimates which are shown in Table 12.2 with an asterisk.[9] The last column of Table 12.2 computes the net loss in property taxes incurred by Hamilton County by subtracting the property taxes paid by Cincinnati from the foregone property taxes computed in column four.

To offset these expenses, Cincinnati is one of the most aggressive cities in using the municipal stadium to generate tax revenues. Not only is there a city payroll tax, but the city imposes a 3 percent stadium use tax on tickets as well as a 25 cent-per-ticket admissions tax for all events at the stadium. The revenues from these tariffs are shown in Table 12.3.

The payroll expenditures were not available for the years 1970 and 1971 because the financial reports for these years aggregated the expenditures too much to acquire these data. Given that the payroll during these years was modest, the amount of the payroll tax revenues generated is relatively small. The admissions and use tax revenues are estimated because the city has an agreement with the Reds and Bengals not to make this information public. The two sports' attendance figures were estimated by taking the Reds' annual attendance and adding it to the capacity of the stadium for football for the Bengals' games. The implicit assumption is that the Bengals sold out every game during the period. For the 3 percent use tax, each ticket was assumed to cost $5 during the 1970s and $10 during the 1980s. While the 1980 assumption may overestimate the

---

9.   Direct municipal expenditures are from *Financial Report for the Year Ended December 31* for the fiscal years 1973, 1974, 1975, 1976, 1977, 1978, 1979, 1980, 1981, 1982, 1983, 1984, 1985, 1986, 1987, 1988. Property tax data are from a private conversation with Robert E. Wachendorg, downtown reappraisal director, County of Hamilton, on 24 April 1987.

average ticket price for Reds' games, it more than likely underestimates the price of Bengals' tickets.

By combining the last column of the previous three tables (Direct Municipal Expenditures, Net Foregone Property Tax, and Municipal Stadium Tax Revenues), it is possible to estimate the municipal subsidy to the Reds and Bengals. This is done in the fifth column of Table 12.4. In the last column of Table 12.4, the cash flows in column five are discounted to get the present value of those cash flows in 1969.

From Table 12.4 the conclusion can be drawn that over the first twenty years of operation, the Bengals and Reds received a subsidy that equaled a combined one-time lump sum payment of $4,846,388 in 1969. This figure assumes that Riverfront Stadium would have been constructed by a private party and considers the unpaid foregone property taxes as an opportunity cost derived from the public ownership of the stadium. Since the Cincinnati archives still have the property tax assessments for the land and improvements previously on the Riverfront site, it is possible to compute the subsidy, assuming the land remained in its pre-stadium use.

Table 12.5 alters the foregone property tax calculations by taking the 1969 property tax assessment and allowing for a 6 percent growth rate in the evaluation. The assumption in Table 12.5 is that the land upon which Riverfront is built would have remained in its pre-stadium (private) use. The same property tax rates are also assumed. So that a comparison can be made, it is also assumed that the city would have obligated itself to the same property taxes it paid to Hamilton County.

It is interesting to note that by assuming no development would have occurred at the Riverfront Stadium site, the property taxes paid by the city to Hamilton County dominates the foregone property taxes through the 1970s. During this period, the municipal development of the area actually generated more property taxes than the original use. The profit and loss column of Table 12.5 assumes the city would have earned the same tax revenues from payroll, admissions, and usage taxes, as well as the same lease payments. The last column shows the present value of the annual cash flows. The sum of this column shows that the sum of these present values assuming the stadium site would not have been developed, is less than half of the sum of the present values assuming a private party would have built the stadium.

Using the more conservative property tax calculations, Riverfront Stadium approaches an investment with positive accumulated values. The accounting practices, however, have changed so often over this period that consistency is hard to achieve. If these changes are accounted for, the stadium may earn a positive accumulated present value. For example, lawyers for the Bengals[10] have argued that much of the direct subsidies reported in later years are revenues generated by the parking structure beneath the stadium, which is used by

---

10. Robert G. Stachler and W. Stuart Dornette, *Riverfront Stadium Finances, 1970–1988*, a document dated 20 October 1989, filed with the case of *Cincinnati Bengals, Inc. v. City of Cincinnati*.

weekday business clients. These funds are first credited to the general fund and then transferred to the stadium account, making funds that were earned by the stadium investment appear to be subsidies. When this adjustment is made, the negative $2.2 million subsidy may be reduced significantly.

Table 12.1
Riverfront Stadium
Operating Profits and Losses and Direct Municipal Subsidy
(1969–1989)

Year	Operating Profit (Loss)	Direct Municipal Subsidy
1969		($2,547,103)
1970	$1,212,000	$0
1971	$147,000	$0
1972	$2,131,000	($1,850,000)
1973	$2,230,400	($1,850,000)
1974	$1,700,500	$0
1975	$2,056,700	($800,000)
1976	$2,487,800	($1,000,000)
1977	$2,546,900	($1,000,000)
1978	$2,129,900	($1,000,000)
1979	$2,447,100	$0
1980	$1,194,100	($4,200)
1981	($493,844)	($880,226)
1982	$861,837	($1,007,719)
1983	$960,012	($1,428,675)
1984	($715,128)	($1,558,995)
1985	$760,374	($2,259,726)
1986	$284,000	($2,496,000)
1987	$557,000	($2,561,000)
1988	$2,401,000	($3,283,000)
1989	$1,652,000	($3,240,000)

Table 12.2
Riverfront Stadium
Direct and Indirect Property Tax Expenses
(1969–1988)

Year	Property Tax Rate	Property Tax Valuation	Foregone Property Taxes	City Expenditures for Property Taxes	Net Foregone Property Tax
1969	0.04862	$2,532,100	($123,111)	$82,074*	($41,037)
1970	0.04944	$8,304,360	($410,568)	$273,712*	($136,856)
1971	0.046864	$8,228,920	($385,640)	$257,093*	($128,547)
1972	0.043974	$10,715,590	($471,207)	$314,138*	($157,069)
1973	0.044406	$10,715,590	($475,836)	$329,335	($146,501)
1974	0.045522	$10,715,590	($487,795)	$332,715	($155,080)
1975	0.042939	$10,715,590	($460,117)	$313,870	($146,247)
1976	0.05044	$10,715,590	($540,494)	$326,064	($214,431)
1977	0.0481	$10,715,590	($515,420)	$309,792	($205,628)
1978	0.04744	$13,118,500	($622,342)	$335,120	($287,222)
1979	0.04734	$13,118,500	($621,030)	$333,326	($287,704)
1980	0.05598	$13,118,500	($734,374)	$399,664	($334,710)
1981	0.0546	$12,679,660	($692,309)	$382,796	($309,514)
1982	0.05436	$12,679,660	($689,266)	$390,004	($299,262)
1983	0.0588	$12,679,660	($745,564)	$416,446	($329,098)
1984	0.06024	$13,333,580	($803,215)	$440,504	($362,711)
1985	0.06014	$13,333,580	($801,882)	$435,781	($366,101)
1986	0.06024	$13,333,580	($803,215)	$436,000	($367,215)
1987	0.06904	$13,333,580	($920,550)	$498,000	($422,550)
1988	0.06672	$13,333,580	($889,616)	$603,000	($286,616)

Table 12.3
Riverfront Stadium
Tax Revenues Derived from Stadium Operations
(1970–1988)

Year	Stadium Payroll	City Payroll Tax Rate	Payroll Tax Revenues	Two Sport Attendance Figures	Stadium Use Tax (25¢)	3% Admission Tax	Municipal Stadium Tax Revenues
1970		0.017		2,196,968	$549,242	$329,545	$878,787
1971		0.017		1,894,522	$473,631	$284,178	$757,809
1972.	$150,730	0.017	$2,562	2,004,859	$501,215	$300,729	$804,506
1973.	$195,322	0.02	$3,906	2,411,001	$602,750	$361,650	$968,307
1974.	$240,983	0.02	$4,820	1,484,128	$371,032	$222,619	$598,471
1975.	$316,238	0.02	$6,325	2,709,003	$677,251	$406,350	$1,089,926
1976.	$348,472	0.02	$6,969	3,023,108	$755,777	$453,466	$1,216,213
1977.	$328,161	0.02	$6,563	2,913,138	$728,285	$436,971	$1,171,818
1978.	$834,253	0.02	$16,685	2,925,897	$731,474	$438,885	$1,187,044
1979.	$532,927	0.02	$10,659	2,750,333	$687,583	$412,550	$1,110,792
1980.	$582,403	0.02	$11,648	2,820,646	$705,162	$846,194	$1,563,003
1981.	$592,628	0.02	$11,853	1,293,313	$323,328	$387,994	$723,175
1982.	$679,354	0.02	$13,587	1,523,288	$380,822	$456,986	$851,395
1983.	$767,322	0.02	$15,346	1,583,819	$395,955	$475,146	$886,447
1984.	$833,146	0.02	$16,663	2,252,430	$563,108	$675,729	$1,255,499
1985.	$831,084	0.02	$16,622	2,312,651	$578,163	$693,795	$1,288,580
1986.	$844,000	0.02	$16,880	2,170,464	$542,616	$651,139	$1,210,635
1987.	$820,000	0.02	$16,400	2,663,237	$665,809	$798,971	$1,481,368
1988.	$928,000	0.02	$18,560	2,550,560	$637,640	$765,168	$1,421,368

Table 12.4
Riverfront Stadium
Total Profit (Subsidy) from Stadium and Present Value of Cash Flows
(1969–1988)

Year	Direct Municipal Subsidy	Net Taxes	Municipal Tax Rev. From Stadium	Total Profit (Subsidy)	Present Value of Profit (Subsidy)
1969	($2,547,103)	($41,037)	$0	($2,588,140)	($2,588,140)
1970	.... $0	($136,856)	$878,787	$741,931	$692,876
1971	.... $0	($128,547)	$757,809	$629,262	$549,416
1972	.. ($1,850,000)	($157,069)	$804,506	($1,202,563)	($984,407)
1973	.. ($1,850,000)	($146,501)	$968,307	($1,028,194)	($785,872)
1974	.... $0	($155,080)	$598,471	$443,390	$318,506
1975	..... ($800,000)	($146,247)	$1,089,926	$143,679	$96,413
1976	.. ($1,000,000)	($214,431)	$1,216,213	$1,782	$1,116
1977	.. ($1,000,000)	($205,628)	$1,171,818	($33,809)	($19,758)
1978	.. ($1,000,000)	($287,222)	$1,187,044	($100,178)	($54,582)
1979	.... $0	($287,704)	$1,110,792	$823,088	$417,830
1980	.... ($4,200)	($334,710)	$1,563,003	$1,224,094	$578,577
1981	..... ($880,226)	($309,514)	$723,175	($466,565)	($207,160)
1982	.. ($1,007,719)	($299,262)	$851,395	($455,585)	($190,204)
1983	.. ($1,428,675)	($329,098)	$886,447	($871,326)	($342,368)
1984	.. ($1,558,995)	($362,711)	$1,255,499	($666,206)	($246,599)
1985	.. ($2,259,726)	($366,101)	$1,288,580	($1,337,247)	($466,736)
1986	.. ($2,496,000)	($367,215)	$1,210,635	($1,652,580)	($540,071)
1987	.. ($2,561,000)	($422,550)	$1,421,368	($1,502,370)	($459,721)
1988	.. ($3,283,000)	($286,616)	$1,421,368	($2,148,248)	($615,504)
			Accumulated Net Present Value		($4,846,388)

Table 12.5
Riverfront Stadium
Present Value of Cash Flows Using Alternative Property Values
(1969–1988)

Year	Alternative Property Evaluation	Foregone Property Taxes	Net Property Taxes	Direct & Indirect City Outlay	Profit (Loss) from Stadium	Present Value Using Alt. Assumption
1969	$2,532,100	($123,111)	($41,037)	($2,588,140)	($2,588,140)	($2,588,140)
1970	$2,684,026	($132,698)	$141,013	$141,013	$1,019,801	$952,373
1971	$2,845,068	($138,363)	$118,731	$118,731	$876,540	$765,317
1972	$3,015,772	($142,813)	$171,325	($1,678,675)	($874,169)	($715,587)
1973	$3,196,718	($158,638)	$170,698	($1,679,302)	($710,996)	($543,430)
1974	$3,388,521	($178,887)	$153,828	$153,828	$752,299	$540,407
1975	$3,591,832	($185,610)	$128,260	($671,740)	$418,185	$280,616
1976	$3,807,342	($239,838)	$86,226	($913,774)	$302,438	$189,456
1977	$4,035,783	($251,583)	$58,210	($941,790)	$230,028	$134,430
1978	$4,277,930	($272,944)	$62,177	($937,823)	$249,220	$135,788
1979	$4,534,605	($299,605)	$33,721	$33,721	$1,144,513	$580,997
1980	$4,806,682	($389,714)	$9,949	$5,749	$1,568,753	$741,483
1981	$5,095,083	($418,118)	($35,322)	($915,548)	($192,373)	($85,416)
1982	$5,400,788	($457,908)	($67,904)	($1,075,623)	($224,227)	($93,613)
1983	$5,724,835	($544,840)	($128,374)	($1,557,049)	($670,602)	($263,498)
1984	$6,068,325	($614,001)	($173,497)	($1,732,492)	($476,993)	($176,561)
1985	$6,432,425	($674,280)	($238,499)	($2,498,225)	($1,209,645)	($422,200)
1986	$6,818,370	($742,942)	($306,942)	($2,802,942)	($1,592,306)	($520,374)
1987	$7,227,472	($936,619)	($438,619)	($2,999,619)	($1,518,439)	($464,638)
1988	$7,661,120	($995,660)	($392,660)	($3,675,660)	($2,254,292)	($732,918)

Accumulated Net Present Values..............($2,198,476)

Chapter 13
Foxboro Stadium

HISTORY

Foxboro Stadium in Foxboro, Massachusetts, is part of a sports complex that includes the New England Harness Raceway. The stadium is a football-only facility built by Stadium Realty Trust, a private firm. Although the stadium is privately owned, it is included in this survey because it receives a property tax abatement.

The stadium was financed from the sale of more than 400,000 shares of Stadium Realty Trust stock.[1] The primary backing for the stock was a thirty-year lease with the New England Patriots. The stadium received its name, Schaefer Stadium, from the Schaefer Brewery, which bought over $1,000,000 in Stadium Realty Trust stock in return for the rights to the name of the stadium and exclusive beer sale at the stadium.[2]

Late in 1981, the Sullivan family became owners of the Patriots and the stadium. The new owners renovated the stadium completely, improving the rest room facilities and adding luxury suites, and a video scoreboard.[3] The family also changed the name of the stadium to Sullivan Stadium.

Many of the renovations carried out by the Sullivan family after they purchased the stadium were required because of the low quality of the original construction. One report indicated that major repair and renovations were needed to maintain the stadium immediately after opening.[4] These costs included a staff

---

1. Private correspondence with New England Patriots, dated 20 May 1983.
2. *The NFL's Official Encyclopedic History of Professional Football* (New York: Macmillan, 1977), 459.
3. Private correspondence with New England Patriots, dated 20 May 1983.
4. Terrence Cullinan, Eric Duckstad, and James S. Van Dias, *Sacramento Sports Complex Needs and Implementation Recommendations—Discuss Draft* (Sacramento, CA: SRI Project ECC-4082, May 1975), 78.

of eighteen to twenty plumbers to open clogged toilet lines because the sewer lines were undersized.[5] This, and similar problems, led one group of observers to surmise that the per-game operating costs were twice that of other major league stadiums.[6]

In 1988, the Sullivan family sold the Patriots and the stadium to different parties. The franchise was sold to electric shaver magnate Victor Kiam, and the stadium was purchased by a partnership, called K-Corp. At that time, the stadium name was changed for the third time in eleven years to Foxboro Stadium. In 1992, Kiam sold the team to a St. Louis syndicate and in late 1993 Robert Kraft, one of the partners in K-Corp., purchased his partner's share to own the stadium outright.[7]

In early 1994 Foxboro Stadium's future was cloudy. The new franchise owners stated they intended to keep the team in Foxboro, but rumors persisted that the team may move. One destination mentioned was Hartford, Connecticut. When St. Louis lost in its 1993 bid for an NFL expansion franchise, speculation that the St. Louis-based syndicate would want to move the franchise closer to their home circulated. These rumors ended in January 1994 when Robert Kraft, owner of Foxboro Stadium, purchased a controlling interest in the franchise. By purchasing the team, Kraft united ownership of the team and the stadium for the first time since 1988.

CONSTRUCTION COSTS

With a football seating capacity of 61,457 and a cost of construction of $6.7 million, Foxboro Stadium has the lowest cost per seat of any modern stadium. This figure may be misleading, however, because the low cost may have been at the expense of quality. Almost immediately after completion another $1.3 million in improvements were undertaken.

SUBSIDY ANALYSIS

In that Foxboro Stadium is owned and operated by a private party, the financial records regarding the stadium's operation are privileged information and are beyond the scope of this study.

The Patriots reimburse the city for game-day expenses such as police and sanitation expenses linked to the stadium's operations. As such, the team does not impose any operating expenses on the Boston suburb.

As mentioned earlier, Foxboro granted the Patriots a property tax abatement in return for its relocation to the Boston suburb. The stadium and the land

---

5.   Ibid.
6.   Ibid.
7.   Private conversation with Stacey James, New England Patriots, 30 Decmber 1993.

carried a 1985 property tax valuation of $27,900,381,[8] and in 1990, the valuation was $29,853,397.[9] In computing the historical valuations, which were not available, it was assumed the 1985 valuation depreciated at a rate of 6 percent a year. For the five years between 1985 and 1990, the almost $2 million difference in values was amortized at a rate of $400,000 a year.

The property tax rate in Foxboro is volatile, ranging in 1987 from .0225 to .01171 in the 1990. In order to estimate the foregone property taxes derived from Foxboro Stadium, the property tax rates for the years 1986 to 1990 were averaged. This gave an average tax rate of 0.159. Table 13.1 shows the result of these computations.

Instead of property taxes, the Patriots pay a tax on each ticket sold. In 1987, the levy was at 67 cents per ticket but was to be adjusted to reflect changes in the Boston Consumer Price Index.[10] More recent communication with the town administrator indicates that the per ticket tax rate is still 67 cents.[11]

Table 13.2 computes the admission tax revenues by assuming the admission tax rate is tied to the national Consumer Price Index in years before 1986. The third column of Table 13.2 subtracts the lost property tax revenues computed in Table 13.1 from the ticket tax revenues to estimate the annual subsidy or profit from the tax abatement to the stadium owners. As can be seen by reviewing this column, the city has never earned enough in ticket taxes to make up for the property tax abatement.

The last column of Table 13.2 discounts the annual net subsidies to get the present value of Foxboro's losses through 1990 due to the stadium. The negative ANPV, combined with the fact that there have been no years in which ticket tax proceeds were larger than the property tax abatement, indicates the city has indeed subsidized the Patriots. The subsidy is the equivalent of about a $1 million grant for the stadium's operations over the first twenty seasons the facility has been in use.

Since the stadium probably would not have been built without the tax abatement, it is not likely that the alternative use would have been so highly valued as a stadium, thus the subsidy computations overstate the costs of the foregone property taxes. Indeed, if the alternative use of the stadium site had a value less than $25 million in 1990, with appropriate discounts for earlier years, the ANPV would be positive.

8. Private conversation with Foxboro Assessor's Office, 4 June 1987.
9. Private conversation with Foxboro Assessor's Office, 30 August 1991.
10. Private conversation with Andrew Gala, Foxboro town administrator, 4 June 1987.
11. Private conversation with Foxboro Town Administrator's Office, 30 August 1991.

Table 13.1 Foxboro Stadium Foregone Property Taxes (1971–1990)			
Year	Property Tax Rate	Property Tax Valuation	Foregone Property Taxes
1971	0.0159	$11,732,757	$186,715
1972	0.0159	$12,481,657	$198,633
1973	0.0159	$13,278,358	$211,312
1974	0.0159	$14,125,913	$224,800
1975	0.0159	$15,027,567	$239,149
1976	0.0159	$15,986,773	$254,414
1977	0.0159	$17,007,206	$270,653
1978	0.0159	$18,092,772	$287,928
1979	0.0159	$19,247,630	$306,307
1980	0.0159	$20,476,202	$325,858
1981	0.0159	$21,783,193	$346,658
1982	0.0159	$23,173,610	$368,785
1983	0.0159	$24,652,777	$392,324
1984	0.0159	$26,226,358	$417,366
1985	0.0159	$27,900,381	$444,007
1986	0.0217	$28,300,000	$614,110
1987	0.0225	$28,700,000	$645,750
1988	0.0117	$29,100,000	$341,052
1989	0.0119	$29,500,000	$352,230
1990	0.0117	$29,853,397	$349,583

Table 13.2
Foxboro Stadium
Admission Tax Revenues and Present Value of Cash Flows from Stadium
Investment
(1971–1990)

Year	Admissions Tax	Total Profit (Subsidy)	Present Value of Profit (Loss)
1971	$118,446	($68,269)	($68,269)
1972	$122,352	($76,281)	($71,950)
1973	$129,968	($81,344)	($71,049)
1974	$144,225	($80,575)	($65,278)
1975	$157,407	($81,742)	($61,459)
1976	$166,488	($87,926)	($61,217)
1977	$177,229	($93,424)	($60,098)
1978	$190,802	($97,126)	($57,599)
1979	$212,285	($94,022)	($51,289)
1980	$240,993	($84,865)	($42,525)
1981	$265,991	($80,667)	($37,503)
1982	$282,298	($86,487)	($37,320)
1983	$291,379	($100,945)	($40,445)
1984	$303,780	($113,586)	($42,221)
1985	$315,927	($128,080)	($44,233)
1986	$315,927	($298,183)	($95,448)
1987	$315,927	($329,823)	($95,562)
1988	$315,927	($25,125)	($6,986)
1989	$315,927	($36,303)	($9,222)
1990	$315,927	($33,656)	($7,923)
Accumulated Net Present Value			($1,027,593)

Chapter 14
Rich Stadium

HISTORY

The migration of NFL teams to the suburbs continued with the Buffalo Bills moving from Buffalo's Memorial Stadium to Orchard Park, New York. The move was controversial. As mentioned in chapter 4, the City of Buffalo spent $750,000 in 1960 preparing the twenty-three year old stadium for the Bills and another $1.5 million to add a second deck that the Bills demanded in 1964. Although the city financed the expansion with long-term bonds, the Bills agreed only to a five-year lease with ten one-year options.

The Bills, however, were still unhappy with their Depression-era downtown stadium and began looking for a suburban replacement. In 1971 they signed a twenty-five-year lease with Erie County to occupy a football-only stadium if it could be ready in time for the 1973 season.

Despite the area's harsh winters, Rich Stadium is not domed. Erie County rejected the original plan for a domed stadium when it was estimated such a structure would cost $74 million.[1] When the New York State Urban Development Corporation estimated that a bare bones open stadium could be built for about $20 million, the county legislature authorized the construction of a facility providing they could get a long-term lease from the Bills and the total bids would be less than $23.5 million.[2] The lease was contingent upon the construction bids being less than $23.5 million. When initial bids fell some $5 million less than this amount,[3] final approval was granted and construction

---

1. "Bids Under $20 Million Signal Stadium's Start," *Engineering News Record* 188, no. 6 (April 1972): 35.
2. Ibid.
3. Ibid.

began in April 1972.[4] This left about fifteen months for construction, and there was some concern whether the facility would be completed in time for the 1973 season. The lease contained several references concerning this possibility and a penalty clause reducing the county's percentage of the gate receipts if the deadline were not met. For the twenty-five-year term of the lease, the county would receive 9 percent of the gate receipts from the first 500,000 patrons if the stadium was completed on time and only 8 percent if it was not ready by opening day 1973.[5]

For the first two months, the stadium project was ahead of schedule, but a labor dispute stopped work for seven weeks in the summer of 1972.[6] The delay prompted the county legislature to authorize another $338,000 to add men and capital during the winter. By June 1973, 600 workers were completing the stadium, almost twice the 350 that were originally planned.[7] With this additional effort, the stadium opened on schedule.

CONSTRUCTION COSTS

The added push to get the stadium completed in time contributed to some cost overruns. The final cost to Erie County was $22 million.[8] While this was below the $23.5 million set as an upper limit by the Erie County Legislature, it was almost 19 percent above the original bids that totaled $18.5 million.

The Bills spent $3 million on private suites, scoreboard, landscaping, and offices.[9] In 1984, the Bills replaced the stadium club with private suites at an undisclosed cost.[10]

SUBSIDY ANALYSIS

Erie County leases the stadium directly to the Bills, who bear the operating costs of the facility. Therefore, the operating costs of the stadium are not incurred by the county. However, the City of Orchard Park incurs the game-day expense of traffic control.[11] The costs of the stadium to Erie County and

---

4. "Owner Gambles $338,000 on Stadium Completion," *Engineering News Record* 190, no. 7 (June 1973): 16.

5. Ibid.

6. Ibid.

7. Ibid.

8. *The NFL's Official Encyclopedic History of Professional Football* (New York: Macmillan, 1979), 454.

9. Ibid.

10. Undated private correspondence with Buffalo Bills public relations department.

11. Private conversation with Terrence Campbell, city assessor of Orchard Park, 23 June 1987.

Orchard Park are the debt service and the foregone property taxes. Table 14.1 reviews these.

Orchard Park and Erie County have several sources of revenue at the stadium. Table 14.2 enumerates these. The Orchard Park Assessor originally placed the stadium on the city's property tax roles, arguing that the stadium was operated by the Bills and should not be treated as tax-exempt property. The city lost the issue in court when the court held that since the county built the stadium it was exempt from property taxes, even if the Bills operate the stadium.[12] In 1987, the city assessor estimated the loss in revenues from the court order to be $2.33 million for 1986.[13] The third column in Table 14.1 estimates these foregone revenues, discounted by the Producer Price Index. The last column in Table 14.1 adds the two sources of costs for Erie County to get the total direct and indirect municipal outlays.

The Bills pay property taxes on the improvements of the stadium they added for their use. These include a practice facility on the stadium grounds and the luxury boxes at the stadium. The property taxes on these improvements amount to $23,000 a year.[14] The only other source of municipal tax revenues is a 25 cent admissions tax on each ticket that generates about $80,000 a year in revenue if the stadium sells out for every Bills game. Erie County receives a portion of the gate receipts or a flat $500,000-a-year rent, which ever is greater.[15] The county receives 9 percent of the first $5 million in gate receipts, 4 percent for the next $2.5 million, and 2 percent for receipts more than $7.5 million. The gross receipts do not allow for any deduction for visitor or league shares, but it does not include the 25 cent admissions tax on each ticket.

The rent paid in excess of the minimum can be applied toward any future years when the percentage does not support the $500,000 minimum. Thus, if the Bills pay $600,000 in rent one year, the $100,000 over the minimum can be applied to the minimum rent any year the team fails to draw enough interest to warrant $500,000 in lease payments. Over the life of the lease, the Bills are obligated to pay $2.5 million more than the minimum. Therefore, the Bills are obligated to pay $17.5 million over the life of the lease [(25 years x $500,000 per year) + $2.5 million]. The Bills are obligated to continue the lease until the $17.5 million minimum has been paid.

Between the years 1973 to 1983, the rent was not to exceed 90 percent of the debt service for those years. After 1983, the rent was not to exceed the county's expenditures for debt service and repairs. These terms virtually guarantee that the Bills will not reimburse the county for all the costs the county incurred in building the stadium. The fifth column of Table 14.2 corroborates this inference. The net municipal receipts fell short of the municipal costs in each of the ten years in Table 14.2.

---

12. Ibid.
13. Ibid.
14. Ibid.
15. Erie County, New York, County Legislature, *1971 Minutes*, Meeting for 23 September 1971, 831–874.

The last column of Table 14.2 discounts the subsidies back to 1976. These calculations indicate that the during the first ten years of the stadium's existence, Erie County and Orchard Park subsidized the Bills an amount equal to a lump sum payment of almost $16.5 million. Given that the annual subsidies have been around $3 million a year for the last four years surveyed and show no signs of getting smaller, this subsidy will probably get larger as time goes on.

In all likelihood, Rich Stadium would not have been built without government participation. In that case, the above calculations overstate the amount of the municipal subsidy to the Bills because it assumes the stadium would be privately owned and property taxes would be paid on the stadium valuation. In reality, the alternative usage would have carried a lower property valuation than the stadium. Indeed, the taxes generated by the property tax levies on the Bills' property at the stadium and the ticket tax recover what would be equal to foregone property taxes on an alternative usage valued to almost $4.6 million. To assume the alternative usage of the stadium site would be equal to or less than this is defensible. If this is true, then the only source of a subsidy to the Bills is the amount by which the lease payments fall short of the debt service. Table 14.3 computes the subsidy using this alternative assumption.

The alternative assumption reduces the magnitude of the subsidy from almost $16.5 million to almost $7 million. Although there is a greater variance in the size of the annual subsidies, there does not appear to be any trend for the reduction of the annual subsidy. The conclusion from this analysis is that the subsidy to the Bills between the years 1977 and 1986 is the equivalent to a lump sum payment equal to somewhere between $7 million and $16.5 million and is unlikely to get larger with time.

Table 14.1
Rich Stadium
Direct and Indirect Municipal Outlays
(1977–1986)

Year	Total Debt Service	Foregone Property Taxes	Direct and Indirect Municipal Outlay
1977	$1,521,105	$1,345,926	$2,867,031
1978	$1,898,880	$1,451,111	$3,349,991
1979	$1,859,280	$1,612,592	$3,471,872
1980	$1,843,855	$1,829,629	$3,673,484
1981	$1,802,605	$1,998,518	$3,801,123
1982	$1,785,530	$2,079,259	$3,864,789
1983	$1,742,630	$2,112,592	$3,855,222
1984	$1,723,905	$2,157,037	$3,880,942
1985	$1,679,355	$2,243,259	$3,922,614
1986	$1,658,980	$2,333,333	$3,992,313

Table 14.2
Rich Stadium
Municipal Receipts and Present Value of Cash Flows from Stadium Investment
(1977–1986)

Year	Bills' Property Taxes	Municipal Stadium Revenue	Total Municipal Revenue	Total Profit (Subsidy)	PV of π or (Loss)
1977	$23,000	$525,680	$628,680	($2,238,351)	($2,072,163)
1978	$23,000	$566,690	$669,690	($2,680,301)	($2,282,075)
1979	$23,000	$724,342	$827,342	($2,644,530)	($2,053,835)
1980	$23,000	$971,688	$1,074,688	($2,598,796)	($1,803,034)
1981	$23,000	$1,035,490	$1,138,490	($2,662,633)	($1,618,047)
1982	$23,000	$636,202	$739,202	($3,125,587)	($1,669,196)
1983	$23,000	$851,285	$954,285	($2,900,937)	($1,382,741)
1984	$23,000	$742,262	$845,262	($3,035,680)	($1,283,796)
1985	$23,000	$660,161	$763,161	($3,159,453)	($1,199,731)
1986	$23,000	$1,019,846	$1,122,846	($2,869,467)	($1,089,615)

Accumulated Net Present Value   ($16,454,233)

Table 14.3
Rich Stadium
Present Value of Cash Flows Using Alternative Development
Assumption
(1977–1986)

Year	Municipal Cash Flows with Alternative Assumption	Present Value of Municipal Cash Flows (alternative assumption)
1977	($995,425)	($939,967)
1978	($1,322,190)	($1,161,137)
1979	($1,134,938)	($918,442)
1980	($872,167)	($654,539)
1981	($767,115)	($529,643)
1982	($1,149,328)	($726,287)
1983	($891,345)	($530,317)
1984	($981,643)	($552,051)
1985	($1,019,194)	($583,153)
1986	($639,134)	($310,971)
Accumulated Net Present Value		($6,906,507)

Chapter 15
Louisiana Superdome

HISTORY

Attempting to describe the construction of the Louisiana Superdome is as large a task as the building itself. The Louisiana voters approved a 1966 state constitutional proposition that formed the Louisiana Superdome Authority by a three to one vote. The proposition allowed the state to borrow $35 million for a structure to house major league sports, provide accommodations for trade shows, conventions and special entertainment events.[1]

The referendum, however, was passed with no stadium design nor site selected. Eight years later, Bernard Levy, executive director of the Louisiana Stadium and Exposition Commission, said, "That $35 million was just a wild-hair guess. They had no site selected for the project. They had no architectural plans drawn. They were thinking of a 55,000-seat stadium. They hadn't included parking facilities . . . it would have been another Astrodome as originally envisioned."[2]

Not satisfied to have just another Astrodome, Louisiana governor John McKeithen argued for a larger, more versatile, and more costly facility than the Astrodome, which was seen as siphoning money away from Louisiana. When complaints about the costs began, McKeithen retorted, "We're not going to let a couple of million dollars stop us."[3]

Good to his word, McKeithen did not let more than $125 million over the original $35 million stop construction of the stadium. The 346 percent of

---

1. Jerry Kirshen, "Let Me Make One Thing Clear," *Sports Illustrated*, 7 June 1971, 35.
2. "Super Headache," *Newsweek*, 29 April 1974.
3. Kirshen, "Let Me Make One Thing Clear," 35.

additional expenses were attributed to inflation and changes in the design of the facility that were meant to increase the capacity of the stadium.[4]

To say the stadium was built despite the increased cost is not to say there was no controversy surrounding the Superdome. Between November 1966, when the proposition passed, and August 1971, when the ground was broken, the state had to field over twenty suits regarding the stadium. There was enough discontent over the financing and alleged fraud in the proposed construction of the stadium that many in the state legislature wanted to give the state's voters a second chance to vote on the project on the June 1971 ballot. The debate was sufficiently emotional that two state senators were reported to have "squared off on the floor of the legislature."[5]

The stadium became an issue in the 1971 Louisiana gubernatorial election. Because of term limit legislation, McKeithen was not able to run for re-election. One of the candidates in the Democratic primary to replace McKeithen, John Schwegmann, claimed that the Superdome was "a clear case of fraud and deception."[6] The financing of the stadium was the root of Schwegmann's complaint. The original bond issue was to be backed by a 4 percent tax on hotel and motel bills in both Orleans and Jefferson Parish, with the State of Louisiana explicitly excluded from putting up its credit to support the bonds.[7]

As the expected costs of the facility grew far beyond the $35 million appropriated in the bond issue, the state entered into an agreement to lease the stadium at an annual rent equal to any shortfall the Louisiana Superdome Authority might incur in servicing the increasing debt to construct the facility.[8] While this may have violated the spirit of the referendum, it did not violate the letter of the law since the state's credit was not used to secure the debt.

Charges of fraud included allegations of kickbacks from construction companies and the use of state deposits to force Louisiana banks to buy bonds that financed the purchase and preparation of the land.[9] Another revelation that came out during the gubernatorial campaign was that the relatives of the Superdome's 1971 executive director, Dave Dixon, owned real estate directly across from the proposed Superdome site.[10] Questions were also raised about the awarding of the scoreboard contract to Ad Art. Ad Art, the highest bidder

---

4. House Select Committee on Professional Sports, *Inquiry into Professional Sports, Part 1*, 96th Cong., 2d sess., 1976, 494.
5. Kirshen, "Let Me Make One Thing Clear," 35.
6. Ibid.
7. House Select Committee on Professional Sports, *Inquiry Into Professional Sports*, 489.
8. Lawrence D. Shubnell, John E. Petersen, and Collin B. Harris, "The Big Ticket: Financing a Professional Sports Facility," *Government Finance Review* 10, no. 12 (June 1985), 9.
9. Kirshen, "Let Me Make One Thing Clear," 38.
10. Ibid.

for the project, was partly owned by Blake Arata, the New Orleans' city attorney.[11]

Schwegmann's run for governor garnered enough support to disrupt the financing of the stadium. In mid-July 1971, a syndicate led by Chase Manhattan Bank was prepared to underwrite the bonds, but the syndicate dissolved when Schwegmann warned that if he were elected governor, he would use his power to derail the Superdome project.[12] The dissolution of the Chase syndicate prompted a local banker to use his bank's resources to collaborate with a bank in Little Rock, Arkansas, to sell $113 million in bonds on 11 August 1971.[13] The sale of the bonds permitted the construction to begin.

The start of the construction did not bring an end to the Superdome controversy. The stadium's design called for a foundation of 2,670 precast and prestressed fourteen-inch square piles. In early summer 1972, it was reported that 8 percent of these piles had been rejected.[14] A consulting firm predicted that "one undetected broken pile could precipitate a failure of the superstructure."[15] The Superdome's advisory committee made up of three Louisiana State University deans "unequivocally recommend[ed] that additional remedial measures be taken to insure protection against (a) differential settlement and its attendant maintenance and failure problems and (b) failures in the structure resulting from possible undetected broken piles."[16] The Superdome's administration chose instead to heed the advice of its architects, who argued that all the suspected piles had been rejected and that a pile failure would not cause the structure to fail.[17]

For the stadium to be financially self-sufficient, it was estimated that it would have to earn between $26,000 and $35,000 in daily rental income.[18] To earn this magnitude of income, the Superdome had hoped to secure a franchise in both Major League Baseball and the National Basketball Association.

The NBA was an easier league to attract than Major League Baseball. In the 1975 NBA expansion, New Orleans received a franchise, called the Jazz. During the first five seasons, the Jazz set one game attendance records when selected teams drew many tens of thousands of spectators. In general, however, the support for the Jazz was weak, and in 1980, they relocated to Salt Lake City.

---

11. "Super Headache."
12. "A Financial Hero in New Orleans," *Business Week*, 18 September 1971, "Names and Faces" column.
13. Ibid.
14. "Superdome Battle Stirs New Orleans," *Business Week*, 27 May 1972, 22.
15. "New Orleans Superdome Going Up Despite Foundation Arguing," *Engineering News Record* 188 (15 June 1972): 12.
16. Ibid.
17. Ibid.
18. House Select Committee on Professional Sports, *Inquiry Into Professional Sports*, p. 504 gives an estimate of $26,000 a day; "Let Me Make One Thing Perfectly Clear," p. 35, projected a breakeven point of $35,000 a day.

Superdome officials claim that Major League Baseball gave assurances that New Orleans would receive a franchise.[19] In testimony before a congressional committee, the secretary-treasurer of the Superdome, William Connick, estimated that the facility would need rent of $9,000 a game to make it feasible to host a baseball team.[20] When informed that baseball commissioner Bowie Kuhn had testified that a baseball franchise would be able to pay no more than $7,000 a game in rent, Connick indicated that $7,000 would not only be acceptable, but also that $7,000 would not be an absolute minimum. Connick disclosed that the Superdome would be willing to have a lease similar to the one Milwaukee had concluded with the Braves and Brewers.[21] The Milwaukee County Stadium had a lease that called for the Brewers to use the stadium rent free until the team drew 1.2 million fans a year (see chapter 2). Despite the Superdome's willingness to negotiate a favorable lease, Major League Baseball has repeatedly declined the invitation to locate in New Orleans. The most recent rejection occurred in 1990 when the National League spurned New Orleans for an expansion franchise.

Any shortfall of revenues relative to expenses cannot be fully described as a subsidy to sports teams that resided in the Superdome. The stated purpose of the facility was to stimulate growth in the New Orleans' central business district. This goal is supported by the design of the structure. The main arena not only has provisions for a playing field, but it includes outlets for gas, steam, electric, telephone, and television so the facility can be used for major conventions. The Superdome also has four ballrooms. Each room averages 19,000 square feet and can be divided into twenty meeting rooms.[22]

To some extent, the plan to rejuvenate the downtown area has been achieved. Built in a depressed area of town, the stadium replaced an aged railroad freight yard. In the first decade after the Superdome's construction, the number of hotel rooms in New Orleans increased from 6,500 to 20,000.[23] Since many of these rooms are built near the Superdome, the hotels replaced a decaying neighborhood, but at considerable cost.

---

19. House Select Committee on Professional Sports, *Inquiry Into Professional Sports*, 491.
20. Ibid., 503.
21. Ibid.
22. "Louisiana Superdome Quick Facts," a fact sheet distributed by Facility Management of Louisiana Superdome. Received in a private, undated correspondence from Bill Curl, Facility Management of Louisiana.
23. House Select Committee on Professional Sports, *Inquiry Into Professional Sports*, 501.

CONSTRUCTION COSTS

The total cost of building the Superdome finally stopped increasing at $163.5 million.[24] It is not appropriate to consider this total cost as a cost of a sports facility because of the facility's features designed for the convention trade.

SUBSIDY ANALYSIS

Louisiana's contribution to the Superdome does not end with construction costs. The Superdome continues to be a major expense for the state since its completion, as well. Financial records are not available for the first year of operations, but from congressional testimony, it can be inferred that the Superdome ran a deficit of between $6 million and $8 million. Much of this deficit was debt service.[25]

Financial data are available beginning with fiscal year 1977, the second year of service for the Superdome, through 1984.[26] These statements are greatly disaggregated, allowing for detailed analysis. Because several lessons can be learned from closely examining the Superdome's financial statements, the analysis in this chapter will deviate somewhat from the pattern followed in other chapters.

Tables 15.1 and 15.2 duplicate the reports of operating revenues and operating expenses, respectively. Table 15.3 shows the non-operating revenues and costs. The last row of Table 15.3 combines the operating losses and non-operating losses to get the total (variable and fixed) losses for each of the years shown.

Several entries in the tables require explanation. One of the unique clauses in the lease between the New Orleans Saints and the Superdome is that the Saints pay rent for their office space at the Superdome. For fiscal years 1977 to 1981, this rent was included under "other." For subsequent years, this growing source of revenue was given its own line item.

For fiscal years 1976 and 1977, the first two years of its existence, the Superdome was managed by a public agency. Beginning with fiscal year 1978, the Superdome was managed by a private firm, Facility Management of Louisiana (FML). FML is a subsidiary of Facility Management Group, which has similar affiliates operating sports and entertainment facilities in New York, Florida, and California. Several changes in the payment for services occurred with the change in management. The almost $6.5 million paid to contractors in fiscal year 1977 was part of FML's duties and were included in the management

---

24. Ibid.
25. Ibid., 499.
26. *Louisiana Stadium and Exposition District Combined Statements of Revenues and Expenses.* Made available through a private correspondence with Bill Curl of the Facility Management of Louisiana.

fees to FML. Since these fees never exceeded $2 million, the switch to a private management firm saved the Superdome approximately $4.5 million annually.

Depreciation represents much of the "total loss" in Table 15.3. Since depreciation is an accounting expense, not a financial one, it should be subtracted to determine the financial cash flow of the Superdome. The last row in Table 15.3 does this. This is what will be used as the estimate for direct state expenditures.

From all aspects on the financial statements, the Superdome is a super money loser. The operating losses have ranged between $3.3 million to $5.4 million. Nor does there appear to be any trend for these numbers to be decreasing. The operating losses for fiscal year 1984 is less than the loss for fiscal year 1983, but the loss for fiscal year 1984 is the second highest in the survey.

Total rental income has remained relatively constant, increasing only 41 percent over the eight years shown. At the same time, the gross national product deflator increased over 94 percent. In real terms, the rental income in 1984 was approximately 28 percent less than the rental income in 1977.

The only source of rental income that grew in real terms over the survey period was that received from the Saints. The impact of the Saints on the financial well-being of the Superdome is evident from these tables. The NFL strike year of 1982 falls into fiscal year 1983. Rental revenues from football fell more than $200,000 in the fiscal year, the largest drop in football rental income in the survey. In real terms, the football revenues in 1983 were the lowest of any in the period.

The effect of the football strike on operating income was apparent as well. Concession revenues fell by more than $400,000 or 37 percent. Income from the stadium club and parking also declined. In total, operating revenues fell by approximately $1 million.

The impact of the Saints on the local economy is implied by the revenues from the hotel occupancy tax, shown in Table 15.3. Although the convention revenues increased by 69 percent in fiscal year 1983, the largest increase observed, the hotel occupancy tax fell for the only time in eight years. One implication of this is that NFL football games may draw more out-of-town visitors to the city than do conventions. Obviously, this one observation is not enough evidence for a proof, but it does provide sobering data for those considering construction of a facility to stimulate an economy through the convention and tourist trade. This certainly warrants further study.

The total financial losses for the Superdome also increased in fiscal year 1983. This increase in total losses reversed a trend of continuously declining losses. The only other year in which total losses increased was in fiscal year 1981, the year the Jazz relocated to Utah.

The trend in hotel occupancy tax revenues did not appear to change when the Jazz left for Salt Lake City. The data suggest that the hotels gain as football fans decide to make a weekend outing of attending a Sunday NFL game, but there is no such impact on hotels from the mostly weekday NBA schedule.

The conclusion that is evident from these financial records is that the professional sports teams that play (or have played) in the Superdome pay sufficient rents to cover the operating costs they impose upon Superdome authorities.

Total losses have been trimmed by more than 55 percent from 1977 to 1984. These gains, however, are due to increases in the hotel occupancy tax and interest income. Whether the hotel occupancy tax revenues should be included in determining the financial viability of the Superdome is debatable. If the Superdome was self-supporting, the hotel tax revenues could be spent on other civic projects or the hotel tax could be eliminated, allowing hotel guests to have more to spend on their visits. In this sense, the Superdome is a drain on civic funding and/or tourism.

Supporters of the Superdome argue that if the Superdome had not been constructed, the conventions, tourists, and hotels would not have been attracted in the first place. Thus, the Superdome, while a drain on the local treasuries of New Orleans and Jackson Parishes, has contributed more to these treasuries than it has taken out. One such study has estimated the economic impact of the Superdome on the Louisiana economy to be $2.678 billion for the first ten years of its existence.[27] While the analysis in this economic impact study is suspect (for reasons to be discussed later), the evidence supports the later argument. Much of the more than 100 percent increase in the hotel occupancy tax revenues comes from the growth in the hotel room inventory built since the Superdome opened.

The Superdome is exempt from property taxes. In 1986, the property tax rate was $132.32 per $1,000 of assessed valuation.[28] Applying this rate to the 1986 assessed valuation of $16,896,580[29] means the public ownership of the Superdome cost local governments the equivalent of $2,235,755.47 in foregone property taxes in 1986. In 1992, the property tax rate had risen to $176.92 per $1,000 of assessed valuation, but the assessment was virtually unchanged.[30]

Historical data on the Superdome's assessment are not available. Using the method employed in earlier analyses, the assessment is reduced by 6 percent annually to get the new tax base. Since property tax rates are not available for New Orleans before 1986, it was assumed that the property tax rate remained unchanged over the years. For the years 1986 to 1990, the difference between

27. Eddystone C. Nebel III, project director, *The Economic Impact of the Louisana Superdome (1975–1985)*, economic impact study conducted by the Division of Business and Economic Research, University of New Orleans, 1985, 11.

28. Conversation with Ellis Smith, New Orleans's Tax Assessor's Office, 3 March 1986.

29. Ibid.

30. Private conversation with Ray Burgess, deputy assessor of New Orleans, 27 July 1992. In the candid conversation, Mr. Burgess admitted that the assessments on exempt property "are given about as much thought as they deserve." Since there are no revenues generated from these properties, the assumption is they do not get much attention.

the 1986 rate and the 1992 rate were interpolated. Table 15.4 shows the property tax estimates working with these assumptions.

A closer look at the assessed valuation of the Superdome is instructive. The 1986 assessed value of the land on which the Superdome is located is $896,580, which means the market value of the land is $8,965,800.[31] This brings into question the previously mentioned economic impact study. That study estimated that the value of the land on which the Superdome is built at $100 million.[32] Using this number, the value of the land increased by more than $86 million. This increased value, in turn, is figured as a gain to the State of Louisiana. In reality, the land looks to have a market value less than the price the state paid for it. While some of this discrepancy may be the fault of the assessor, since exempt property is not assessed as often as taxable property, for the economic impact study to have an error factor more than ten places the validity of the whole study in serious doubt. Unfortunately, such errors are typical in economic impact studies.

Table 15.5 condenses the information from Tables 15.3 and Table 15.4 to get the direct and indirect government outlays derived from the Superdome. The outlay of $7 million for 1975 and 1976 is based upon the previously mentioned congressional testimony that the loss in these years was between $6 million and $8 million. Since there is no entry for tax expenses in Table 15.1, it is assumed that no taxes are generated directly by the Superdome. Thus, the outlays shown in the last row of Table 15.3 are assumed to be the state's subsidy of the Superdome.

In the likely event that the Superdome has continued to be a money loser, Table 15.5 underestimates the present value of the loss the Superdome imposes upon Louisiana.

The point should be made again that the ANPV of negative $47,729,356 does not mean Louisiana has subsidized the professional sports teams this amount. The design of the Superdome, with its many amenities and meeting rooms, means that the state subsidy of $47,729,356 is more appropriately debited to an urban renewal project of which the Saints and, while they played there, the Jazz were only one component.

---

31. Ibid.
32. Nebel, *The Economic Impact of the Louisiana Superdome*, 16.

Table 15.1
Louisiana Superdome
Operating Revenues
(1977–1984)
(in thousands of dollars)

Fiscal Year

	1977	1978	1979	1980	1981	1982	1983	1984
Football Rental	$576.8	$703.8	$638.2	$741.1	$768.9	$899.7	$669.8	$1,185.7
Convention Rental	$229.2	$170.5	$333.7	$291.6	$342.8	$314.3	$532.7	$363.0
Basketball Rental	$193.3	$240.9	$181.8	$7.5	$126.6	$94.4	$20.5	*
Musical Event Rent.	$109.9	$88.7	$228.2	$258.1	$279.8	$403.7	$284.4	$172.7
Baseball Rental	$34.0	$22.0	*	$32.0	$38.4	$32.1	$16.6	$33.7
Other Event Rent.	$156.6	$351.0	$335.5	$219.4	$133.2	$204.1	$183.4	$264.3
Reimbursed Costs	$1,462.5	$1,361.0	$1562.9	$1,418.0	$1,353.7	$1,514.5	$1,152.8	$1,886.6
Total Rent Inc.†	$2,762.3	$2,937.9	$3,280.3	$2,967.8	$3,043.3	$3,462.7	$2,860.2	$3,906.0
Concess. Revenue	$833.2	$943.4	$1,007.8	$889.1	$1,013.2	$1,106.6	$689.5	$1,293.5
Parking Revenue	$782.6	$1,113.1	$1,222.4	$1,272.8	$1,604.3	$2,109.6	$2,099.9	$2,047.1
Box Rentals	$429.5	$444.7	$532.4	$654.5	$699.6	$704.0	$736.3	$797.8
Guided Tours	$392.0	$534.1	$549.0	$516.7	$546.0	$476.5	$416.1	$404.9
Adver'g &Broadc'g Rev	$307.3	$309.9	$337.1	$258.9	$297.7	$292.2	$310.5	$364.8
Stadium Club	$111.2	$51.7	$59.5	$57.8	$48.4	$73.7	$57.4	$60.0
Office Space Rent.	*	*	*	*	*	$96.9	$153.4	$246.1
Promo of Spec'l Ev.	*	*	*	$155.1	*	*	*	*
Other	$172.2	$94.5	$121.4	$115.2	$141.0	$12.1	$10.9	$18.8
Total Non-Rental Income†	$3,027.9	$3,491.3	$3,829.6	$3,920.0	$4,350.2	$4,871.5	$4,474.0	$6,232.4
Total Operating Rev.†	$5,790.3	$6,429.2	$7,110.0	$6,887.7	$7,393.5	$8,334.2	$7,334.3	$10,138.5

† Columns may not sum to the total due to rounding.
* No line item entry for this fiscal year.

Table 15.2
Louisiana Superdome
Operating Expenses
(1977–1984)
(in thousands of dollars)

Operating Expenses

	1977	1978	1979	1980	1981	1982	1983	1984
Salaries & Wages	$860.9	$3,390.2	$3,979.4	$4,249.7	$4,750.2	$5,407.3	$5,142.6	$5,810.6
Contractor Payments								
Operations & Security	$3,528.2	$1,124.1	*	*	*	*	*	*
Building Engineering	$2,840.5	*	*	*	*	*	*	*
Parking Facilities	$61.8	*	*	*	*	*	*	*
Utilities	$1,939.9	$2,202.3	$1,844.3	$1,830.2	$2,134.2	$2,923.5	$2,588.9	$2,877.5
Insurance	$635.7	$852.3	$894.4	$898.3	$674.5	$517.6	$408.2	$484.7
Mgmt. Fees	$503.5	$1,096.2	$1,431.3	$1,551.1	$1,735.6	$1,903.1	$1,395.1	$1,632.4
Legal Fees	*	$685.6	$783.6	$592.5	$532.3	$304.5	$327.3	$487.4
Repairs/Maint.	$399.7	$570.3	$687.3	$973.5	$995.1	$1,059.4	$1,334.9	$1,594.7
Advertising & Public Relations	$154.6	$181.3	$185.2	$83.3	$75.7	$64.5	$74.6	$100.9
Direct Event Expense	*	*	*	*	*	*	104.1	469.6
Other	$221.0	$570.8	$602.4	$800.1	$439.5	$484.8	$203.0	$192.3
Total Operational Expenses†§	$11.1	$10.7	$10.4	$11.0	$11.3	$12.7	$12.2	$14.3
Operating Loss†§	$5.4	$4.2	$3.3	$4.1	$3.9	$4.3	$4.8	$4.2

† Columns may not sum to the total due to rounding.
* No line item entry for this fiscal year.
§ In millions of dollars

Table 15.3
Louisiana Superdome
Non-Operating Revenues and Expenses
(1977–1984)
(in thousands of dollars)

Fiscal Year

	1977	1978	1979	1980	1981	1982	1983	1984
Non-Operating Income								
Hotel Occupancy Tax	$4,659.3	$5,704.4	$6,763.4	$7,619.0	$8,644.2	$9,140.7	$8,828.1	$9,421.8
Interest Inc.	$198.3	$273.9	$661.7	$948.7	$1,102.7	$1,447.8	$1,072.9	$1,046.0
Total Non-Operating Income†§	$4.9	$6.0	$7.4	$8.6	$9.8	$10.6	$9.9	$10.5
Non-Operating Expenses								
Interest Exp.	$7,535.0	$7,859.0	$7,830.1	$7,623.8	$7,449.7	$7,196.7	$6,976.4	$6,718.0
Depreciation & Amortization	$5,056.7	$5,084.4	$5,113.9	$5,466.6	$5,516.5	$5,631.9	$5,061.5	$5,045.7
Legal Settlements	*	*	*	*	$1,795.0	$335.8	$297.4	$175.8
Total Non-Operating Expenses†§	$12.6	$12.9	$12.9	$13.1	$14.8	$13.2	$12.3	$11.9
Total Loss§†	$13.1	$11.21	$8.8	$8.6	$9.0	$6.9	$7.3	$5.7
Total Loss Minus Depreciation†§	$8	$6.11	$3.67	$3.13	$3.48	$1.27	$2.24	$0.65

† Columns may not sum to the total due to rounding.
* No line item entry for this fiscal year.
§ In millions of dollars

Table 15.4
Louisiana Superdome
Foregone Property Taxes
(1975–1990)

Year	Tax Valuation	Property Taxes
1975	$8,900,908	($1,177,768)
1976	$9,434,962	($1,248,434)
1977	$10,001,060	($1,323,340)
1978	$10,601,123	($1,402,741)
1979	$11,237,191	($1,486,905)
1980	$11,911,422	($1,576,119)
1981	$12,626,107	($1,670,687)
1982	$13,383,674	($1,770,928)
1983	$14,186,694	($1,877,183)
1984	$15,037,896	($1,989,814)
1985	$15,940,170	($2,109,203)
1986	$16,896,580	($2,235,755)
1987	$16,896,580	($2,361,297)
1988	$16,896,580	($2,486,839)
1989	$16,896,580	($2,612,380)
1990	$16,896,580	($2,737,922)

Table 15.5
Louisiana Superdome
Accumulated Present Value of Cash Flows
(1975–1990)

Year	Direct Municipal Subsidy	Foregone Property Taxes	Direct & Indirect Municipal Subsidy	PV of π or (Subsidy)
1975	($7,000,000)	($1,177,768)	($8,177,768)	($8,177,768)
1976	($7,000,000)	($1,248,434)	($8,248,434)	($7,562,514)
1977	($8,000,000)	($1,323,340)	($9,323,340)	($7,770,090)
1978	($6,110,000)	($1,402,741)	($7,512,741)	($5,689,312)
1979	($3,670,000)	($1,486,905)	($5,156,905)	($3,532,501)
1980	($3,130,000)	($1,576,119)	($4,706,119)	($2,919,475)
1981	($3,480,000)	($1,670,687)	($5,150,687)	($2,894,774)
1982	($1,270,000)	($1,770,928)	($3,040,928)	($1,555,521)
1983	($2,240,000)	($1,877,183)	($4,117,183)	($1,931,908)
1984	($650,000)	($1,989,814)	($2,639,814)	($1,138,960)
1985		($2,109,203)	($2,109,203)	($875,568)
1986		($2,235,755)	($2,235,755)	($798,663)
1987		($2,361,297)	($2,361,297)	($768,153)
1988		($2,486,839)	($2,486,839)	($736,721)
1989		($2,612,380)	($2,612,380)	($704,774)
1990		($2,737,922)	($2,737,922)	($672,655)

Accumulated Net Present Value ....($47,729,356)

Chapter 16
Minneapolis Metrodome

HISTORY

The movement to replace the Metropolitan Stadium (the Met) in Minneapolis, Minnesota began in the early 1970s, fifteen years after it was completed. The first proposals were generated in response to pressure by the Minnesota Vikings. The Vikings were dissatisfied with the Met's low seating capacity and the open air nature of the stadium, which the Vikings felt hurt attendance during the winter football season.

The Vikings' contract to occupy the Met expired in 1975, which prompted Minneapolis to undertake a feasibility study that was completed in 1973.[1] The proposal called for a $51 million downtown stadium with a capacity of 70,000 to 75,000. A positive aspect of the downtown location cited by the study was that the parking lot designed for 4,000 to 5,000 cars could be used to alleviate a downtown parking shortage during the week.[2] The facility was to be designed so it could house expositions and conventions as well as sporting events. The study also called for a major traffic artery into Minneapolis to be realigned to pass under the stadium, making it more accessible to suburban patrons. Three more feasibility studies were completed in 1973. Two called for some form of a downtown stadium, while another was to upgrade the University of Minnesota's Stadium.

The Met was operated by the Metropolitan Sports Area Commission (MSAC), which represented the communities of Minneapolis, Bloomington, and Richfield. The MSAC could not make an expenditure larger than $5,000 without permission of the constituent communities. Obviously, the $51 million exceeded this spending limit.

---

1. "City Studies Proposal for $51 Million Stadium," *Engineering News Record* 190 (11 January 1973), 15.
2. Ibid.

The Minnesota Legislature introduced three proposals in 1973 to form a new sports commission with a wider geographic representation than the existing commission. The new commission would be charged with improving the existing stadium or building a new stadium to keep the Vikings in the Minneapolis metropolitan area. A Special Committee on Sports and Cultural Facilities convened in 1973 to hold hearings on the merits of the legislative proposals. The first to testify at these hearings was Max Winter, president of the Vikings.

Winter complained that the facilities at the Met were inadequate, citing that it had the smallest capacity in the NFL at that time. Winter projected that the small capacity would doom the Vikings to operating losses in 1975.[3] Winter laced a threat of leaving Minneapolis for another city with heavy doses of altruism. He complained that the small capacity at the Met caused the visitor's share received by the Vikings' opponents to be small.[4] He argued for a facility with a capacity between 70,000 and 80,000 and estimated the new facility's cost to be about $30 million. Winter wanted a domed stadium, saying franchises in the upper Midwest regions of Green Bay, Chicago, Detroit, and Minneapolis "are most in need of protecting fans and players from the weather."[5] Surprisingly, none of these franchises played in a domed stadium at the time, and now only Detroit does in addition to Minneapolis.

Winter's charity went beyond his concern for NFL franchises. He said the Vikings would play in any facility in the Minneapolis metropolitan area, including the University of Minnesota's Memorial Stadium, but they preferred a new stadium in downtown Minneapolis or St. Paul to benefit the city's downtown area. Winter's concern for his fellow man continued when he dismissed several alternatives to public funding a new stadium, including the selling of bonds to season ticket holders, such as the Dallas Cowboys had done to finance their stadium. He argued that selling a $2,000 bond would eliminate the "man in the street from attending Vikings' games." Winter's benevolence ended when considering options to a new stadium. Without a new facility, he said the Vikings would raise ticket prices from $7 to $8 to reduce the losses they would earn in the small Met.

The Met was located on land with an estimated market value greater than the outstanding debt on the Met. Winters used this fact to argue that a new stadium would present no additional tax burden. He theorized that the Minnesota Twins would be happy to take over the debt payments for the Met if the Vikings moved out, since they would be acquiring a facility worth more than the payments.

The assumption that a new stadium would be built for the Vikings and that the Twins would remain at the Met dominated the testimony of those who appeared before the committee. Gerald Moore, chairman of the MSAC, testified, "In all likelihood the Twins will remain as the major tenant in the facility [the

---

3. Minneapolis Minnesota Metropolitan Council, "Recommendations for a Metropolitan Sports Commission" (24 January 1974, Microfiche), 26.
4. Ibid.
5. Ibid.

Met] even if the Vikings should decide to move to another facility."[6] The committee concluded, "It is a generally accepted fact that Metropolitan Stadium is an excellent baseball facility."[7]

The only person to counter this conclusion was Calvin Griffith, president of the Twins. In his 25 October testimony before the committee, Griffith indicated "that a new stadium was definitely needed or that there should be extensive remodeling of Metropolitan Stadium."[8] Among the improvements Griffith sought was increased seating capacity (although the capacity of the Met was rarely a constraint at Twins games), installation of escalators, a better public address and lighting systems, and improved concessions and restroom facilities. Griffith was disappointed that all the talk of a new stadium centered on the Vikings' needs. His solution was to build a new football stadium next to the Met, make his recommended improvements to the Met, and add a movable roof, much like the one that Kansas City abandoned, that would move between the two facilities.

The committee recommended that a new sports commission be formed representing the seven counties surrounding the Minneapolis metropolitan area. The assumption that the sports franchises had to be kept for the good of the region was addressed in the first paragraph of the committee's recommendations: "This area struggled to obtain big league sports. There is a danger of losing these valuable franchises."[9] The committee recommended that the new commission take over the operation of the Met and the Sports Arena and assume all the outstanding debt related to these facilities. The committee concluded that the new stadium should be self-sufficient and that the portion of the private sector benefiting from the stadium's construction should contribute "to the maximum extent possible."[10]

Several expansions were made in a futile attempt to try to placate the Vikings by raising the capacity to 49,700 for football. The expansions were poorly designed and had little architectural reference to previous construction. As a result, the sight lines for football were poor, and the stadium had a jerry-built appearance. To add to the Met's misery, the $5,000 restriction on capital expenditures hamstrung the MSAC from making needed capital expenditures. Far from being the "excellent baseball facility," that the review committee saw, the Met had the reputation of being the worst maintained stadium in Major League Baseball.[11] In 1980, a railing on the third deck broke away, creating a safety hazard.

Following the committee's recommendation, the Minnesota Legislature formed the Metropolitan Sports Facility Commission (MSFC) in 1977 to build

---

6. Ibid.
7. Ibid., 5.
8. Ibid., 34.
9. Ibid., 5.
10. Ibid., 5–8.
11. Philip Lowry, *Green Cathedrals* (Cooperstown, NY: Society of American Baseball Research, 1986), 61.

and operate a stadium in the Minneapolis metropolitan area. By 1982, the Met became the first modern stadium to be replaced.

The new stadium, the Metrodome, was a domed facility, using air pressure to support a fiberglass roof of the type that is used in the Carrier Dome and the Hoosierdome. The facility has been plagued with several problems, including roof collapses, and in one case a thunderstorm caused the roof to rip.

CONSTRUCTION COSTS

The Metrodome cost $52.7 million to complete in April 1982. This was accomplished through two economy measures to keep the cost of the stadium close to the $51 million projected in 1973. First, the 1973 plans were for a stadium with a capacity in the low 70,000 range, the Metrodome has a capacity of 63,000 for football and 55,000 for baseball. Second, the use of the fiberglass roof reduced the cost from the original plan which called for a traditional solid roof.

SUBSIDY ANALYSIS

The Metrodome is able to earn enough in rents, concessions, and fees to cover the operating costs of the stadium. As Table 16.1 shows, the Metrodome has earned an operating profit in each of its ten years of operation.[12]

A definite pattern exists between the professional success the Twins enjoy and the operating profits the Metrodome earns. In 1988, when the Twins finished second in their division, the Metrodome earned the highest operating profits in its history. In 1991, when the Twins won the World Series, the Metrodome had its second highest operating profits. The 1987 operating profit appears to counter this trend. The Twins won the World Series in that year, but operating profits were the lowest of the last five years of the survey. A lawsuit settlement of almost $1.4 million,[13] and a twenty-four–day NFL strike during 1987 account for this anomaly. The Twins and Vikings, it seems, pay the variable costs they impose upon the MSFC.

The state legislation that formed the MSFC allowed the issuance of bonds to cover the construction costs and gave the MSFC several revenue sources so that

---

12. Data for Table 16.1 comes from State of Minnesota, Financial Audit Division, Office of the Legislative Auditor, *Financial Statements and Management Letter for the Year Ended December 31,* for 1982, 1983, 1984, 1985, 1986, 1987, 1988, 1989, 1990, 1991. While the MFSC also owns an indoor arena, the Met Center, neighboring the Metrodome, was essentially operated by the Minnesota North Stars hockey franchise before they relocated to Dallas beginning in the 1993 season.

13. State of Minnesota, *Financial Statements and Management Letter for the Year Ended December 31, 1987,* footnote 6(b).

the payment of the debt service would not become the state's burden. These levies and the operating profits have been successful in paying the debt service.

One of the revenue sources was a tax of up to 10 percent on liquor and hotel and motel rooms within the city. The tax was to be imposed as needed to cover the debt service on the Metrodome's bonds. Every year the Minneapolis City Council estimates the amount of money that the MSFC will need to meet the debt service on the stadium's bonds and sets the tax rate to accumulate the needed amount. Insofar as the patrons of the city's hotels and motels and consumers of liquor do not visit the Metrodome, there is a cross-subsidy to those who use the facility. As Table 16.1 indicates, the magnitude of this cross-subsidy has been diminishing over time, and no tax revenues were required by the MSFC to finance the debt service since 1984. The hotel and liquor taxes paid in 1985 and 1986 are late receipts incurred in prior years.

Since the hotel and liquor tax receipts are not generated from stadium operations, and if the city did have such a tax and no stadium, the revenues could be used for other purposes; these taxes are treated as a subsidy to the stadium operations.

A more direct tax that finances the debt service is a 10 percent tax on the price of tickets to Metrodome events. This includes not only games by the Twins and the Vikings, but those by the University of Minnesota as well. The revenues from this tax are included in operating revenues, but in the last four years, the size of these revenues have been larger than the amount of the annual debt service. The operating profits not used to pay fixed costs is credited to several interest-bearing contingency accounts for future payment of the debt service. These reserve accounts are well funded and, in 1991, earned more than $1.1 million in interest, about 33 percent of the debt service that year.

A final source of revenues is the proceeds from the sale of the Met in 1984. On the recommendation of the Special Committee on Sports and Cultural Facilities the new Sports Commission acquired the Met and the Met's debts. In 1984, the MSFC received $10,721,934 from the sale of the Met.

Foregone property taxes are difficult to measure. The assessor attempted to get the Metrodome included in the tax base but, like many of his counterparts in other cities, lost the case that the stadium should be taxed because it was primarily used by profit-seeking firms. The city and county do tax the $5 million in private property that the teams keep at the stadium. This provides about $500,000 in revenues annually. To the extent that the alternative use of the stadium site would have had value greater than this amount and the amount that the ticket tax exceeds the debt service, the accumulated net present value in the last column of Table 16.1 may be an overestimate.

The net accumulated present value of negative $43,500 is not significantly different from zero. The structure of ticket taxes appears to be creating enough revenues to pay variable and fixed costs from stadium users. While there was a cross-subsidy from hotel and liquor consumers to stadium consumers in the early years, this contingency tax did not seem to be necessary once the proceeds from the sale of the Met were realized. While ten years is not enough time to draw decisive conclusions, Table 16.1 gives strong evidence that the Metrodome bears watching as one of the few financial success stories in stadium investments.

Table 16.1
Minneapolis Metrodome
Operating Profits, Cash Flows, and Present Value of Cash Flows
(1982-1991)

Year	Operating Profit	Liquor/Hotel Tax Revenues	Proceeds from Sale of Met	PV of π or (Subsidy)
1982	$1,947,552	$3,263,819		($3,263,819)
1983	$23,223,574	$3,228,765		($2,777,193)
1984	$4,470,633	$2,519,330	$10,721,934	$6,047,810
1985	$3,802,761	$57,762		($36,522)
1986	$3,455,455	$25,639		($13,776)
1987	$5,224,274	$0		$0
1988	$8,224,893	$0		$0
1989	$6,148,930	$0		$0
1990	$5,472,771	$0		$0
1991	$6,831,656	$0		$0

Accumulated Net Present Value.......($43,500)

Part II
Data Analysis

Chapter 17

Summary and Analysis of Financial Data

Chapters 2 through 16 presented financial data for fifteen stadiums. The data were studied in several forms, including planned and actual construction costs, operating profits, calculations of outlays and revenues and, for fourteen stadiums, and the municipality's accumulated net present value of the cash flows (ANPV) generated by the stadium investment. The stadiums in the previous chapters were selected because sufficient data were available to compute the ANPV for the stadium. In some of the categories, data on other stadiums were also available. In this chapter, these additional data are included when appropriate. Several generalizations can be made for each of these categories of financial analysis.

CONSTRUCTION COSTS

Projected construction costs chronically are underestimated. Table 17.1 contrasts the anticipated and the actual construction costs for sixteen stadiums, including many in the subsidy study.

Table 17.1 construction costs are for the original stadium structure and related facilities, such as parking lots and scoreboards. The figures do not include any subsequent renovations (except Yankee Stadium, where the cost is of the renovation that took place in the mid-1970s).

Whenever possible, a publicized construction cost estimate is used. In cases in which these data were not available, the size of the construction bond issue is used. In those cases in which a significant amount of time elapsed between the passage of a bond issue and the completion of the stadium, the stadium was not included. For example, Candlestick Park in not included because almost a decade elapsed from the time the original $5 million bond issue was passed and the stadium was completed for more than $15 million.

The data in Table 17.1 supports the allegation that early estimates are poor indicators of the final cost of the stadium. The actual construction cost was an average of 73 percent above the projected construction cost. The range was from a .4 percent overestimate for Three Rivers Stadium to a 367 percent underestimate for the Superdome.

Although the Superdome represents the most significant underestimated construction cost, it is not an anomaly. The renovation of Yankee Stadium cost more than three times the original estimate. The construction cost of RFK Stadium was more than two-fold over projected costs, even after measures were taken to allow the Armory Board to lease, rather than purchase, the stadium land. Even if the Superdome is excluded from the analysis, the construction costs of the stadium projects listed on Table 17.1 were, on average, 67 percent above the projected costs.

It is possible to test to see if the figures in the projected column and the actual column are statistically significantly different from each other. Using the test for the difference of two means,[1] it can be shown that the likelihood that these two series are from the same distribution is less than 2 chances out of 100.

SUBSIDIES

Sufficient data were gathered and presented to estimate ANPV for fourteen stadiums. These figures are summarized in Table 17.2.

Over the years studied, the stadiums have an aggregate negative ANPV of $119,009,396. This means that the teams occupying these facilities received an aggregate subsidy of $119,009,396 to play in municipal stadiums. This represents approximately $391,478.28 for each of the 304 years included in the survey.[2] The average is misleading in this case, however, because of the wide variation in the ANPVs. The values range from a positive $8 million to negative $70 million.

Alternative subsidy calculations were made in four cases in which it was possible to determine the predevelopment property values and when it was reasonable to argue that the stadium would not have been constructed by a

---

1. This test was introduced earlier as

$$z = \frac{\mu_a - \mu_b}{\sqrt{\dfrac{s_a^2}{n_a} + \dfrac{s_b^2}{n_b}}}$$

Where:
   • μ_a and μ_b represent the means of the actual costs ($51,692,558) and the projected costs ($29,818,000), respectively.
   • s_a and s_b represent the standard deviations of the two distributions, $39,739,990 and $24,382, respectively.
   • n_a and n_b represent the number of data points for each period, fifteen each.
2. Milwaukee County Stadium, for which it was not possible to compute an ANPV, is included in the subsidy analysis discussed in this paragraph.

private party. These stadiums and their alternative assumption ANPV are shown in Table 17.3.

The alternative assumptions increase the magnitude of the ANPV significantly. This is not surprising, since much of the subsidy in many cases consists of foregone property taxes.

For the analysis in the remainder of this chapter, the data in Table 17.2 will be used.

Per Capita Subsidy

Table 17.4 summarizes the per capita subsidy in order of increasing levels of subsidy. The per capita subsidy is calculated by dividing the subsidy in Table 17.2 by the population of the city when the stadium was started or when the first game was played. The exceptions are Baltimore, in which the 1950 population is used, and Erie County (Orchard Park) in which the 1970 population was used. Population data were not available for Foxboro.

The figures in Table 17.4 represents the lump sum tax (or wealth increase in the case of Dodger Stadium) that would have been assessed to every citizen of the city at the time the stadium was built or put in service. Excluding the Superdome from the analysis, the average subsidy is $13 (with a standard deviation of $13, as well).

The high end of the distribution is dominated by facilities that are financed, partially at least, by entities larger than the city. New Orleans' Superdome, for example, began the trend toward state financing of stadiums. The Oakland–Alameda Coliseum Complex is financed in part by Alameda County, and Atlanta–Fulton County Stadium is a joint city–county venture. Orange County was to participate in the financing of Anaheim Stadium, but the county backed out. It is not clear, however, how one accounts for a one-third contribution by a county, for example, in these computations, but when these considerations are taken into account, the variation in the distribution of the per capita income would be less than is reflected in Table 17.4.

SUBSIDY ANALYSIS

Table 17.2 shows that most municipal stadium investments earn a negative ANPV. The presence of a subsidy can be examined from many perspectives. The direction of this inquiry will be to determine the nature of the subsidy first. This analysis will be useful in determining who benefits from the subsidy. The affect that certain demographic conditions have on the size of the subsidy will be measured. The chapter will conclude by attempting to predict the future direction of specific stadium subsidies.

The Nature of the Subsidies

In the most hopeful case, the city will earn enough in rent to cover the game-day costs as well as costs of maintaining the stadium (in what follows, these will be called operating expenses or variable costs), as well as the cost of construction and debt service (fixed costs).

In the probable event that revenues do not cover all the costs of the stadium, two possibilities exist. The least favorable prospect would be that the stadium earns such a meager income for the municipality that it does not cover even the operating expenses. A middle ground, in which the stadium does earn enough in revenues to recover operating expenses, but not all the fixed costs, is possible also.

The distinction between the two is important in more than the size of the city's deficit. If the city is not earning enough to recover the fixed costs but is covering the operating costs of the stadium, the city authorities are acting rationally by keeping the team in the stadium. Even though a subsidy exists, it is smaller than if the city had to pay the debt service without any of the revenues net of operating expenses. If, on the other hand, the stadium tenants do not pay enough to cover the operating costs they impose on the city for using the facility, the city would be better off not having the team play in the stadium unless there are sufficiently large external benefits to justify the subsidy.

Operating Costs. Teams in public stadiums usually cover the variable costs imposed upon their municipal landlords. In more than 70 percent of the years for which operating profits were available, including data that are not reported in chapters 2 through 16, the cities earned more income from the teams than the cities paid in operating expenses. The implication is that, in most cases, the cities are acting rationally by hosting franchises in their stadiums.

Fixed Costs. Covering a stadium's operating costs does not mean the teams are paying the full costs of the stadiums. The increasingly large costs of modern facilities make it unlikely that stadiums will earn enough to cover debt service expenditures.

Relationship Between Investment Size and the Subsidy

Four of the five stadiums with the highest ANPV (either positive present values or lowest negative present values) are those for which the cities incurred little, if any, construction expenditures. Dodger Stadium is a private facility, with public participation limited to infrastructure improvements. Similarly, construction costs were not included in the ANPV of Buffalo's War Memorial Stadium since it was not built to host professional sports.

The next highest ANPV belongs to Foxboro Stadium, also built with private funds. The negative ANPV for Foxboro Stadium is attributable to the foregone property taxes the public sector loses due to a tax abatement on the stadium property. Denver's Mile High Stadium was privately constructed to house a minor league baseball team. The facility was donated to Denver by a private syndicate when renovations were necessary to raise the stadium to NFL standards.

The fifth member of the low subsidy species, the Metrodome, also supports the hypothesis that there is a negative relationship between construction costs and the size of the subsidy. When adjusted for inflation, the Metrodome is the lowest cost publicly built stadium in the survey. When the low construction cost is combined with the fact that the Metropolitan Sports Facilities Commission, operators of the Metrodome, received a $10 million cash inflow from the sale of the old Metropolitan Stadium, the Metrodome required a tax subsidy in only the first three years of its first decade.[3] If this trend continues, the Metrodome could become a model of how to construct a municipal stadium with a minimum municipal subsidy.

To test if a relationship exists between the municipal costs and municipal subsidy, a regression test was conducted using the subsidy (in dollars) as the dependent variable and the municipal fixed costs (in 1977 dollars) and the years of data in the survey as the independent variables. The last independent variable was used to adjust for the number of years the facility has been generating a subsidy. If the stadium is earning a subsidy in each of the years, the magnitude of the subsidy will be directly related to the number of years in the survey. The regression is described by the following equation:

$$ANPV = a + b(\text{Construction Costs}) + c(\text{Years in Survey})$$

The results of the regression analysis are given by:

N	R^2(adjusted)	F-ratio	Constant	Coefficient (t-ratio) Construction Costs	Years
14	74.7%	20.22	4,766,817.8 (.6834)	0.2353 (5.7404)	-367,885.97 (-1.336)

The chance of the data occurring randomly is less than 1 in 1,000, although the adjusted R^2 of .747 indicates that about one-fourth of the variation in subsidies is caused by some factor other than construction costs and years in the survey.

The coefficient for construction costs has the predicted sign. The implication is that for every dollar in fixed investment in a stadium, the city can expect to incur a present value subsidy of about 23.5 cents. In other words, it will only recover about 76.5 cents of the construction costs, at least through the period of life shown in the survey. The probability that the true value of the construction cost coefficient is zero, given this distribution, is less than 1 in 10,000.

The sign of the coefficient for the years covered in the survey is negative, which is counter to the assumptions made before the regression was run. The

---

3.   If the proceeds of the sale of the Met are excluded from the cash flows, the ANPV for the Metrodome is approximately negative $7.5 million.

level of significance for the years' coefficient is low. The probability that the true value of the years' coefficient is zero is about 20 percent.

The implication of the negative sign, if indeed it is significant, is that the longer a stadium operates the smaller the subsidy. This means the operations of a stadium for a professional sports team covers the variable costs and a portion of the initial investment, so that the subsidy gets smaller as time passes. This is further evidence that stadium operators are rational, and that the magnitude of the subsidy is related to the size of the construction costs.

Subsidy Incidence

Since a subsidy exists in most cases, a welfare question arises: to whom does the subsidy go and from whom? It is generally thought, with no scientific evidence, that a wealth transfer from higher- to lower-income households is preferred to one that goes the other way. Because the desirability of the direction of wealth transfers is beyond the scope of this study, it will not dwell on the finer points of welfare economics. Instead, the analysis will focus on the direction of the wealth transfer and the likely beneficiaries of the stadium subsidy to the team.

Basically, three parties may gain from a subsidy to a sports team. Obviously, the first party to receive the subsidy is the team owner, but he may have to share a portion of this with the fan, in the form of lower ticket prices or with his players, in the form of higher salaries. How much of this subsidy he will have to pass on to the fan will depend upon two factors: (1) the nature of the subsidy, and (2) the price elasticity of demand for the team's tickets. The nature of the subsidy is important in determining whether the subsidy reduces fixed or variable costs. As with the city's decision to rent the facility, fixed costs do not enter into a team's output or pricing decision. A lease that subsidizes a team through a reduction of fixed costs will only serve to increase a franchise's profits (or reduce their losses). In a case where there is free entry, this may attract more firms, but this hardly describes either Major League Baseball or the NFL.

A subsidy that reduces the team's marginal costs will serve to reduce prices.[4] Such a subsidy will make it less costly to admit fans to the game. Since each fan represents more profit, the team owner will reduce the ticket price to encourage more fans to attend a game. The reduced ticket price will represent a transfer of some of the subsidy from the team owner to the fan.

The evidence in the earlier section of this chapter supports the argument that little, if any, of the subsidy is passed on to fans. In most cases, the subsidy to the team is in the area of construction costs and property taxes on the stadium. These are fixed costs, so little if any of the subsidy will be passed on to the fan.

---

4. Here "marginal cost" is meant to be the additional cost of admitting one more fan, rather than the cost of an additional game. The latter is meaningless since the number of games is fixed by the league.

Even if the subsidy is one that affects marginal costs, exactly by how much the prices fall depends upon the price elasticity of demand for the tickets. A larger part of any given subsidy will be passed on to fans the more unresponsive the quantity demanded is to price changes. Given that most teams play in cities where they are the only major league franchise in that sport, the demand curve for the team's games may, at first, seem to be inelastic.[5] When one views, however, the monies spent on sports as discretionary expenditures for entertainment, a variety of alternatives arise so the demand is more responsive to changes in price than might first be thought. The result is that there is little likelihood that a significant amount of the subsidy will be passed to the team's patrons.

The recent escalation of players' salaries might lead one to believe that some of the subsidy to team owners is transferred to players. Because of the fixed cost nature of the subsidy, however, this is not likely.

The chance for desirable wealth transfer (in the conventional meaning of the term) is slim. If the city's tax structure has any proportional characteristics at all, or if the subsidy results in reduced aid programs to low-income people, it is likely low-income citizens will pay some share of the subsidy. The inequitable nature of the subsidy is made even more compelling if one makes the reasonable assumption that the poorest segments of an economy cannot afford to attend most sporting events at any price. The income of team owner, player, and frequent fan will most certainly be higher than the poorest elements of the city's economy. No matter how the subsidy is divided there is likely to be a perverse (in the conventional sense) transfer of income created by the stadium subsidies.

Relationship Between Subsidies and Relocation and Expansion Factors

As mentioned in the introductory chapter, Frank Jozsa, Jr. studied the economic motivation of existing professional team relocation and the placement of expansion franchises. Jozsa found that the demand for franchise sites was directly related to a city's population and per capita income. In addition, there was a positive relation between the proportion of blacks living in a city and the attractiveness of the location to NFL franchise owners. When expansion sites were considered, cities with successful professional sports franchises in other sports were favored over those that had no track record with professional sports.[6]

To test Jozsa's hypothesis, a regression equation was run to see if a relationship existed between the magnitude of a stadium's ANPV and the

---

5. When two teams in the same sport "share" a territory, the schedules are devised to minimize direct competition. This, combined with fan loyalties, leads to little economic competition from crosstown rivals.

6. Frank P. Jozsa, Jr., "An Economic Analysis of Franchise Relocation and League Expansions in Professional Team Sports, 1950–1975" (Ph.D. diss., Georgia State University, 1977), 137–141.

presence of "desirable" characteristics. If the city's population, income levels, and demographics are favored by franchise owners, the city should find itself in a stronger bargaining position that may allow the city to secure better lease terms. Since the team would be willing to pay a higher rent for a preferred location, the ANPV of the stadium investment would be higher. Thus, larger cities with higher incomes should be able to negotiate better lease terms than smaller, poorer cities. For expansion teams, cities that are hosting sports franchises should realize higher ANPVs.

The New Orleans Superdome was eliminated from the study because of its position as an outlier of municipally owned stadiums. Dodger Stadium was eliminated from the analysis because it is a private stadium. Foxboro was excluded from this portion of the analysis because population data were not available. It was not possible to observe the effect upon football leases made by the proportion of blacks in a community because the subsidy survey included too few stadiums that were used exclusively by NFL franchises.

An ordinary least squares regression was conducted, using the ANPV of the stadium investment as the dependent variable. The city's population, income, and existing franchises served as independent variables. The regression is described by the following equation:

$$ANPV = a + b(Population) + c(Income) + d(Sport)$$

Where:
- ANPV is the estimate in chapters two through sixteen and summarized in Table 17.2.
- Population is the total population of the SMSA for the host city in the closest decennial census to the date when the stadium opened.
- Income is the per-capita monetary income for the host city as reported in the closest decennial census to the date the stadium was opened (in nominal dollars).
- Sports is a dummy variable to reflect the presence of a professional sports franchise in another sport at the time the stadium was constructed. A value of one was assigned to a city if it hosted at least one other major league sports team (in another sport) when the stadium was built.

The coefficients are the number of dollars the ANPV increases (the subsidy decreases) if the related variable increases by one unit. Positive signs of the coefficients will support Jozsa's hypothesis.

The results of the regression equation are given below:

N	R²(adjusted)	F-ratio	Coefficient (t-ratio)			
			Constant	Population	Income	Sports
11	0.2%	1.01	-21,267,550 (1.81)	0.136219 (0.027)	1,042.63 (.046)	10,809,952 (1.08)

The regression equation does not yield conclusive results, but they do not lend strong support to Jozsa's findings. The coefficients have the predicted signs, but the magnitude of the coefficients is not large enough to consider any of them statistically significant. The collection of the independent variables does a poor job of explaining the variation in subsidy sizes. The adjusted R^2 of 0.2 percent implies that other factors account for more than 99 percent of the variation of stadium subsidies.

The lack of a large F-ratio or statistically significant coefficients does not, by itself, discredit Jozsa's findings. The small number of data points may preclude getting any significant relationships.

A second argument in defense of Jozsa is that the nature of the test is indirect at best. The regression tests the relationship between the city's demographics and the size of the subsidy, not the team's willingness to pay a higher rent for the stadium. If the team is not required to pay higher rents, they will not.

The team's elasticity of demand for cities with the favored characteristics may be high. While it is true that franchises look for certain features when deciding where to locate, there may be several cities that possess such qualities. The "one-buyer" position of professional sports teams to locate in a territory could give the team the bargaining edge when negotiating lease terms with a city. If the managers of the stadium are unwilling or unable to negotiate a lease that will reduce the subsidy to the franchise, the size of the subsidy may not be a function of the city's characteristics.

Jozsa's research does not estimate the value of each of the favored characteristics to the team. This would be useful for cities that want to assess the amount of market power they possess when negotiating a lease. Franchises also would find the information useful to compare cities' profit potentials more scientifically. Unfortunately, such analysis is not likely to be forthcoming shortly. Finances of professional sports teams are closely guarded data, and the number of observations is so small that statistical significance may prove elusive.

LONG-TERM OUTLOOK FOR STADIUM INVESTMENTS

The chance that the stadium projects earn a positive ANPV over their life falls into three groups. The first group is the handful of stadiums that either presently have a positive ANPV or are likely to have a positive ANPV by the end of the stadium's useful life. The second group are those facilities that probably will never recover their costs of construction but are earning enough in rents to cover their operating costs. The last group is for those stadiums that were so ill advised that they not only fail to cover their fixed costs, but are running operating losses as well.

Four stadiums fall into the positive, or near positive, ANPV category. The one unambiguous member is Dodger Stadium. The other three are Mile High Stadium, Baltimore's Memorial Stadium, and the Minneapolis Metrodome.

Mile High Stadium has been profitable from 1981–1989. These profits, however, are discounted twenty-two years so that each dollar of current profit increases the ANPV by only about 25 cents. Ironically, Mile High Stadium may be reaching the end of its functional life and that could put the stadium investment into the black. The Colorado Rockies National League expansion team will play its home games in a new stadium once it is constructed. Such a gesture to one professional team usually leads to expectations by the other team, in this case the Broncos, for a new facility. If this were to happen soon, and if Mile High Stadium sold for around $10 million, the final NPV of the municipal investment could be positive.

Similarly, if Baltimore's Memorial Stadium is sold in the next two to three years, the project undertaken in the mid-fifties might earn a positive NPV. The stadium's operations earned a profit in all but one of the last six years stadium accounts were reported. When discounted at the low interest rates appropriate for a project undertaken in the mid-1950s, every dollar of profit in 1985 still represented about a 40 cents gain in ANPV.[7]

Memorial Stadium was retired as the Orioles' home field after the 1991 season. It remains standing as a potential interim field for any NFL franchise that locates in Baltimore. If the profitable trend continued through the 1991 season, the negative ANPV could be in the $1 million to $1.5 million range. A sale price of approximately $8 million by 1995 could bring Baltimore's investment in Memorial Stadium to a positive NPV.

Minneapolis' Metrodome has already been discussed. The ANPV of negative $43,500 after ten years is the smallest of any publicly built stadium in the survey. The one limitation to the facility's ability to achieve a positive ANPV is that while the stadium has not received any tax subsidy over the last seven years, thus eliminating any municipal negative cash flows, there appears to be no way for the civic owners to receive a positive cash flow from the investment. The $43,500 subsidy, therefore, may be the steady state until the facility is sold. While the trend of the first decade is encouraging, the Metrodome is in the early stages of its existence, and cash flows for stadiums are highly volatile.

One example of the volatile nature of stadium finances is Anaheim Stadium. In 1988, "The Big A" appeared to be one of those stadiums that could, by the end of its life have attained a positive NPV. By adding the Rams to its list of tenants, the stadium had earned large profits each of the years during the early 1980s. If this trend had continued for another ten to fifteen years, it is

---

7. The last year Baltimore kept separate financial records for Memorial Stadium was 1985.

conceivable that Anaheim Stadium might have had a positive NPV of cash flows at the end of its life.

After 1988, however, the stadium became self-sufficient, so the city receives no revenues (nor incurs any costs) from the stadium operations. The negative ANPV is likely to get more negative as there is no municipal income to offset the accumulating foregone property taxes. Thus, Anaheim Stadium, once a strong candidate to be in the first group now appears to be a second tier investment: one that will never earn a positive present value but which covers its operating costs regularly.

Foxboro Stadium falls into the second category, as well. Although it did not cost the city any direct expenditures to construct or maintain, the private facility imposes a financial loss on the city in the form of foregone property taxes. Like Anaheim Stadium's new arrangement, the foregone property taxes will accumulate with time, and there is no provision for the stadium to earn any direct revenues for the city.

RFK Stadium is another facility that should be included into the second group. The Redskins pay sufficient rent to cover the operating costs now that the stadium's construction bonds have been paid. Jack Kent Cooke's unsuccessful attempt to move the team to Northern Virginia in late 1992, however, may signal the approaching end to RFK Stadium.

Several stadiums are more rightly placed in the second category, although arguments can be made for placing them in another as well. Jack Murphy Stadium earned progressively smaller deficits until 1984, when it ran an operating surplus sufficiently large enough to cover its debt service. Since 1984, Jack Murphy Stadium has earned positive net revenues in three of the six years surveyed. But the size of the net cash flows are relatively small, and when discounted significantly, it means that Jack Murphy Stadium is unlikely to ever reach a positive NPV.

The Oakland–Alameda Coliseum Complex is an example of a facility that had its fate altered significantly by a policy change. In 1985, the complex had a small chance of reaching a positive NPV at the end of its useful life. However, in 1986 the sports authority negotiated a new lease with the A's that allowed the franchise to keep more of the concession revenues. This change caused the city and county to go from earning a positive net cash flow of as much as $2 million in some years to losing $1.5 million annually. Since the civic authorities have not received any of their annual $1.5 million contribution to the complex back since the new lease was signed, it appears the Oakland–Alameda Coliseum Complex will slip into the third group of stadiums.

When speaking of chronic money losers, one must include the Louisiana Superdome. The ANPV for the Superdome exceeds $70 million and grows each year, as the facility cannot earn enough to pay its operating expenses.

Atlanta–Fulton County Stadium amassed a large negative ANPV in the early years, but the size of the subsidy declined from the mid-1970s to the mid-1980s. This trend was reversed in the last part of the 1980s for two reasons. First, the stadium was enlarged in 1986, and there is no evidence that the revenues increased sufficiently to cover this additional expense. Second, the Braves negotiated a new contract that limited the municipal portion of the gate receipts.

This places Atlanta–Fulton County Stadium decidedly in the third category of stadiums.

Although it has the second largest (least negative) ANPV studied, Buffalo's Memorial Stadium will never have a positive NPV. The Buffalo Bills abandoned the facility after the expansion, leaving the city with no revenues to pay the debt service related to the expansion. The Bills did their new landlords, Erie County, no favor by vacating Buffalo. Rich Stadium, the Bills' new home, loses at least $1 million every year in the survey.

One thing is sure when projecting the tendency of stadium subsidies. The size of the subsidies are highly dependent upon the lease terms, and any prediction is subject to major revisions if there is even a modest change in the conditions of the lease. Since there is no precedent for a lease renegotiation to favor the city, the predictions in this analysis probably consist of best-case scenarios.

Table 17.1
Projected vs. Actual Stadium Construction Costs

Stadium Name	Projected Costs	Actual Costs	Amount over (Under) Budget	Percent over (Under) Budget
Atlanta-Fulton County Stadium	$18,000,000	$18,500,000	$500,000	3%
Houston Astrodome	$18,000,000	$45,350,000	$25,500,000	142%
Indianapolis Hoosierdome	$69,600,000	$80,000,000	$10,400,000	15%
Kansas City, Missouri Harry Truman Sports Complex	$43,000,000	$54,000,000	$11,000,000	26%
Louisiana Superdome	$35,000,000	$163,500,000	$128,500,000	367%
Milwaukee County Stadium	$5,000,000	$5,768,365	$768,365	15%
Minneapolis Metrodome	$51,000,000	$52,700,000	$1,700,000	3%
New York Shea Stadium	$15,000,000	$25,000,000	$10,000,000	67%
New York Yankee Stadium	$24,000,000	$98,500,000	$74,500,000	310%
Orchard Park, New York Rich Stadium	$20,000,000	$22,000,000	$2,000,000	10%
Philadelphia Veterans Stadium	$30,000,000	$48,000,000	$18,000,000	60%
Pittsburgh Three Rivers Stadium	$45,170,000	$45,000,000	($170,000)	(.4%)
San Diego Jack Murphy Stad.	$27,500,000	$28,000,000	$500,000	2%
Seattle, Washington Kingdome	$40,000,000	$67,370,000	$27,370,000	68%
Washington, D.C. RFK Stadium	$6,000,000	$21,700,000	$15,700,000	262%
Total	$447,270,000	$775,388,365	$328,118,365	73%

Table 17.2			
Summary of Present Value Calculations			
Stadium Name	Years in Survey	Accumulated Present Values	Comments
Baltimore Memorial Stadium	32	($2,922,206)	•'83 is the only loss from '80-'85. •Separate financial acc'ts end in '85. •Stadium closed for baseball at the end of the '91 baseball season.
Buffalo War Memorial Stadium	20	($836,021)	•No original construction costs included. •PV of cash flows represents loss on expansion. Bills vacated stadium at end of '72 season. Bonds for expansion matured in '79.
Denver Mile High Stadium	22	($2,010,631)	•No municipal construction costs. •PV of cash flows includes loss on '77 expansion. •Profitable in last nine years.
Los Angeles Dodger Stadium	34	$7,992,568	•Limited participation by municipal authorities in the development of property. •Stadium built at Dodgers' expense. •PV includes tax income on Dodger-owned land, stadium, and operations.
Washington, D.C. RFK Stadium (District of Columbia Stadium)	25	($10,780,339)	•Data are missing for fiscal years '63, '65 –'67. •Subsidy includes $19.8 million paid by D.C. and federal government. •Stadium earned a profit in the last eight years of the survey.
Anaheim Stadium	25	($4,268,715)	•Revenues exceed costs (including debt service) in five of the last seven years. •Stadium has been self-sufficient since '89.
Atlanta–Fulton County Stadium	22	($16,547,623)	•Losses smaller in '80s then increased after renegotiated lease with Braves. •Data not available after '87 due to aggregation with county zoo and arena. •Ceased operation as a home for Falcons after the '91 season.

Table 17.2 (continued)			
Stadium Name	Years in Survey	Accumulated Present Values	Comments
Oakland-Alameda Coliseum Complex	25	($10,534,636)	•Losses incurred since lease extension negotiated with A's. •Sports complex includes arena.
San Diego Jack Murphy Stadium	23	($9,000,723)	•Four of last seven years have been profitable.
Cincinnati Riverfront Stadium	20	($4,846,388)	•Municipal subsidy includes revenues from stadium parking structures.
Foxboro, MA Foxboro Stadium	20	($1,027,593)	•Privately constructed. •Subsidy is foregone property taxes.
Orchard Park, N.Y. Rich Stadium	10	($16,454,233)	
Louisiana Superdome	16	($47,729,356)	•Cost of construction includes facilities related to convention center.
Minneapolis Metrodome	10	($43,500)	•Includes proceeds from the sale of Met. •No tax revenues used to finance the stadium during the last seven years.

Table 17.3 Accumulated Present Values of Stadium Investments Using Alternative Development Assumptions		
Stadium Name	Alternative Accumulated Present Values	Comments
Atlanta–Fulton County Stadium	($9,926,936)	
Baltimore War Memorial Stadium	$1,342,626	• alternative present value calculations were positive in fourteen of the last sixteen years surveyed.
Cincinnati Riverfront Stadium	($2,198,476)	
Orchard Park, NY Rich Stadium	($6,906,507)	

Table 17.4
Per-Capita Subsidies

City	Per-capita Subsidy
Los Angeles	$4
Minneapolis	$0
Buffalo	($1)
Baltimore	($3)
Denver	($5)
Cincinnati	($11)
San Diego	($13)
Washington	($15)
Orchard Park	($17)
Oakland	($30)
Anaheim	($30)
Atlanta	($33)
New Orleans	($83)

Chapter 18
Non-Financial Data and Analysis

Chapter 17 summarized the financial data in chapters 2 through 16, and concluded that stadium investments fall into three classes of financial health. A few are able to earn their municipal owners a profit by covering the operating costs and the fixed costs of debt service and foregone property taxes. The second category consists of those stadiums that do not earn a profit but, through their use, come close to breaking even. The vast majority of the stadiums built in the last three decades fall into the third category: facilities whose income covers the operating costs of hosting a team but not the fixed costs. Finally, a few stadiums were so badly advised that they not only fail to cover the fixed costs, but they also fail to cover the operating costs.

Supporters of stadiums, and the subsidy to the professional sports teams that reside in them, argue that a facility and the franchises bring many improvements in the quality of life to a city and its residents. Representative Wilmer Mizell, a former Major League Baseball player, made the point in a 1971 speech on the floor of Congress:

...through baseball, opportunities have been afforded to young men who otherwise would not have been able to fully enjoy the American dream...

Baseball builds character into young men who are going to be the leaders of the future. This leadership development and character building comes about in many ways, some of which may not seem very important in that sense while a boy is playing a game. But these are the things that stick with a boy when he becomes a man.[1]

---

1. Quoted in Senate Committee on the District of Columbia, *Future Use and Financing of RFK Stadium*, 92d Cong., 1st Sess., 1971, 2–4.

Mizell continued to say that baseball increased a player's appreciation for competition. It was Major League Baseball's role in transmitting these values, he concluded, that led Congress to grant baseball an anti-trust exemption.

Another rationale for stadium subsidies is the effect of the stadium upon economic growth. Supporters of stadium construction argue that the stadium attracts funds that would be spent outside the city limits. In this way, the city gains by creating jobs, which in turn means more money is spent again in the city through a multiplier process. Those who oppose municipal funding of stadiums argue that most expenditures by patrons of stadiums are just funds that would have been spent in the city on some other form of entertainment. As such, the stadium adds very little to the city's growth.

In the case where a stadium does increase a community's quality of life, and/or spur economic growth, a public subsidy of a stadium may be justified. These benefits to society, although provided by a privately owned stadium, are such that a private stadium developer will not be compensated for providing them. Since a private developer incurs all stadium construction costs but receives only a portion of the benefits, the private sector would invest less than the optimal amount in stadiums without a subsidy to reimburse the developer for the public good he has created.

Two approaches are usually undertaken to measure the external impact of a stadium. The first, either *ex-ante* or *ex-post*, attempts to measure the amount of "new" spending generated by a sports franchise and then apply some multiplier. This technique will be referred to as the "projection method." A second type of economic impact study is to attempt to measure, *ex-ante*, the impact of stadiums or a team on an economic indicator. This technique will be referred to as the "statistical technique." This chapter will report, in order, on estimates made using both of these methods.

The qualities of leadership and character that Mizell referred to in the quote at the start of this chapter are virtually impossible to quantify. One quantifiable effect of an improvement in the character of youth and the quality of life, is reported crime. If a professional sports team contributes to building character among a city's population, then it might be possible to discern a fall in the frequency of crime in that city. The analysis attempts to link the presence of a major league sports franchise to changes in the reported crime rate.

The discussion of statistical evidence (for both economic indicators and crime) concludes with a caveat regarding limitations of statistical studies in general. This warning applies to all regression analysis whether the studies are looking for relationships between a sports team and employment, crime, or sunspots. The chapter will conclude with an indirect test of the return on stadium investment by looking at the results of mayoral elections following the construction of a stadium.

EMPLOYMENT

Economic growth can come in three forms. The first is the game-day expenses. Proponents of stadium investments argue that the expenditures for tickets and concessions spur the economy by creating jobs for stadium employees and demand for local products. The implicit, and unrealistic, assumption in this argument is that all these jobs are newly created and that the employees of the stadium would be unemployed without the stadium investment. More realistically, many of the game-day expenses would have been spent in some other form of entertainment, most likely in the city. To the degree that this occurs, game-day expenses are only a diversion of funds from one firm in the city to another. While the residents of a city may be better off with an added option of how to spend their entertainment dollars, this does not necessarily translate into greater expenditures. To the extent that the team has a regional following, however, the spending by the fans who live outside the city limits could increase the economic activity within the city. This, however, does not translate into 100 percent of the game-day expenses as being new spending.

The second source of increased economic activity is the spur to ancillary industries, such as hotel and restaurant trades. In many cases during stadium site location, a downtown area was selected in hopes of converting a blighted area into an attractive site catering to stadium patrons. The success in achieving this depends upon the site's location relative to existing establishments and the ability of the resident team(s) to generate a regional following. Even if the results are auspicious, this increased economic activity may be at the expense of decreased business in hotels and restaurants in other nearby areas.

A third source of growth is the increased economic activity derived from the major league franchise elevating the perception of the city by those who live outside the city. Team(s) can make the city more attractive to vacationers, convention planners, and firms choosing a city in which to locate if they offer the amenity of major league sports. Not only is the city's name mentioned daily in the media during the team's season, but the presence of a sports team in a smaller city means employees being asked to transfer from larger towns will not have to sacrifice attendance at major league events if they move to the new city.

The projection method of estimating these indirect benefits focuses on the first two causes of growth. The technique first estimates the number of dollars spent at the stadium. This exercise is fraught with difficulties. Naive estimates treat all dollars as new dollars to the local community. More realistic studies realize that many of those expenditures are really redirected from other local entertainment and related ventures. Typically, multipliers are applied to the dollar expenditure estimates generated with the above techniques so that the stadium appears to be a major force in the local economy.

Such analysis is not performed unvaryingly. The process is loaded with judgment calls that, not surprisingly, go in favor of the side commissioning the study. A comparison by Robert Baade and Richard Dye of several studies using the "projection" technique illustrates the diversity in approaches:

A study on the impact of the Pirates on the Pittsburgh area uses a multiplier of only 1.2 for goods and services and 1.6 for wages and salaries. They are careful to include only wages paid to Pirate employees who actually live in Pittsburgh. A study commissioned by the Philadelphia Sports Consortium uses a multiplier of 1.7 obtained from independent research of the Wharton Econometrics model of Philadelphia. The author of a study of the impact of a Class A baseball stadium for

South Bend, Indiana, represents as "conservative" a multiplier of 3.0. This, despite the well-established result that the smaller the city, the smaller the portion of respending that stays inside the area. A team-financed study on the impact of Chicago baseball asserts a multiplier of 3.2.[2]

Perhaps in few other areas of empirical statistical work does the phrase "believing is seeing" fit more appropriately.

The second method is to estimate, using statistical techniques, the relationship between the presence of a stadium or franchise and relevant economic indicators. The first of these studies to receive widespread recognition was by Mark Rosentraub and Samuel Nunn.[3] In a model that they admit has limitations, the authors compared the economic impact of the stadiums in the suburban communities of Irving and Arlington, Texas, with the growth of surrounding communities to see if the two host suburbs grew substantially faster than their neighbors. The authors concluded that the two communities had difficulties "in capturing the economic benefits of an investment in professional sports,"[4] with the growth that was expected in the two suburbs spilling over into the different suburban cities within the regions.[5] This conclusion supports those who would use a low multiplier in such suburban situations but also support those who look at stadiums as engines of economic growth.

Robert Baade co-authored two of the most quoted studies using statistical techniques. In a 1988 article, Baade combined with Richard Dye to test the third source of economic growth: that a stadium or sports franchise so influences the outside perception of the city, that economic activity is attracted to the metropolitan area.[6] Their test consisted of regressing three measures of manufacturing activity, manufacturing employment, value added, and new capital expenditures, against the presence of a stadium, an NFL franchise, and a Major League Baseball franchise. The eight cities used in the survey were small to medium markets of the type that would gain in prestige by attracting a major league sports franchise.[7] The ratio of the population in the SMSA relative to

---

2. Robert A. Baade and Richard F. Dye, "Sports Stadiums and Area Development: A Critical Review," *Economic Development Quarterly*, no. 2 (August 1988): 270. Also see William Fulton, "Desperately Seeking Sports Teams," *Governing*, I, no. 6 (March 1988), for a discussion of the disparity in numbers used in these studies.

3. Mark S. Rosentraub and Samuel R. Nunn, "Suburban City Investment in Professional Sports: Estimating the Fiscal Returns of the Dallas Cowboys and the Texas Rangers to Investor Communities," *American Behavioral Scientist*, 21 no. 3 (February 1978).

4. Ibid., 412.

5. Ibid.

6. Robert A. Baade and Richard F. Dye, "An Analysis of the Economic Rationale for Public Subsidization of Sports Stadiums," *The Annals of Regional Science*, 22 (July 1988), 37-47.

7. The cities included in the survey were Buffalo, Cincinnati, Denver, Miami, New Orleans, San Diego, Seattle, and Tampa Bay.

the population in a neighboring multi-state region and a trend analysis were used to control the measures of manufacturing activity. Each of these measures had their own regression equation. The survey period ran from 1965 to 1978. If a stadium existed, or a football or baseball team played at the city, continuously during the survey period, that component was dropped from the analysis.

Of the thirty-six non-zero possibilities remaining in which the influence of the presence of a stadium or football or baseball franchises could be measured, only five were so strong that the correlation would occur randomly less than five times in 100. Of these five, one was negative. Three of the four positive significant correlations occurred in one city, San Diego.[8] No aggregate analysis of this data was performed. "On the basis of this evidence," Baade and Dye concluded, "the assertion that a major-league-sports identity is a decisive factor in the location or operation of manufacturing business is suspect."[9]

Equally suspect, however, may be the authors' analysis and statistical techniques. Of the forty-eight control coefficients (population and trend for each of three independent variables in eight cities) only seventeen were significant. While this is almost twice the incidence of the significance of the stadium and team coefficients, of the seventeen significant coefficients of the control variables, twelve, or more than two-thirds, were negative. This reflects the declining importance of the manufacturing sector in many parts of the country. The significance of this to these findings is that in the eight cities surveyed, the majority of significant trend and population coefficients were negative, while 80 percent of the significant stadium and team coefficients were positive. Indeed, three of the four significantly positive stadium or team coefficients occurred in those equations that had negative trend coefficients (although not significantly so).

With the small number of observations in each equation, the low incidence of significant coefficients of any type is not surprising. As a time series from 1965 to 1978, each equation is estimated with fourteen data points. Such a paucity of data points is rarely conducive to significant findings. There is no explanation in the 1988 article as to why the data series survey ended in 1978. The addition of another eight to ten years of data would have increased the number of observations and could have changed, materially, the number of significant findings.

In the study, at least nine other stadium and team coefficients had potential for being significant.[10] If additional observations found all nine coefficients to be significant, a total of fourteen stadium and team coefficients would be significant out of a possible thirty-six. Of these fourteen coefficients, ten would indicate a positive relationship between a stadium or a sports team and manufacturing activity. By comparison, seven control coefficients are "near

8. Baade and Dye, "An Analysis of the Economic Rationale for Public Subsidization of Sports Stadiums," 44–45.
9. Ibid., 45.
10. "Potential for being significant" is defined as having a t-ratio of 1.5 or more in absolute value terms.

significant," making a total of twenty-four out of a possible forty-eight. Of the twenty-four significant, or near significant coefficients, fourteen show negative relationships. Thus, more observations may show that stadiums and sports teams seem to help cities "buck the trend" of declining manufacturing activity.

The small number of observations also means that there is a limited opportunity to distinguish trends during the two periods of team and non-team or stadium and non-stadium tenure. For example, the Miami Dolphins were founded in 1966. The study then has one non-Dolphin observation to compare with thirteen data points during the "Dolphin era." To attempt developing a trend when the control year consists of one data point is questionable at best.

The low incidence of significance in all coefficients may also be explained by the close relationship between the presence of a stadium and a sports franchise of franchises. For example, San Diego's Jack Murphy Stadium opened in late 1967 for the Chargers. This means that the time series contains only two non-stadium years. In addition, the time series includes only one full year, 1968, to measure the impact of only the stadium on the San Diego economy. In early 1969, the Padres began playing in San Diego. If an increase in manufacturing activity occurred in 1969, was it the result of the stadium or the Padres? Such problems, which statisticians refer to as multicollinearity, lead to artificially low levels of significance.

Including a stadium coefficient in the regression creates other problems, as well. The attraction theory does not attribute the elevation of the city's status to the stadium. One would not expect, for example, that St. Petersburg, Florida (not one of the cities included in the study), would experience a boost in manufacturing activity because it built a stadium that, for the most part, remains a secret to the general public because it does not have a major league tenant. The elevation of status occurs when the city acquires a major league franchise. This misinterpretation of the attraction theory, combined with the possibility of multicollinearity, argues strongly for dropping the stadium variable from the analysis. Similarly, the study includes as part of the stadium coefficient the renovation of the stadium. Thus, Denver's expansion of Mile High Stadium in 1968 may have been a cause for increased civic pride within Denver, but it was not well known outside the region and would hardly qualify as a business magnet.

Finally, measuring economic activity by changes in the manufacturing sector is questionable. First, it is only one component of the economy. To say that manufacturing activity is a proxy for measuring economic growth is to overlook other sectors of the economy, such as the service sector. Many observers dismiss service sector jobs as low-paying but doing so overlooks such industries as insurance, education, finance, and entertainment. While it is a major segment in the economy, manufacturing employment is declining in absolute and relative terms in the United States. Few far-sighted civic leaders will opt for recruiting manufacturing firms, which are becoming less labor intensive, if they can get a service sector firm that hires the same number of employees.

Even in the best of circumstances, Baade and Dye's study would capture only short-term effects. With manufacturing this would be dangerous in that neither relocation nor changes in manufacturing activity occur instantaneously. Yet, the survey was attempting to measure the change in manufacturing activity caused by stadiums that were built in 1976 (Seattle and Tampa Bay) and 1975 (New Orleans) with a time series that concluded in 1978. Similarly, it would be a real coup if a change in manufacturing activity registered with a time series that ended in 1978 when teams started in 1976 (the Seattle Seahawks and Tampa Bay Buccaneers) and 1977 (the Seattle Mariners).

Professor Baade, alone, conducted another study that concluded that a professional sports team precipitates a decline in the income growth rate in the host community.[11] Using similar techniques to those in the survey he conducted with Dye, Baade used a ratio of income in the host city's SMSA to the level of income of the surrounding census region to see if a stadium or team creates economic growth relative to the surrounding area. Baade repeated the regression for retail sales in the same study.[12]

In both cases, Baade found a low incidence of positive significant relationships. Indeed, the findings support the argument that a professional sport team or a stadium reduces SMSA income relative to that of the surrounding region. When adjusted for population, by taking the SMSA's population as a fraction of the region's population, thirteen non-zero possibilities existed. Of these, six significant outcomes (at the 95 percent confidence level) were found. Five of the six were negative, indicating that the presence of a team or a stadium was related to a decline in relative SMSA income.[13] Baade inferred from his findings that a stadium does not create jobs; instead, jobs are "diverted from the manufacturing economy to the service economy, or from higher-skilled to lower-skilled (and lower-paid) occupations."[14]

Many of the same technical problems that plagued the Baade and Dye study reappeared in this study by Baade. While the income equation for each city now consisted of nineteen data points instead of the fourteen used in the Baade and Dye survey, a nineteen-year period still gave relatively few data points on which to build any degree of confidence where long-run phenomenon such as incomes

---

11. Robert Baade, "Is There an Economic Rationale for Subsidizing Sports Stadiums?," *Heartland Institute Policy Study* 13 (23 February 1987). The cities used in the income study were Cincinnati, Denver, Detroit, Kansas City, New Orleans, Pittsburg, San Diego, Seattle, and Tampa Bay.

12. The cities observed in retail sales were Atlanta, Buffalo, Cincinnati, Denver, Miami, New Orleans, San Diego, Seattle, and Tampa Bay. The substitution of cities was due to available data .

13. Baade reports that "in no instance did a positive, significant correlation surface among stadiums, professional sports, and city income as a fraction of regional income." (Baade, "Is There an Economic Rationale for Subsidizing Sports Stadiums?" 15). However, in reviewing the results of the equations in the appendix of this paper, there is a sufficiently strong relationship between the Padres and San Diego's relative income to warrant a significant relationship.

14. Baade, "Is There an Economic Rationale for Subsidizing Sports Stadiums?" 18.

are concerned. When the cities' data were aggregated, only the population coefficient is significant even if the standard of significance is reduced to the 80 percent confidence level.[15] An opponent of a stadium project could argue that Baade's findings show there is no positive relationship between stadium and team presence and income. That conclusion, however, is a far step from saying the presence of stadium or a team causes the city's income to decline relative to regional income.

Data for the retail sales study were available for only four years (1967, 1972, 1977, 1982). The regression aggregated the data for nine cities to get thirty-six observations. In this equation, when population was treated as a ratio of SMSA population relative to regional population, only the population and the football coefficients were significant at the 99 percent and 80 percent confidence level, respectively. Similar criticisms can be made regarding the conduct of the regression analysis on retail sales as was made concerning the income study. There are thirty-six total observations, which relieves some of the criticism regarding the dearth of observations. In this equation, however, the data points themselves may have influenced the results.

The years of 1967 and 1968 are generally regarded to be one of the strongest in the American economy. Unemployment was at 3.7 percent, while inflation was less than 3 percent.[16] Mean duration of unemployment was at it lowest point during this period as well. These variables get increasingly larger in each of the observation years, with 1982 having the highest unemployment rate and the highest average mean duration of unemployment of the four observation years. Thus, a flattening of retail sales might be expected during the survey period due to the deterioration of the overall economic conditions. This is a flaw in the analysis over which Baade had not control, since these are the only years for which the data are available. It is clear, however, that the lack of growth in economic activity attributable to stadiums and franchises in this analysis may be explained, at least in part, by the slowing economic activity throughout the economy over this fifteen-year period.

A stadium opponent might argue that Baade's use of the city's income as a ratio of the regional income takes the general decline in the economy into account. This adjustment is not as strong as it appears, however, if one accepts that the representation of low skilled workers and minorities is higher in inner cities than in the surrounding regions and that these are the groups most likely harmed during a recession. This criticism can also be leveled at the income regression analysis.

Besides the technical problems present in these studies, city residents must engage in some curious decision making for Baade's findings to be true. If the number of jobs does not change when a stadium and team are introduced into a city's economy, the franchise will attract employees only by providing an opportunity superior to the positions the workers held before the stadium was

---

15. Ibid., Table A-2, 25.
16. Council of Economic Advisors, *Economic Report of the President, 1984* (Washington, D.C.: U. S. Government Printing Office, 1984).

built. If the number of jobs increases, the city's income should increase since more people are working than before.

Perhaps an explanation that accommodates both Rosentraub and Nunn's and Baade's conflicting conclusions is that the jobs that are created by the stadium are low skilled, but these positions are filled by workers who otherwise were unemployed and lived outside the SMSA before the stadium was built. These individuals were attracted to the city by the offer of new job opportunities. This will lower income in the host city relative to the control area. If the immigrant came from the control area, it may also raise the income in that locality. The net result is that the ratio of host city income to surrounding area income falls, but the area did experience economic growth.

To test Baade's hypotheses we ran two regression equations for cities from 1958 to 1984. The first equation tested for a relationship between a major league professional sports team and service employment. The second was run to determine the effects of a professional sports team on non-agricultural employment.

Service Employment

One of the sectors of a local economy that may be directly affected by the introduction of a sports team is the service sector. By testing for the relationship between sports teams and service employment, we may take the first step in testing not only a professional team's impact on the local economy, but also Baade's hypothesis that a stadium's major influence on the economy is through service employment. The following regression equation was derived to test the presence of an impact on service employment from population and a Major League Baseball and/or an NFL franchise.[17]

$$\text{Service Employment}_t = a(\text{Population}_t) + b(\text{Football}_t) + c(\text{Baseball}_t)$$

Dummy variables were used for the presence of football and baseball franchises. Employment is recorded in thousands of individuals employed in the service industry in the metropolitan area. The regressions were run using the Data Desk computer program.[18] Table 18.1 reports the results of the regressions which were calculated for various size cities.[19]

---

17. U. S. Department of Labor, Bureau of Labor Statistics, *Employment, Hours, and Earnings, States and Areas, 1939–1982* (Washington, D.C.: Bureau of Labor Statistics, 1984).

18. Paul F. Velleman and Agelia Y. Velleman, *Data Desk Version 1.11* (Ithaca, N. Y.: 1986).

19. Service employment data were not available for all cities. Cities and years included in the regression equation were Anaheim (1958–1981), Cincinnati (1964–1982), Cleveland (1964–1982), Dallas (1970–1982), Detroit (1972–1982), Hartford, Connecticut (1972–1982), Houston (1972–1982), Kansas

The evidence strongly supports a link between the three independent variables and employment in the service sector. The R^2 for each equation is good, and the F-ratio suggests that the chances of the independent variables having such an impact on service employment by chance is far less than one percent.

The independent variables also have a significant impact on the service industry employment that grows as population grows. The only coefficient that is not significant to the 95 percent confidence level is the football coefficient for cities with a population less than 500,000, which is significant to the 92 percent confidence level.

A one-unit increase in the relevant independent variable will cause service employment in the metropolitan area to increase by one thousand times the coefficient, if everything else is held constant. An NFL franchise in a city of 500,000 or fewer people will raise service employment by more than 23,000 workers. A Major League Baseball team will raise service employment by more than 40,000 workers in the smallest cities. In larger cities (those with fewer than three million citizens), the impact of a football and baseball franchise on the service industry grows to more than 55,000 and 44,000, respectively. Baseball's influence on service sector employment is stronger than football's in smaller cities, but this pattern reverses itself in the larger cities. The baseball coefficient for "all" cities is suspect since all data points for cities with population greater than three million have both baseball and football franchise. It is important to note these changes do not represent replacement jobs but are instead additional jobs in the community.

The evidence supports Rosentraub and Nunn's study. If one assumes that professional sports teams in smaller cities generate the same number of jobs as their counterparts in larger cities, the differences in the impact a sports team makes in different-sized cities can be explained by the inability of smaller metropolitan areas to "capture" all the economic growth stimulated by the sports franchise.

Baade's findings do not fare as well as Rosentraub and Nunn's. The number of jobs created in the service sector is larger than one could reasonably expect would come solely from the operation of the stadium and its major league tenants. This indicates that the service industry grows, a hypothesis furthered by Baade, but it grows by more than the low-income concessionaires, as implied by Baade.

Non-Agricultural Employment

Baade's argument, that a sports stadium diverts the economy from its pre-stadium path to one more oriented to low-paying service jobs, could still be

---

City (1970–1982), Los Angeles (1958–1964), New Orleans (1964–1982), New York (1958–1972), Pittsburgh (1958–1982), San Francisco (1958–1982), St. Louis (1970–1982).

valid if the stadium stimulated service industry employment at the expense of employment in other sectors of the local economy. To test this hypothesis, the effects of population, Major League Baseball, and NFL franchises on non-agricultural employment were measured. If non-agricultural employment for a city held steady at the same time service industry employment grew, Baade's argument would be supported.

Table 18.2 reports the results of the regression equation:[20]

$$\text{Non-agricultural Employment}_t = a(\text{Population}_t) + b(\text{Football}_t) + c(\text{Baseball}_t)$$

The R^2 and F-ratio both indicate that the equation explains a significant amount of the change in the non-agricultural employment among cities. The chance of the variables having these values and not being related is much less than one percent.

The coefficients are to be interpreted as before. A one-unit increase in the independent variable will cause non-agricultural employment to increase by one thousand times the coefficient, with everything else held constant. Thus, a football team can be expected to add more than 54,000 jobs to the non-agricultural sector of a metropolitan area surrounding a small city (less than 500,000 population), and a baseball team will add almost 200,000 jobs to such a metropolitan area. In a large metropolitan area (around a city with a population less than 3,000,000), the combined impact grows to more than 620,000 jobs. While these numbers are larger than can realistically be assumed, the t-ratios are large, indicating that the chance of the actual impact of sports franchises on non-agricultural employment being zero is virtually zero itself.

Football has a large and significant impact on the employment of a larger city, but the impact is not statistically different from zero until the upper limit of population is increased to 2,000,000. The t-ratios for football in cities of less than 2,000,000, less than 3,000,000 and "all" categories is larger for non-agricultural employment than for service employment. Football loses its attraction effect in small cities. While the absolute numbers are large, the level of significance, given by the t-ratio, is very weak. This may be explained, in part, by the small number of data points that cause the coefficients' standard of errors to be large over the range of the smaller cities.

---

20. Data for non-agricultural employment were available for Anaheim (1958–1982), Atlanta (1970–1982), Baltimore (1978–1982), Boston (1970–1982), Buffalo (1958–1982), Cincinnati (1964–1982), Cleveland (1964–1982), Dallas (1970–1982), Denver (1970–1982) Detroit (1972–1982), Green Bay (1960–1982) Hartford, Connecticut (1972–1982), Houston (1970–1982), Indianapolis (1960–1982), Kansas City (1970–1982), Los Angeles (1958–1982), Miami (1958–1982), Milwaukee (1967–1982), Minneapolis (1972–1982), New Orleans (1964–1982) New York (1958–1982), Philadelphia (1970–1982), Pittsburgh (1958–1982), San Francisco (1958–1982), St. Louis (1970–1982), Tampa (1972–1982), and Washington, D. C. (1958–1982).

In every category of population, the t-ratios are stronger for baseball impact on non-agricultural employment than for service employment. Baseball has a significant impact on non-agricultural employment for every population category observed. This is probably a result of baseball's long and more or less continuous summer schedule. The smallest t-ratio for a baseball coefficient in Table 18.2 indicates that the probability of the impact measured by the regression equation happening randomly is less than one percent. Again, the smallest cities do not seem capable of keeping all the employment gains within the city limit, although the maximum impact baseball has on non-agricultural employment comes for those cities below 750,000 in population.

The analysis supports baseball's ability to attract business. Unlike the service employment data, baseball has a greater impact on the cities with a population in the smaller to middle range. The indication is that the city has been elevated in the minds of those who live outside, and this change in perception has increased the likelihood that firms and workers will locate in the city, even if their line of work is unrelated to sports.

Baade's hypothesis fails to explain the pattern shown in Table 18.2. All the coefficients shown in Table 18.2, except the impact of football on cities of less than 1,000,000, are larger than the service industry coefficients in absolute and statistical significance. A sports team not only causes the service industry to grow but causes non-agricultural employment to grow as well. Often the growth in the non-agricultural sector is more than twice that of the service sector.

CRIME

Congressman Mizell's view of baseball's impact on youth was positive. The presence of sports teams not only gives a city's youth an opportunity to see and follow positive role models, but it reinforces living by rules and consequences. The presence of a sports team also gives the city's youth a socially acceptable activity (watching a professional sports contest) in place of less desirable activities.

Another view holds that the dynamics of a large city are sufficiently complex that a single change, such as adding a sports team, cannot have a significant impact on crime. This school of thought would look more to predictors like income and family stability.

To test the correlation between sports teams and crime, the following equation was estimated:

$$\text{Crime Index}_t = a(\text{Population}_t) + b(\text{Football}_t) + c(\text{Baseball}_t)$$

Data were gathered on crime and population for thirty cities between 1958 and 1984, with the exception of 1959 when no crime data could be found.[21] The crime index refers to the Federal Bureau of Investigation's compilation of reported crimes.[22] When the data for suburban communities were included with a larger nearby city, the suburb was deleted from the study for that year.

Population data were available with the crime statistics in many cases. When no data were available, the decennial census data were used and the years in between were interpolated. To ensure a sufficient number of data points and variation in population and crime, all cities for which reliable data were available were aggregated into one sample. Then the sample was disaggregated into groups by population size to determine if the impact of a sports team on the crime rate differed with population size. Table 18.3 shows the results of the regression.

The coefficients represent the increase in the number of indexed crimes for each unit increase in the independent variable, with everything else held constant. These numbers are more than likely an overstatement of the actual impact. For example, it is not probable that the introduction of an NFL team into a city of less than 500,000 would increase the number of reported crimes by more than 35,500 cases.

In general, the results indicate that the independent variables in the equation explain a significant amount of the variation in crime events among data points, but that city size is by far the strongest explanatory variable. For cities with a population of less than 500,000, factors other than the three variables in this

---

21. Cities used in the survey included Anaheim, California; Arlington, Texas; Atlanta Georgia; Baltimore, Maryland; Boston, Massachusets; Buffalo, New York; Cleveland, Ohio; Dallas, Texas; Denver, Colorado; Detroit Michigan; Green Bay, Wisconsin; Hartford, Connecticut; Houston, Texas; Indianapolis, Indiana; Kansas City, Missouri; Los Angeles, California; Miami, Florida; Milwaukee, Wisconsin; Minneapolis, Minnesota; New Orleans, Louisiana; New York, New York; Oakland, California; Philadelphia, Pennsylvania; Pittsburgh, Pennsylvania; San Diego, California; San Francisco, California; St. Louis, Missouri; Tampa, Florida, and Washington, D.C. Cities that have hosted teams for which the crime index could not, at least partially, be found included Arlington, Texas (1958–1960, no index found); Buffalo, New York (1981, no index found); New East Rutherford, New Jersey (all years, no index available for East Rutherford); Houston, Texas (1981, no index available); Kansas City, Missouri (1960, no index available).

22. United States Department of Justice, Federal Bureau of Investigation, *Uniform Crime Reports for the United States* (Washington, D.C.: U. S. Department of Justice, for years 1958, 1959, 1960, 1961, 1962, 1963, 1964, 1965, 1966, 1967, 1968, 1969, 1970, 1971, 1972, 1973, 1974, 1975, 1976, 1977, 1978, 1979, 1980, 1981, 1982). Crimes included in the crime index are murder, forcible rape, robbery, aggravated assault, burglary, larceny-theft, motor vehicle theft, and arson.

regression equation explain 64 percent of the variation in the crime index, but the strong F-ratio indicates that the probability of the relationship between the dependent variables and the independent variable occurring by chance is less than one percent, even in this weakest case.

An NFL franchise's influence on crime remains relatively constant in absolute terms as the city size grows up to one million residents. The t-statistic of 3.03 for the football coefficient in cities with less than 500,000 population indicates that the probability of no relationship between crime and an NFL franchise is less than one percent. The statistical significance of the relationship between crime incidence and an NFL franchise grows as population grows up to one million, as the increased number of data points reduces the standard error of the coefficient. The absolute and statistical significance of the relationship between crime and an NFL team declines as the size of the city's population increases beyond one million. Indeed, when all the data points are considered, there is a negative, albeit statistically insignificant, relationship between crime and football. The pattern of an increasingly and then decreasingly strong relationship between crime and football supports the argument that the acquisition by a smaller city of a professional football team changes the perception of the city in the eyes of outsiders and that may attract crime.

The influence of a Major League Baseball franchise on crime is far more ambiguous than an NFL franchise. The absolute impact rises as population grows from cities of less than 500,000 to cities of less than 750,000 people. In cities of more than 750,000 people, the relationship between baseball and crime trends downward as the cities get larger. The last row in Table 18.3, which reports a stronger relationship between crime and a baseball franchise for all cities than for cities of fewer than three million inhabitants, is probably a spurious correlation. All observations of cities with populations greater than three million included a baseball team. With no variation in the independent variable, the impact a baseball franchise has on crime in the largest cities is probably confused with the impact of population on the crime in these larger cities.

Excluding the case of all cities, the only statistically significant relationship between a Major League Baseball franchise and increased crime is for cities of fewer than 750,000 people. The probability of baseball's affect on crime as estimated by this equation for the cities of less than 750,000 occurring by chance is less than 3 percent. This is another piece of evidence for the argument that sports franchises elevate the outside perception of small cities.

CAVEAT EMPTOR ON STATISTICAL TECHNIQUES

While the statistical method is more defensible and uses empirical evidence instead of subjective assumptions about new spending and multipliers, it is not without shortcomings. As any statistics student learns, correlation, which is what Baade and Dye, and we have measured, is not causation for a number of reasons.

First, there may be spurious correlation. That is, two variables will appear to be related when in fact they are independent. Surveys with small sample sizes are susceptible to this. Second, two variables may be affected by a third variable not in the equation. In this case, the third, unmeasured variable is the causal factor that is affecting both variables in the equation, making it appear that the two are related. Third, the direction of the causation is not possible to discern. Are more jobs related to the presence of a baseball franchise because the baseball franchise elevates the image of the city and attracts new firms and visitors, or is a quickly growing urban center a magnet for sports franchises? The studies reported here are unable to answer this question.

A PUBLIC CHOICE TEST OF STADIUM INVESTMENT

Perhaps one indirect technique of measuring the external benefits of the stadium investment would be to look at the response of the "stockholders." If information markets are efficient, then voters will know they are better or worse off with a stadium. Do the citizens who finance the subsidy think they are getting a good value? If the officials who propose the stadium make the area poorer with an insufficient benefit, would the public not be able to perceive this and vote the scoundrels out of office? Here the evidence appears to be as ambiguous as the statistical data.

A search of the national print media from 1953 to 1990 located only one incident where the stadium, once built and occupied by a franchise, played a role in the following mayor's election. In 1955, Baltimore mayor Thomas D'Alesandro overcame a nervous collapse, his son's involvement in a teenage vice scandal, and his wife's admission that she accepted $11,000 from a contractor to defeat Samuel Hopkins.[23] Hopkins, who ran on a reform platform, won endorsements from both of Baltimore's newspapers. These endorsements were no match against D'Alesandro's campaign cards that consisted of the Orioles' home schedule and the claim, "50 Years of Progress in Eight Years."[24] Clearly Baltimore's voters thought the stadium that brought the Orioles to town was a worthwhile investment.

In 1990, Oakland mayor Lionel Wilson lost his bid for a fourth term because Wilson miscalculated the Raiders' support in Oakland. This discontent, though, was not directed at the Oakland–Alameda Coliseum Complex, but rather the deal Wilson had struck with the Raiders in face of the increasing problems Oakland was having in funding "basic" services of police and schools.

These other issues point the way for determining why stadium investments have been a non-issue in all other mayoral elections. The pluralism present in urban voters means that the size of a stadium investment, while not trivial, represents one issue among others, such as race relations, education, personal integrity, abortion rights, and party affiliation. The voter is asked to vote for a

---

23. "Big Leaguer," *Time*, 16 May 1955.
24. Ibid.

"bundle" of issues when voting for candidates, and a candidate's position on a stadium may be secondary when compared to these other issues.

When the stadium issue is isolated during a referendum, public acceptance for stadium investments is more easily measured. From 1965 to 1985, stadium issues calling for facilities to be built with no private participation were passed routinely in locales as diverse as Buffalo, Philadelphia, Cincinnati, Seattle, Indianapolis, and San Diego. Recall, that stadium proponents in the San Diego race explicitly projected that the stadium could not pay for itself, and the measure still carried with 72 percent of the vote. The rationale of the support of these referenda was the stadium's impact on economic growth and quality of life.

Since 1985, however, the public has become more grudging in its approval of stadium projects. Stadium proposals, some that include financial participation by franchises, have been defeated in Miami, Cleveland, Phoenix, Santa Clara County (in northern California), San José, and twice in San Francisco. The recent resistance to stadiums may be due to buyers' remorse because of disappointment in how other stadium projects fell short of expectations, but there could be other reasons, as well. First, even with franchise participation, the civic outlay is greater today than twenty years ago. A modest proposal calls for public sector expenditures exceeding $100 million. While there does not appear to be a significant increase in subsidies to franchises when the price tag increases, the voters' perception is that it must.

Second, the competition for state and municipal funds has increased over the last decade. The limitation on traditional tax sources combined with the federal government's reduction of funding to local projects makes the opportunity cost of a stadium investment more compelling. While voters may perceive a stadium to be a worthwhile investment, they may view the return on additional school, hospital, police, and fire services to be higher. When the projects are forced to compete in an era of decreased funding opportunities, the stadium investment loses. With the level of aggregation done in this research it is not possible to determine the voters' motivations in rejecting stadium proposals. This could be a fruitful area for joint research among economists and political scientists.

SUMMARY

The lack of congruence and confidence in the answers gathered using the traditional projection and statistical methods indicates that no general conclusion can be offered concerning a sports team's economic impact on the host community. The question has been addressed only recently by semi-objective research, and perhaps an analysis will evolve that will quell most of the criticisms of the embryonic research. The process will probably involve a detailed study of cases to note the specific pattern of growth in differing urban settings. Researchers may have to be content, as often is the case, with the fact that a universal answer may not exist to the question of how much growth a professional sports team generates.

A franchise will bring significant economic growth to an area only if it can serve as a magnet to business and visitors who otherwise would not have considered the city as a destination. A franchise can serve as a powerful promotional tool. Having the city's name in all the nation's print and broadcast sports reports is a strong asset. A promotional tool, however, is useful in increasing business only if the consumers being interested find the total product attractive.

A stadium may increase the frequency with which the city is considered for corporate locations, conventions, or private vacations, but the city will compete poorly if it has substandard schools, an above-average crime rate, poor police and fire protection, and a hostile tax structure. The stadium, by this reasoning, is like make-up used to tempt willing suitors to earn the city a look by a potential suitor, but for the relationship to mature it must be supported with compatibility in more substantial areas.

Table 18.1
The Relationship Among Service Employment, Population, Baseball, and
Football Franchises
(1958–1984)

Population Size	N	R^2	F-Ratio	Coefficient (t-Ratio)		
				Population	Football	Baseball
<500,000	84	0.85	163	0.00019 (3.97)	23.4696 (1.36)	40.3672 (2.91)
<750,000	173	0.87	389	0.000149 (5.43)	25.7407 (1.7)	56.901 (6.27)
<1,000,000	193	0.87	431	0.000169 (7.42)	24.6032 (1.66)	43.1611 (5.34)
<2,000,000	216	0.88	524	0.000127 (9.1)	47.7333 (4.16)	43.4394 (5.07)
<3,000,000	223	0.89	613	0.000111 (11.7)	57.1019 (5.84)	44.566 (5.25)
All	248	0.93	1077	0.000083 (35.3)	50.5313 (5.14)	69.5384 (6.44)

Table 18.2
The Relationship Among Non-Agricultural Employment, Population, Baseball, and Football Franchises
(1958–1984)

Population Size	$\underline{N}$	$\underline{R^2}$	F-Ratio	Coefficient (t-Ratio)		
				Population	Football	Baseball
<500,000	87	0.90	271	0.00112 (5.93)	54.884 (0.81)	199.654 (3.61)
<750,000	176	0.93	802	0.00093 (9.29)	46.857 (0.843)	314.355 (9.29)
<1,000,000	196	0.93	863	0.0011 (12.7)	22.229 (0.392)	234.591 (7.5)
<2,000,000	219	0.93	903	0.00075 (13.1)	212.421 (4.5)	232.907 (6.57)
<3,000,000	260	0.92	1056	0.0037 (32.5)	370.1 (7.77)	257.194 (4.92)
All	293	0.92	1069	0.0037 (32.1)	485.172 (11.2)	152.629 (3.11)

				Coefficient (t-Ratio)		
Table 18.3 The Relationship Among Crime, Population, Baseball, and Football Franchises (1958–1984)						
Population Size	N	R^2	F-Ratio	Population	Football	Baseball
<500,000	124	0.36	24.2	0.015996 (0.0535)	35561.8 (3.03)	9154.07 (0.79)
<750,000	250	0.56	107.0	0.018325 (1.64)	30635.6 (4.64)	9264.53 (1.89)
<1,000,000	291	0.59	143.0	0.028156 (3.29)	30447.4 (5.14)	2395.38 (0.06)
<2,000,000	337	0.70	260.0	0.051124 (8.95)	18929.0 (3.73)	2496.8 (0.59)
<3,000,000	359	0.79	449.0	0.0613699 (17.9)	13047.0 (2.96)	882.97 (0.02)
All	436	0.81	621.0	0.057786 (32.8)	-115.14 (-0.02)	14525.4 (2.25)

Chapter 19

Comparison of Public and Private Stadiums

Privately and publicly owned and/or operated stadiums exist simultaneously, and as such, they offer fertile ground to test the incentives, if any, provided by private ownership. Proponents of the existence of these incentives argue that the private proprietor, who is responsible for earning (and enjoying) a profit, will more aggressively secure bookings, be more concerned about consumer welfare, and use resources more frugally to meet these ends and in building the facility. This does not imply that public employees are more wasteful or lazy than their private sector counterparts. The argument is that the different incentives offered by private ownership will promote different behavior.

This chapter tests this hypothesis by comparing publicly and privately owned stadiums to determine if there is a significant difference in their construction costs, utilization, customer amenities (as measured by available parking and an independent rating), and for their contribution to team stability.

Sixty-three facilities have been used by Major League Baseball teams and/or NFL franchises in the United States between 1953 and 1992. Of these, nineteen are (or in the case of facilities no longer in existence, were) privately owned, thirty-nine are (were) publicly owned. Three stadiums are (were) owned by universities, and it is not possible to trace the lineage of two sites that no longer exist. The last five stadiums were not included in the survey. The remaining fifty-eight stadiums were included in the study. In each area of analysis, some facilities were deleted because of a shortage of quality data.

Of these stadiums, four have been completed in the last eight years. Joe Robbie Stadium was completed in 1987 by the Miami Dolphins' owner, for whom it was named. In 1991, Major League Baseball's oldest extant ball park, Comiskey Park, was replaced with a new stadium called New Comiskey Park. Two new stadiums were inaugurated in 1992: In April, the Baltimore Orioles baseball franchise moved into Oriole Park at Camden Yards, a new facility in a newly renovated waterfront area; in the autumn, the Atlanta Falcons moved into the Georgia Dome. As the name implies the Georgia Dome was built with state funds, as were Comiskey Park and Camden Yards. While the Dolphins received a property tax abatement on the stadium and structure, the facility was built with private funds and, as such, is considered a private stadium in this survey. These new facilities can be used to see if any conclusions made for the earlier stadiums are still valid in the new era of construction.

CONSTRUCTION COSTS

Twenty-six stadiums were used in analyzing construction costs. Of the thirty-two omitted sites, fourteen were private and eighteen were public stadiums. These sites were excluded because (1) reliable data could not be found; (2) the facilities were built when accurate deflators were unavailable, making inflation adjustment impossible; or (3) they were built concurrently with other facilities and the allocation of costs was not possible.

Original construction costs are supplemented with major renovation costs. When evidence showed renovation had taken place, but reliable data regarding costs are not available, only the original costs and capacities are used. Maintenance costs to replace aging equipment are not included. All cost figures (original, renovation, and expansion) are adjusted by the Composite Index of Construction Costs.[1] As a result, all costs are analyzed in the index's base year (1977) dollars.

Since the index began in 1947, only stadiums constructed after 1946 are included in the analysis of construction costs.

Table 19.1 surveys the construction cost and years for publicly owned stadiums and shows the appropriate deflator value, the construction costs in 1977 dollars, and the average-inflation-adjusted-cost-per-seat (AIACPS) for each publicly owned stadium for which it was possible to compute the value. Information that was not available is indicated with a (n.a.) symbol. Because of the different field configurations for football and baseball, the seating capacities vary greatly in some instances. For multipurpose stadiums, the baseball capacity is used.

Reliable data were found for twenty-two of the thirty-nine publicly owned stadiums listed. The 1977 AIACPS range from a low of $298 for Tampa Stadium to a high of $2,388 for the Houston Astrodome.

Table 19.2 reviews the construction costs for privately built stadiums. Because fourteen of the privately built stadiums were built before the cost index was established, only five private stadiums have computed AIACPS. The private AIACPS ranges from a low of $221 for Foxboro Stadium to a high of $1,187 for Busch Stadium.

---

1. U.S. Department of Commerce, *Construction Review* (July–August 1983): 56. For construction completed after 1982, *Construction Review*, (September–October 1984): 54. For 1987, 1991, and 1992 data, deflators were acquired through a conversation with Sherrita Powell of the Bureau of the Census, September 1993.

The last two entries of each table represent the mean AIACPS and the standard deviation of the AIACPS for each type of ownership. The mean AIACPS for publicly and privately built stadiums is $1,135 and $722, respectively. The standard deviations for public and private stadiums are $476 and $367, respectively.

Using a z-test, the probability that the mean of the private stadiums is the same as the public mean is less than 2 in 100. The evidence supports the argument that privately built stadiums cost less per seat to construct than do publicly built facilities.

An alternative test compares the private mean with the combined mean of $1,059. The z-test estimates that the probability that the private distribution came from the same population as the total distribution is less than 3 in 100.

By comparison, the same z-test comparing the means of the public and private stadium construction costs for the stadiums built before 1985 yields a probability that the two samples come from the same population to be about 4.5 percent. The differential between private and public stadium construction costs appears to have widened still further with the stadiums constructed in the last eight years.

To confirm this inference, another test can be performed to estimate the likelihood that the AIACPS of Joe Robbie Stadium, the one privately built facility in the last eight years, is significantly different from the AIACPS of the three publicly built stadiums. The z-test comes to the conclusion that the probability that Joe Robbie's construction costs would come from the same population represented by the costs of new public stadiums is less than 1 in 10,000. This is an underestimate since the public stadium's distribution is skewed to smaller numbers, and the z-test assumes a normal distribution, but it is unlikely that the skew would increase the probability of Joe Robbie's construction costs coming from the public distribution to the extent that the earlier conclusion could be discredited.

These latter tests discredit the criticism that public stadiums cost more because they, on average, were built after the private stadiums and fan expectations are for fancier, more costly stadiums. The evidence from the new stadiums is that new private stadiums are more economical than their public counterparts.

Since construction contains large fixed costs factors, capacity sizes were compared to see if the difference in mean AIACPS could be explained because private facilities are larger, and they spread the fixed costs over a larger number of seats. The publicly constructed stadiums' average capacity is 57,311 compared to 61,132 of private stadiums. The difference is not statistically signficant. Furthermore the private cost per seat is sufficiently low that the private sector is able to build the 61,132 seat facility for $20,624,126 *less* than the public sector can build the 57,311 facility.

Another possible explanation for the difference in construction costs is a "sunbelt" factor. Sixty percent of the private stadiums are in California, Texas, and Florida. If there are lower labor or other construction costs in those states, the results may be biased. Casual comparison of the construction costs of the privately and publicly built stadiums in similar regions refute this. In Southern

California, for example, the AIACPS for Dodger Stadium is $765 compared to the AIACPS of $1,016 and $1,227 for publicly built Anaheim and Jack Murphy Stadiums. Similarly, in Texas the AIACPS of privately constructed Texas Stadium is $660 while the AIACPS of Arlington Stadium is $1,205.

The mean AIACPS of the privately constructed sunbelt stadiums of Los Angeles; Irving,Texas; and Miami is $871. The mean AIACPS of publicly constructed sunbelt stadiums in Anaheim; Arlington, Texas; Atlanta (Fulton County and Georgia Dome), Houston, San Diego and Tampa is $1,190. The standard deviation of the private sunbelt stadium distribution is $279, while the standard deviation for the public sunbelt stadiums is $639. A z-test estimates that the likelihood that these arrays come from the same distribution is less than one-half of one percent.

Another consideration is that the public stadiums are predominantly downtown sites where real estate and labor costs are higher. Three of the five private stadiums, Irving, Foxboro, and, Joe Robbie Stadiums, are located in the suburbs. The opposite argument may be more valid. Many public stadiums are not located for the comfort and convenience of the patrons of the facility, but rather, the location is influenced by other criterion. Many of the publicly owned stadiums were constructed as part of an urban renewal project. In these cases, the stadium is located in a depressed area with land values below what similar land would sell for in the suburbs.

To test the hypothesis that the the construction costs of privately and publicly owned suburban stadiums are the same, the mean AIACPS of the four publicly owned suburban stadiums in Anaheim; Arlington; Orchard Park; and Pontiac, Michigan, is compared to the mean AIACPS of the three private suburban stadiums. The mean and standard deviation of the public suburban stadiums are $795 and $253, respectively. The private stadiums' mean and standard deviation are $553 and $293 respectively. A z-test indicates that the chance that these means come from the same distribution is about 12.5 percent.

Policy Implications

Chapter 17 showed that the source of the subsidies to sports franchises was the cost of construction. This chapter has illustrated that the cost of construction for private stadiums is about 60 percent of that for public stadiums. The implication is that if public stadiums were built by the private sector, the subsidy would be reduced. Indeed, if publicly built stadiums cost 40 percent less to build (the reduction being the average cost differential between private and public stadiums) every one of the stadiums shown to be a losing investment would have a positive ANPV.

DAYS USED

Sports facilities can be used for other events when the home team is away or during the off season. A more intensively used stadium spreads the debt amortization and routine maintenance over more events. A dark stadium also has no positive socioeconomic impact on the community.

To test if private stadiums are more aggressive in recruiting business, data on the days used was solicited for all stadiums. When available, days used included move-in and move-out days, as the facility was not available for an alternative use on those days. "Days used" also included the use of portions of the facility other than the stadium. Therefore, included in the total are days when the convention center or parking lot was used to host an event. Tables 19.3 and 19.4 show the number of days public and private facilities were used in 1984, respectively. The average number of days used and the standard deviations for each kind of stadium are listed as the last entry of each table. The test does not reveal any difference between the two means at any level of statistical convidence.

These results are not surprising. Few events are of the magnitude to justify a stadium. Furthermore, operators of stadiums, particularly stadiums with no dome, face a shortened season of use. This is especially true of stadiums in the northern part of the country. Another consideration for a stadium with a natural grass field is that the amount of time necessary to repair the turf after a non-sports event so that the sports team, the principal tenants, can use it. These constraints exist regardless of ownership, so little difference in privately and publicly owned stadium usage is expected.

AMENITIES

Comforts for patrons play a crucial role in the decision to attend an event. The easier it is to reach the stadium, the more pleasing the concessions, and the more congenial the facility, the more likely a customer will return for another affair. A lack of these amenities will result in lower attendance and stadium revenues and fewer bookings.

Parking

Ample parking is one of those features that is readily apparent and, when lacking, can ruin an otherwise pleasant outing. On the other hand, too many parking spaces means too many resources are devoted to parking.

Stadium managers of facilities that house both Major League Baseball and NFL franchises face a classic peak load problem. Most NFL teams play before capacity crowds while baseball teams do not. For this reason, owners must be able to provide parking for the football enthusiasts, although doing so will lead to "excess capacity" at most baseball games. One solution could arise if the stadium is located in a business district where neighboring parking facilities could provide an "elastic" supply of parking spaces that expands for peak Sunday NFL demand but contracts for baseball games.

Because of the peak load issue, capacity is used as the appropriate measure for stadiums that host NFL franchises. For stadiums used solely as baseball facilities, average attendance for the first five years the stadium was in use is used as the measure of parking demand. Tables 19.5 and 19.6 show the capacity:parking ratio for private and public stadiums, respectively. Major League Baseball stadiums are similarly shown in Tables 19.7 and 19.8. In total, data on parking facilities were found for forty stadiums (nine private and thirty-one public).

The capacity (for football facilities) or average attendance (for baseball) was divided by the number of parking spots within walking distance of the stadium. Tables 19.5 through 19.7 show the capacity-per-parking-space (CPS) or the average-attendance-per-parking-space (AAPS) for each of the stadiums included in the survey.

Several studies have been made to estimate the number of fans arriving in a car to particular sporting events.[2] One fact working in favor of the stadium manager is that football fans tend to use their cars more intensively, averaging about 3.5 occupants to a car compared to about 2.5 baseball fans per car.[3] Parking demand is further eased by the observation that 5 percent of the fans generally take public transit to the games, while another 5 percent take leased buses. Obviously, these numbers will vary from city to city, but they do provide a basis for analysis. To account for the fans that use mass transit and leased buses, the CPS and the AAPS in Tables 19.5 through 19.8 are reduced by 10 percent.

In order to be considered "acceptable," the CPS had to be between 3.0 and 4.0 for football stadiums. Table 19.9 classifies the NFL stadiums in Tables 19.5 and 19.6 as those with too many, too few, and acceptable parking ratios by this standard.

Table 19.9 reflects that there is little to recommend the parking allowance in either ownership category. There is a tendency for most NFL stadiums to have too few parking spaces in the probable event of a sell-out. A reason might be that the NFL home season usually includes only eight home games, not counting play-offs. Since the stadium is not so intensively used on other occasions, it is questionable to build enough parking for sell-outs when there are only eight each year.

Further examination of Table 19.9 reveals that patrons at a private NFL stadium are more likely to be in a stadium with acceptable parking than if they were in a publicly owned stadium. One-third of the private NFL stadiums have acceptable ratios, while only one-fourth of the public stadiums have acceptable parking facilities. Furthermore, while almost 10 percent of the public facilities do so, none of the privately owned facilities devote too many resources to parking. The conclusions drawn from Table 19.9 are that privately owned

---

2.   J. M. Hunnicutt, "Parking Demand for a Large Downtown Stadium," *Traffic Engineering* 39 no. 10 (July 1969): 48.   Also, John E. Ashwood, "Transportation Planning Consideration for New Stadia," (Report on the advisability of building a major dome stadium in Phoenix, Arizona. Prepared by Howard Needles Tammen & Bergendoff), page V-2.

3.   Hunnicutt, "Parking Demand," 48.

facilities have more appropriate parking facilities than their publicly owned counterparts, and that there is a tendency for public planners to provide for parking spaces which most likely will not be used.

In order to be considered acceptable, a baseball stadium's AAPS needs to be between 2.0 and 3.0. Table 19.10 classifies and summarizes the stadiums in Tables 19.7 through 19.8 as having too many, too few, and an appropriate amount of parking.

The numbers do not speak well of the parking facilities for either type of facility. Out of twenty-two stadiums, only seven have acceptable facilities, while thirteen have devoted too many resources to parking. A look at the percentage of the stadiums with acceptable parking ratios in each ownership category is, as before, revealing. A patron of a privately owned stadium is twice as likely to be attending a facility with acceptable parking ratios than a fan at a publicly owned stadium. One-half of the private stadiums have the appropriate amount of parking spaces, while only one-fourth of the publicly owned stadiums have the acceptable levels. Another way of looking at the data in Table 19.10 is that the privately owned baseball stadiums make up less than 28 percent of the total number of baseball stadiums in the study, but they contribute almost 46 percent of the stadiums with an acceptable parking ratio.

Table 19.11 combines the number of facilities in Tables 19.9 and 19.10 to give a total number in each category by ownership classification. Out of the fifty-seven stadiums considered (some counted twice as both an NFL and Major League Baseball stadium), there are sixteen stadiums that have the appropriate level of parking. This represents 28 percent of the stadiums surveyed. Of the private stadiums, 44 percent had acceptable levels of parking, while only 25 percent of the public stadiums were in this category. Both types of ownership have the same tendency to provide too few spaces in that in each type of ownership 44 percent of the facilities do not have enough parking spaces to cater to the demand of their patrons. The inference is, therefore, that private owners tend to guess more accurately than overly optimistic public owners as to the potential number of fans who will attend a team's home games.[4]

Stadium Rating

In the chronicles of his 1985 journey to all twenty-six Major League Baseball stadiums in use during that year, Bob Wood appraised stadiums on such amenities as layout and upkeep, ball field, seating, scoreboard, food, ball park employees, facilities, and atmosphere.[5] Although any rating system of these qualities is subjective, and there are times when Wood did not let a fact get in the

---

4. Comparison of the proportion of those stadiums that are publicly owned but privately managed does not change the numbers significantly from those found when ownership is the consideration.

5. Bob Wood, *Dodger Dogs to Fenway Franks* (New York: McGraw-Hill, 1985).

way of a good story, his rating system does offer a basis of comparison of the facilities' relative ranking in these areas of amenities.

After rating the stadiums on each of these characteritics, he summed the totals and ranked the stadiums on their total scores. Table 19.12 shows the total scores Wood assigns to them.[6] Private stadiums are signified with an asterisk. Arlington Stadium is classified in this study as a public stadium. Even though the Texas Rangers purchased the facility from Arlington in 1985, this did not allow the team sufficient time to make any adjustments. Conversely, Detroit's Tiger Stadium, which was team owned until the late 1970s, is classified as a public stadium because the public ownership was significantly long enough to make its imprint on the measured amenities.

The mean and the standard deviation for the five privately owned stadiums is 687 points and 34.75 points, respectively. For the twenty-one public stadiums, the mean and standard deviation was 625.95 points and 63.46 points. A z-test estimates the chance of these two average rankings coming from the same distribution is less than one-half of one percent.

In that Wood openly expresses a dislike for domed stadiums, a second test was performed eliminating domed stadiums. This was done because all domed stadiums are publicly owned, and Wood's bias against domes could taint the finding that included all domes. The difference in the means is reduced by dropping domed stadiums from the public sector (the new public mean became 639.4). The z-test estimates the likelihood that the public and private ratings came from the same distribution is less than 2 percent.

The use of Wood's rating system may be putting too much weight on a light-hearted survey from the fan's view. As such, though, the findings may carry more signficance. That the difference in the measured area is so large in a survey in which the observer had no intended bias to prove public or private stadiums superior is perhaps more impressive than if the study was done with the express aim of showing one category superior.

TEAM LOYALTY

Many current sports headlines do not deal with competition among professional sports teams from different cities but are concerned with the competition among cities for professional sports teams. Since the Raiders' case decision, the threat of teams leaving a city has become so real that at least four bills have been introduced in Congress to limit a team's ability to move. Not surprisingly, these proposals were sponsored by congressmen from districts that just lost, or were in danger of losing, a major league sports franchise. Each bill, in some way, placed the burden on the sports franchise to prove certain deficiencies before it is permitted to move.[7]

---

6. Ibid., 13.
7. For a compilation and an analysis of the proposals to restrict franchise relocation see Arthur T. Johnson, "Municipal Administration and Sports

Arthur T. Johnson[8] suggested that another alternative to these costly methods is to tie the franchise owners financially to the community. The purpose of this financial relationship is to create costs for the team owner who moves from the city. One way of ensuring an economic stake in the community is to have team ownership of playing facilities.

Table 19.13 reviews franchise moves from one city to another from 1953 to 1985. Table 19.13 does not reflect intracity moves from one facility to another. In this way, the analysis captures the tendency of franchises to abandon one city for another by ownership of stadium, but it neglects a city's efforts to keep an existing team by building a stadium that the team then occupies rather than relocate. In this respect, the analysis may overstate the stability provided by private ownership.

At first blush, there seems little to support Johnson's hypothesis that financial ties to a community in the form of stadium ownership will promote franchise stability. During the thirty-two years covered in Table 19.13, eighteen moves were made by Major League Baseball and NFL teams. Of these eighteen moves, nine involved a team leaving a private stadium.

Deeper analysis provides a picture more sympathetic to the Johnson's thesis. Of the nine moves from private facilities, six involved teams leaving stadiums during the 1950s and early 1960s that were built in the first decade of the twentieth century. In five of these moves, the teams were moving into stadiums that were going to be built or rebuilt expressly for the team. A seventh move, by the California Angels, was prompted by the the resulting friction between the Dodgers and the Angels because the Angels did not have an ownership interest in Dodger Stadium. Likewise, the Chicago Cardinals football team did not possess an interest in Comiskey Park when they moved to St. Louis' Sportsman's Park. This leaves ten moves to be analyzed. Of these moves, none involved a team leaving a private stadium. It appears that Johnson's theory is supported by recent experience.

The inference of this chapter is unambiguous. The incentives of private ownership are strong enough to influence the manner in which the stadium is built and the ammenities provided and strengthens the franchise's tie to the community. Any community that is interested in promoting sports efficiently and so that it is enjoyable from the fan's standpoint will encourage private ownership of the sports facilities.

Relocation Issue," *Public Administration Review* 43 no. 6 (November–December 1983): 522–525.
8. Ibid.

| Table 19.1 |
| Construction Costs of Publicly Built Stadiums |

Construction Type	Year	Cost	Deflator	Cost in 1977 Prices	Capacity	AIACPS
Anaheim, California						
Anaheim Stadium						
Original	66	$20,000,000	0.454	$44,052,863		
Expansion	79	$31,000,000	1.29	$24,031,008		
Total		$68,083,871			67,000	$1,016
Arlington, Texas						
Arlington Stadium						
Original	65	$1,500,000	0.436	$3,440,367		
Expansion........	71	$20,000,000	0.605	$33,057,851		
Expansion........	78	$4,000,000	1.13	$3,539,823		
Total				$40,038,041	42,392	$944
Atlanta, Georgia						
Atlanta–Fulton County Stadium						
Original	65	$18,500,000	0.436	$42,431,193		
Expansion	75	$1,500,000	0.893	$1,679,731		
Total				$44,110,924	45,000	$980
Atlanta, Georgia						
Georgia Dome						
Original	92	$210,000,000	1.985.	$105,793,451	71,594	$1,478
Baltimore, Maryland						
Memorial Stadium						
Original	54	$6,000,000	0.38	$15,789,474		
Expansion	77	n. a.				
Renovation	80	$10,300,000	1.432	$7,192,737	52,137	
Baltimore, Maryland						
Oriole Park at Camden Yards						
Original	92	$105,000,000	1.985.	$52,896,725	48,000	$1,102
Buffalo, New York						
War Memorial Stadium						
Original	36	n. a.				
Renovation	59	$750,000	0.42	$1,785,714	30,000	
Expansion	63	$1,500,000	0.42	$3,571,429	35,000	
Chicago, Illinois						
New Comiskey Park						
Original	91	$135,000,000	1.97	$68,527,919	43,000	$1,594

Table 19.1
(continued)

Construction Type	Year	Cost	Deflator	Cost in 1977 Prices	Capacity	AIACPS
Chicago, Illinois						
Soldier Field						
Original	26	$10,000,000	n.a.			
Renovation	71	n.a.	0.61		57,351	
Cincinnati, Ohio						
Riverfront Stadium						
Original	70	$38,700,000	0.568	$68,133,803	51,920	$1,312
Cleveland, Ohio						
Cleveland Stadium						
Original	32	$3,500,000	n.a.		78,189	
Renovation	67	$3,000,000	0.471	$6,369,427		
Renovation	74	$3,600,000	0.818	$4,400,978		
Renovation	77	$1,500,000	1	$1,500,000		
Renovation	79	$2,800,000	1.29	$2,170,543		
Denver, Colorado						
Mile High Stadium						
Original	48	n.a.				
Renovation	76	$25,000,000	0.924	$27,056,277		
Renovation	68	$10,000,000	0.496	$20,161,290	75,000	
East Rutherford, New Jersey						
Meadowlands						
Original	76	$300,000,000.		2 stadium complex		
Green Bay, Wisconsin						
Lambeau Field						
Original	n.a.	n.a.				
Renovation	61–70	$3,778,000				
Houston, Texas						
Astrodome						
Original	64	$45,350,000	0.422	$107,464,455	45,000	$2,388
Indianapolis, Indiana						
Hoosier Dome						
Original	84	$80,000,000	1.571	$50,922,979	60,500	$842
Jersey City, New Jersey						
Roosevelt Field						
Original	37	n.a.				

Table 19.1
(continued)

Construction Type	Year	Cost	Deflator	Cost in 1977 Prices	Capacity	AIACPS
Kansas City, Missouri						
Municipal Stadium						
Original	20s	$400,000	n.a.			
Renovation	55	$2,448,880	0.39	$6,279,179	32,561	
Kansas City, Missouri						
Arrowhead Stadium, Royals' Stadium						
Original	72	$54,000,000	0.64	$84,375,000	2 stadium complex	
Los Angeles, California						
Memorial Coliseum						
Original	23	$800,000	n.a.		76,000	
Expansion	30	$900,000	n.a.		105,000	
Miami, Florida						
Orange Bowl						
Original	38	$325,000	n.a.		22,000	
Renovation	45	$88,500	n.a.			
Renovation	47	$300,000	0.31	$967,742		
Renovation	49	$196,000	0.34	$576,471		
Renovation	50	$21,000	0.34	$61,765		
Renovation	54	$13,250	0.38	$34,868		
Renovation	55	$532,737	0.39	$1,365,992		
Renovation	59	$350,000	0.42	$833,333	75,449	
Milwaukee, Wisconsin						
County Stadium						
Original	53	$5,768,369	0.38	$15,179,918		
Expansion	53–76	$18,385,778		$18,385,778		
Total				$33,565,696	55,958	$600
Minneapolis, Minnesota						
Metropolitan Stadium						
Original	56	$5,000,000	0.42	$11,904,762	24,000	
Expansion	61	n.a.	0.41		40,800	
Expansion	64	n.a.	0.422		48,446	
Minneapolis, Minnesota						
Metrodome						
Original	82	$52,700,000	1.541	$34,198,572	54,711	$625
New Orleans, Louisiana						
Superdome						
Original	75	$163,500,000	0.893	$183,090,705	includes conv'n center	

Table 19.1
(Continued)

Construction Type	Year	Cost	Deflator	Cost in 1977 Prices	Capacity	AIACPS
New York, New York Shea Stadium						
Original	64	$26,000,000	0.422	$61,611,374	55,300	$1,114
New York, New York Yankee Stadium						
Reconstruction	76	$98,500,000	0.924	$106,601,732	56,000	$1,904
Oakland, California Oakland–Alameda Sports Complex						
Original	66	$30,000,000	0.454	$66,079,295	2 Facility Complex	
Renovation	80–86	$12,500,000				
Orchard Park, New York Rich Stadium						
Original	73	$25,000,000	0.696	$35,919,540	80,290	$447
Philadelphia, Pennsylvania Veterans Stadium						
Original	71	$48,000,000	0.605	$79,338,843		
Improvements	72	$4,700,000	0.641	$7,332,293		
Total				$86,671,136	66,052	$1,312
Pittsburgh, Pennsylvania Three Rivers Stadium						
Original	70	$45,000,000	0.568	$79,225,352		
Renovation	82	$10,000,000	1.541	$6,489,293		
Total				$85,714,645	55,000	$1,558
Pontiac, Michigan Silverdome						
Original	75	$55,700,000	0.893	$62,374,020	80,638	$774
San Diego, California Jack Murphy Stadium						
Original	67	$28,000,000	0.471	$59,447,983	48,460	$1,227
San Francisco, California Candlestick Park						
Original	60	$15,000,000	0.42	$35,714,286	45,774	
Expansion	71	$16,000,000	0.605	$26,446,281	58,000	
Total				$62,160,567		$1,072

Table 19.1
(continued)

Construction Type	Year	Cost	Deflator	Cost in 1977 Prices	Capacity	AIACPS
San Francisco, California						
Keezar Stadium						
Original	21	n.a.	n.a.		23,000	
Expansion	28	n.a.	n.a.		62,000	
Seattle, Washington						
Kingdome						
Original	76	$67,369,745	0.924	$72,910,979	60,000	$1,215
Tampa Bay, Florida						
Tampa Stadium						
Original	67	$4,600,000	0.471	$9,766,454		
Expansion	76	$10,500,000	0.924	$11,363,636		
Total				$21,130,091	71,000	$298
Washington, D.C.						
RFK Stadium						
Original	61	$21,700,000	0.41	$52,926,829	45,016	$1,176
		Average			57,061	$1,135
		Standard Deviation			11,367	$476

Table 19.2
Construction Costs of Privately Built Stadiums

Construction Type	Year	Cost	Deflator	Cost in 1977 Prices	Capacity	AIACPS
Boston, Massachusetts						
Braves Field						
Original	15	n.a.	n.a.	n.a.	n.a.	
Boston, Massachusets						
Fenway Park						
Original	12	n.a.				
Renovation	34	n.a.	n.a.		n.a.	33,513
Brooklyn, New York						
Ebbets Field						
Original	13	n.a.	n.a		n.a.	31,902
Chicago, Illinois						
Comiskey Park						
Original	10	n.a.	n.a.		n.a.	44,492
Expansion	26–27	n.a.	n.a.		n.a.	55,000
Chicago, Illinois						
Wrigley Field						
Original	16	n.a.	n.a.		n.a	37,741
Cincinnati, Ohio						
Crosley Field						
Original	12	n.a.	n.a.		n.a.	29,468
Irving, Texas						
Texas Stadium						
Original	71	$26,000,000	0.605	$42,975,207	65,101	$660
Detroit, Michigan						
Tiger Stadium						
Original	12	n.a.	n.a.		n.a.	54,226
Foxboro, Massachusetts						
Sullivan (Schaeffer) Stadium						
Original	71	$6,700,000	0.605	$11,074,380		
Renovation	71	$1,500,000	0.605	$2,479,339		
Total				$13,553,719	61,457	$221
Los Angeles, California						
Dodger Stadium						
Original	62	$18,000,000	0.42	$23,809,524	56,000	$765

Table 19.2
(continued)

Construction Type	Year	Cost	Deflator	Cost in 1977 Prices	Capacity	AIACPS
Miami, Florida						
Joe Robbie Stadium						
Original	87	$100,000,000	1.764	$56,689,342	73,000	$777
New York, New York						
Polo Grounds						
Original	11	n.a.	n.a.	34,000		
Expansion	24	n.a.	n.a.	55,000		
New York, New York						
Yankee Stadium						
Original	22	$2,305,000	n.a.	n.a.		
Expansion	37	n.a.	n.a.	n.a.	81,000	
Philadelphia, Pennsylvania						
Shibe Park						
Original	9	n.a ..n.a		n.a.	33,608	
Pittsburgh, Pennsylvania						
Forbes Field						
Original	9	n.a.	n.a	n.a.	35,000	
Seattle, Washington						
Sickes Stadium						
Original	n.a.	n.a.	n.a.	n.a.	n.a	
St. Louis, Missouri						
Busch Stadium						
Original...........66		$27,000,000	0.454	$59,471,366	50,100	$1,187
St. Louis, Missouri						
Sportsman's Park						
Original	9	n.a.	n.a.	n.a.	34,450	
Washington, D. C.						
Griffith Stadium						
Original	11	n.a.	n.a.	n.a.	28,669	
		Average			61,132	$722
		Standard Deviation			8,729	$345

Table 19.3
Public Stadiums
Number of Days Used in 1984

Facility	Days Used	Facility	Days Used
Arlington Stadium	90	Metrodome	120
Memorial Stadium	85	Yankee Stadium	82
Riverfront Stadium	100	Oakland Coliseum	100
Mile High Stadium	120	Rich Stadium	13
Meadowlands	200	Three Rivers Stadium	95
Astrodome	200	Silverdome	130
Arrowhead Stadium	12	Kingdome	190
Royals' Stadium	82	Average	107.13
County Stadium	95	Standard Deviation	54.97

Table 19.4
Private Stadiums
Number of Days Used in 1984

Facility	Days Used
Fenway Park	85
Comiskey Park (old)	95
Wrigley Field	82
Texas Stadium	200
Foxboro Stadium.	13
Dodger Stadium	100
Average	95.83
Standard Deviation	60.06

Table 19.5
Capacity: Parking Ratios
Private Stadiums Used for Football

City	Stadium	Capacity	Parking	Capacity:Park
St. Louis	Busch Stadium	51,392	6,982	7.36
Irving	Texas Stadium	65,101	15,000	4.34
Foxboro	Foxboro Stadium	61,457	16,000	3.84

Table 19.6
Capacity: Parking Ratios
Public Stadiums Used for Football

City	Stadium	Capacity	Parking	Capacity:Park
Miami	Orange Bowl	75,449	3,600	20.96
New Orleans	Superdome	72,675	5,000	14.54
Los Angeles	Memorial Coliseum	92,604	6,500	14.25
Denver	Mile High Stadium	75,000	5,500	13.64
Cleveland	Cleveland Stadium	80,165	6,000	13.36
Baltimore	Memorial Stadium	60,020	4,500	13.34
New York	Yankee Stadium	57,745	5,000	11.55
Atlanta	Atlanta–Fulton Stad.	60,489	6,500	9.31
Pontiac	Silverdome	80,638	9,900	8.15
Green Bay	Lambeau Field	56,267	7,000	8.04
New York.	Shea Stadium	60,000	7,500	8.0
Chicago	Soldier Field	57,351	8,000	7.17
Tampa	Tampa Stadium	71,000	10,000	7.1
Pittsburgh	Three Rivers Stadium	55,350	8,000	6.92
Philadelphia	Veterans Stad.	66,052	12,000	5.50
Oakland	Coliseum	54,587	10,000	5.46
Washington, DC	RFK Stadium	54,398	10,000	5.44
Buffalo	Rich Stadium	80,020	16,000	5.00
Milwaukee	County Stadium	55,896	11,500	4.86
San Francisco	Candlestick	61,246	14,000	4.37
Anaheim	Anaheim Stadium	66,000	16,000	4.13
Kansas City	Arrowhead Stadium	78,198	20,000	3.91
Seattle	Kingdome	65,000	17,000	3.82
E. Rutherford	Meadowlands	76,000	20,000	3.8
Minneapolis	Metropolitan Stadium	48,446	14,000	3.46
San Diego	Jack Murphy Stadium	54,000	17,000	3.18
Cincinnati	Riverfront Stadium	56,200	20,000	2.81
Minneapolis	Metrodome	54,711	20,000	2.74
Houston	Astrodome	50,000	28,000	1.79

Table 19.7
Attendance: Parking Ratios
Public Stadiums Used for Baseball

City	Stadium	Avg. Attendance	Parking	Attendance:Park
New York	Shea Stadium	21,681	7,500	2.89
Baltimore	Memorial Stadium.	12,139	4,500	2.70
Atlanta,	Atlanta Stadium	16,213	6,500	2.49
Pittsburgh	Three Rivers Stadium	17,645	8,000	2.21
Philadelphia	Veterans Stadium	20,834	12,000	1.74
San Francisco	Candlestick Park	18,228	14,000	1.30
Arlington	Arlington Stadium	12,388	10,000	1.24
Minneapolis	Metropolitan Stadium.	16,709	14,000	1.19
Cincinnati	Riverfront Stadium.	23,856	20,000	1.19
Oakland	Memorial Coliseum	9,336	10,000	0.93
Kansas City	Royals' Stadium.	16,902	20,000	0.85
Anaheim	Anaheim Stadium	12,511	16,000	0.78
Seattle	Kingdome	11,739	17,000	0.69
Washington, D. C.	RFK Stadium	6,830	10,000	0.68
Minneapolis	Metrodome	10,988	20,000	0.55
San Diego	Jack Murphy Stadium	7,800	17,000	0.46

Table 19.8
Attendance: Parking Ratios
Private Stadiums Used for Baseball

City	Stadium	Avg. Attendance	Parking	Attendance:Park
Boston	Fenway Park	23,042	3,000	7.68
Chicago	Wrigley Field	13,997	3,000	4.67
Detroit	Tiger Stadium	17,375	7,000	2.48
Cincinnati	Crosley Field	11,683	5,500	2.12
Los Angeles	Dodger Stadium	31,341	16,000	1.96
Chicago	Comiskey Park (old)	14,458	8,000	1.81

Table 19.9
NFL Stadiums
Capacity: Parking Ratios by Ownership Category
(rounded to the nearest tenth of a unit)

	Too Many Spaces 0 to 2.9 CPS	Acceptable 3.0 to 4.0 CPS	Too Few Spaces > 4.0 CPS
Public	3	8	21
Private	0	1	2

Table 19.10
Major League Baseball Stadiums
Average Attendance to Parking Ratios by Ownership Category
(rounded to the nearest tenth of a unit)

	Too Many Spaces 0 to 1.9 AAPS	Acceptable 2.0 to 3.0 AAPS	Too Few Spaces > 3.0 AAPS
Public	12	4	0
Private	1	3	2

Table 19.11
Parking Capacities by Ownership Category

	Too Many Spaces	Acceptable	Too Few Spaces
Public	15	12	21
Private	1	4	4

Table 19.12
Independent Rating of Baseball Stadiums

Stadium Name	Rating	Stadium Name	Rating
*Dodger Stadium	745	Arlington Stadium	635
Royals Stadium	745	Olympic Stadium	625
Milwaukee County Stadium	725	Riverfront Stadium	620
Baltimore Memorial Stadium	725	Veterans Stadium	615
*Wrigley Field	685	Three Rivers Stadium	610
*Fenway Park	685	Shea Stadium	595
Oakland Coliseum	680	Metrodome	580
Jack Murphy Stadium	680	Atlanta–Fulton Co. Stadium	575
Anaheim Stadium	675	Cleveland Mun. Stadium	565
Busch Memorial Stadium	660	Kingdome	555
*Comiskey Park (old)	660	Candlestick Park	555
Tiger Stadium	660	Astrodome	535
Yankee Stadium	655	Exhibition Stadium	535

*Designates a privately owned stadium

Table 19.13
Franchise Moves, 1953–1985
Baseball

Year	Team	Old Stadium	New Stadium	Ownbership Change
1953	Braves	Braves' Field	Milwaukee County Stadium	Private-Public
1954	Browns	Sportsman's Park	Baltimore Memorial Stadium	Private-Public
1955	Athletics	Shibe Park	Kansas City Muni. Stadium	Private-Public
1958	Dodgers	Ebbet's Field	Dodger Stadium	Private-Private
1958	Giants	Polo Grounds	Candlestick Park	Private-Public
1961	Senators	Griffith Stadium	Metropolitan Stadium	Private-Public
1966	Braves	Milwaukee County Stad.	Atlanta–Fulton County Stadium	Public- Public
1966	Angels	Dodger Stad.	Anaheim Stadium	Private-Public
1968	Athletics	Kansas City Muni. Stadium	Oakland–Alameda Coliseum Complex	Public-Public
1970	Pilots	Sicks Stadium	Milwaukee County Stadium	Public-Public
1972	Senators	RFK Stadium	Arlington Stadium	Public-Public

Football

Year	Team	Old Stadium	New Stadium	Ownership Change
1960	Cardinals	Comiskey Park	Sportsman's Park	Private-Private
1961	Chargers	L. A. Coliseum	Balboa Stadium	Public-Public
1963	Texans	Cotton Bowl	Kansas City Muni. Stadium	Public-Public
1976	Giants	Shea Stadium	Meadowlands	Public-Public
1980	Rams	L. A. Coliseum	Anaheim Stadium	Public-Public
1982	Raiders	Oakland–Alameda Coliseum Complex	LA Coliseum	Public-Public
1984	Colts	Baltimore Memorial Stad.	Hoosierdome	Public-Public

Chapter 20
Conclusion

This research was undertaken to determine if local (and now state) governments subsidize outdoor professional sports teams through the leasing of municipally owned sports facilities. If subsidies existed, a second objective was to measure the size of those subsidies. Finally, if stadium financing involves tax dollars that are not recovered through stadium operations, are the municipal landlords acting rationally? That is, is there an explanation for the city subsidizing a private enterprise such as a sports team?

As mentioned in the opening chapter, this research updates studies completed in 1988. The conclusions shared by the two studies are:

- •Direct municipal stadium financing almost always involves a transfer of wealth from the taxpayer.
- •The size of the subsidies are variable.
- •Typically the subsidy takes the form of unrecovered construction costs. Leases on stadiums built before occupancy that cover operating expenses but do not recover all construction costs are rational.
- •Given the nature of the subsidy, it is not likely that the fans receive much, if any, of the subsidy.
- •The justification for stadiums built to receive, or keep, a sports franchise revolves around external benefits the city receives by hosting a professional sports franchise.
- •Evidence supports the existence of these external benefits in some circumstances. The external benefits are not universal.

By comparing the data in this report with the data found in 1988, the following observations can be made, as well:

- •The magnitude of the subsidy is volatile and depends upon the lease terms. Every example of lease renegotiation has resulted in the subsidy to the team increasing.

•For at least two reasons, no study yet undertaken has measured the external benefits derived from professional sports teams: First, assessing the increase in economic activity has proven elusive, second, the impact of any increase in economic activity on a government's treasury will depend upon the tax base implied in that government entity's tax code.

It should be stressed that these findings are neutral with respect to the advisability of stadium investment. The existence of a negative ANPV, in and of itself, does not mean a stadium investment is unwise. While a stadium investment incurred with the intention of securing a major league franchise may not be a prudent financial decision for a private sector investor, the increased leisure time options provided by a team to a city's citizenry, the increased civic pride a successful team brings, and the potential for increased employment under certain conditions provide benefits that are difficult to measure in monetary terms.

These benefits are equally difficult for a team owner to capture. A franchise owner who cannot realize all the benefits of building a stadium will underinvest in stadium facilities. The subsidization of the stadium in which the team plays is a way the team owner can extract the benefits his team brings to the community. This capture of benefits would not be available to the franchise if the stadium was privately owned without property tax abatement.

Insofar as personal values will determine whether the increased employment in the service and non-agricultural sectors and civic pride offset the increased crime and monetary costs, this study cannot determine whether it is appropriate for a city to construct an outdoor sports facility. The purpose of this study is to give city, county, and state planners the opportunity to project the size of any uncovered costs of stadium construction. These projections can then be compared with projected external benefits to see if a stadium is a worthwhile project.[1]

Municipal authorities came out better after this research than before it. Traditionally, the local government leaders charged with stadium planning and team procurement were considered image conscious to the extreme. The quest for personal grandeur, reportedly, clouded their decision making, and the local treasury became an open treasure chest for the team owner. It is true that boondoggles exist. In some cases, local officials, in an attempt to acquire or

---

1. The tendency of proponents and opponents of stadium investment to use only parts of the findings was evident in 1990. When the National League was expanding, opponents of a public stadium project in Denver used my 1988 study to show that a stadium project likely would create a subsidy, without referring to the portion of the study showing that external benefits might accrue that would make the investment well advised. Phoenix interests that argued for a stadium in an attempt to secure one of the National League expansion teams cited portions of the 1988 study that showed that economic growth might accompany a stadium project but ignored the section estimating stadium subsidies.

keep a team, lost control of the project or were dishonest with the taxpayers regarding the cost and benefits of the structure. With the exception of the Superdome, however, all the stadiums for which there has been sufficient information to compute ANPVs have modest negative ANPVs and three publicly owned stadiums may ultimately earn positive ANPVs. The existence of external effects makes the outcome of these investments even better.

POLICY IMPLICATIONS OF FINDINGS

Eminent Domain

When the Colts and Raiders left Baltimore and Oakland, respectively, both cities attempted to use, unsuccessfully, eminent domain, the government's right to acquire private property for the public good, with compensation to the owner to keep the team. In both cases, the tactic was not employed until after the franchises left, so the argument became moot.

Team owners, however, must beware of a danger in promoting the public good generated by the team to justify stadium subsidies. This is not meant to advocate public ownership of sports franchises, but team owners who claim stadiums deserve public support because of the external benefits the teams provide are setting themselves up for a legal challenge for the ownership of their team if they decide to leave the city, and if the city can press the case before the team relocates. A city that has agreed to subsidize a team's stadium because it believed the team owner's claim that the franchise improves the city's economy and image would be justified in using that argument in exercising eminent domain.

Location of Stadiums

Since the resources used in producing a ball game, namely players and a stadium, can be located anywhere, professional sports contests need not be what location theorists call "materials oriented."[2] By contrast, since the major cost of transportation is borne by the consumer once a stadium is built the production of a professional sports event is "market oriented." One of the least ambiguous trips in urban planning is the post-game destination of the sports fan. With games being played mostly at night or on weekend days, most fans go directly home after the contest. The choice of a downtown site that increases the travel time for a majority of the patrons who reside in the suburbs, without any compensating reduction in production costs, seems sub-optimal.

---

2. Examples of materials-oriented firms would be steel and saw mills. For more on location theory and the concept of materials and market orientation, see Walter Isard, *Location and Space-Economy* (New York: John Wiley & Sons and MIT Press, 1956).

Despite the increased transportation costs, downtown locations were selected over other sites in several cases, including Cincinnati, Pittsburgh, Philadelphia, Seattle, Chicago, and Washington, D.C. The decision also received tacit approval from the franchises in that they, at least originally, agreed to play their contests in these structures. The question arises, "Why are stadiums located in the downtown area if it increases consumers' travel time?"

The simultaneous increase in crime and employment caused by the arrival of a sports team is useful in explaining this seemingly irrational behavior. The suburbs are areas of relative wealth when compared with most downtown areas. Increasing employment in the suburbs is not a concern of most policy makers because the residents of the suburbs find their employment elsewhere, usually in the downtown area. They also may not be voters in the city, so the increased employment in a suburb would not increase a city politician's electability. Neither the increased employment nor the increased crime related to a stadium and professional sports team(s) are attractions for the suburbs. Indeed, many suburbs take pride in their no, or slow, growth policies. Add to this the study's findings that a suburb cannot capture all the benefits of a stadium investment and one is left with the conclusion that a downtown location for stadiums may be optimal.

For a depressed inner city, the unemployment and incidence of crime is already high. The increase in employment related to a stadium and sports team will be more valuable and the increased crime less objectionable in the downtown area. Thus, the rational place to locate the stadium in a city with a depressed center district would be downtown. The residents of the suburbs are willing to commute the extra distance to keep the stadium "out of their neighborhood," and the residents of the inner city are aided by the increased economic growth.

The evidence is consistent with this explanation. Those cities mentioned previously that built new downtown stadiums in the past twenty-five years were cities with noticeable deterioration in the central business district. Cities that were experiencing relatively healthy economies in central business districts, such as Dallas and Los Angeles, did not place a high value on the stimulation created by stadiums. Sports teams in these cities moved into stadiums located in the suburbs of Arlington, Irving, and Anaheim.

Regional Planning

The findings of Rosentraub and Nunn are borne out by this study. The economic growth noticeable in small cities is too large to be contained in a small suburban economy. This leads to a potential free rider situation. Neighboring suburbs will not contribute to, nor act interested in, a stadium project, if they feel they can receive the benefits of economic growth without incurring the formidable costs of building the facility.

For that reason, suburban cities that are interested in constructing a stadium might do well to do so under a regional plan. The relatively successful Metrodome in Minneapolis is one such example. A regional approach to financing a stadium would allow the host city to receive some compensation for the costs inherent in the stadium from the cities that benefit from a team playing their home games in the area.

FUTURE DIRECTIONS OF RESEARCH

Most research raises as many questions as it answers. This study is no exception.

Economic Impact of a Professional Sports Franchise

While this study finds that in certain environments a professional sports franchise can bring a significant boost to the local economy of small cities, the specifics remain unclear, and doubts concerning methodology exist. Before an objective analysis of the advisability of stadium funding can be performed, more resources must be devoted to measuring the external economic benefits of teams and stadiums.

So that city planners and financial advisors can more precisely project if a stadium project is worthwhile, they must be able to project not only what economic benefits might accrue in different environments, but the magnitude of those benefits, when they are likely to arrive, where geographically they are likely to occur, and which sectors of the economy will be benefited or (in some cases) harmed. This information is useful in determining how to adjust the tax base so that those who benefit from the construction of the stadium would be identified as those who would help finance the project. As mentioned in chapter 18, the studies in this area, including this one, have been too aggregated and have used too few data points to be convincing or useful.

Census data are disaggregated now by SIC code. These may provide a wealth of data for researchers as they attempt to identify the fields affected by professional sports, the geographic regions that can be affected, and the magnitude of the boost.

Lease Terms and Subsidies

This study has shown a definite sensitivity of the subsidy's size to changes in the lease terms. The search for any correlation between terms of a stadium lease and the civic subsidy to the sports team may prove fruitful. By identifying the clauses, if they exist, that reduce the cost of the stadium to the city would allow the city to receive the benefits of the stadium investment at a lower cost.

Subsidies and Indoor Arenas

This research focused on one part of the professional sports spectrum. By concentrating on only outdoor sports, the study neglected the arenas used for the indoor sports by the NBA and the National Hockey League (NHL). The municipal involvement in indoor sports arenas was not included in this research so that a complete study could be made of the outdoor stadiums, which represent a more significant and specialized investment than the indoor facilities. While football and baseball stadiums grab more headlines than do indoor arenas, a study of the financial impact on local treasuries and the economic external impact of indoor facilities may have more general appeal than this study that looked at the impact of the larger outdoor sport stadiums.

Many cities that do not host NFL or Major League Baseball franchises have indoor arenas for NBA and NHL teams. That the initial investment in indoor arenas is smaller and more facilities are more diversifiable means that many "second tier" cities will build an indoor arena. The study on indoor arenas would be related to this study in more than the obvious way. Many of the second tier cities, such as Sacramento, San José, Phoenix, and San Antonio use the presence of an indoor sports team as an argument to team or league executives for locating the more exclusive and prestigious outdoor sport franchises in their cities.[3]

---

3. Remember Jozsa's findings that the presence of a professional sports team in another sport is one of the factors search committees look for in selecting franchise locations.

Bibliography

BOOKS

Alchian, A. A. "Corporate Management and Property Rights." In *Economic Forces at Work*. Edited by Daniel K. Benjamin. Indianapolis, IN: Liberty Press, 1977.

Baade, Robert. "Is There an Economic Rationale for Subsidizing Sports Stadiums?" Chicago, IL: Heartland Institute, 1987.

Berry, Robert C., William B. Gould IV, and Paul D. Staudohar. *Labor Relations in Professional Sports*. Dover, MA: Auburn House, 1986.

Brite, Robert L. *Business Statistics*. Menlo Park, CA: Addison Wesley, 1980.

Demmert, Henry G. *The Economics of Professional Team Sports*. Lexington, MA: D. C. Heath, 1973.

Golenbock, Peter. *Bums*. New York: Putnam, 1984.

Hilton, George W. "Comiskey Park." In *Insider Baseball*. Edited by L. Robert Davis. New York: Charles Scribners' Sons, 1983.

Isard, Walter. *Location and Space-Economy*. New York: John Wiley & Sons and MIT Press, 1956.

Jozsa, Frank P., Jr. "An Economic Analysis of Franchise Relocation and League Expansions in Professional Team Sports, 1950–1975," Ph.D. diss., Georgia State University, 1977.

Lowry, Philip J. *Green Cathedrals*. Cooperstown, NY: Society of American Baseball Research, 1986.

McKenzie, Richard. *Restrictions on Business Mobility*. Washington, D.C.: American Enterprise Institute, 1979.

The NFL's Official Encyclopedic History of Professional Football. New York: Macmillan, 1977.

Noll, Roger, ed. *Government and the Sports Business*. Washington, D.C.: Brookings Institute, 1974.

Reidenbaugh, Lowell. *Take Me Out to the Ball Park*. St. Louis, MO: Sporting News, 1983.

Shannon, Bill, and George Kalinsky. *The Ballparks*. New York: Hawthorne
    Books, 1975.
Smith, Adam. *An Inquiry Into the Nature and Causes of the Wealth of Nations*.
    Edited by Edwin Cannan. Vol. 2. Chicago: University of Chicago
    Press, 1976.
Sullivan, Neil J. *The Dodgers Move West*. New York: Oxford University
    Press, 1987.
Toman, Jim, and Dan Cook. *Cleveland Municipal Stadium*. Cleveland Land-
    mark Series, Volume II. Cleveland, OH: Cleveland Landmark Press,
    1981.
Veeck, Bill, and Ed Linn. *Veeck as in Wreck*. New York: G. P. Putnam's Sons,
    1962.
Wood, Bob. *Dodger Dogs to Fenway Franks*: New York: McGraw-Hill, 1985.

FINANCIAL REPORTS

City of Anaheim, California. Finance Director. *Financial Report, City of
    Anaheim for fiscal years* 1967, 1968, 1969, 1970, 1971, 1972, 1973,
    1974, 1975, 1976, 1977, 1978, 1979, 1980, 1981, 1982, 1983, 1984,
    1985, 1986, 1987, 1988, 1989, 1990.
City of Atlanta. City Controller. *City Finances Report of the City Controller
    for the Year Ending December 31, 1967*.
City of Atlanta. Department of Finance. *Annual Financial Report for the Fiscal
    Year Ended December 31*, 1974, 1975, 1977, 1979, 1981.
City of Baltimore. Director of Finance. *Annual Financial Report for Fiscal Year
    Ended June 30*, 1954. 1955, 1956, 1957, 1958, 1959, 1960, 1961,
    1962, 1963, 1964, 1965, 1966, 1967, 1968, 1969, 1970, 1971, 1972,
    1973, 1974, 1975, 1976, 1977, 1978, 1979, 1980, 1981, 1982.
City of Buffalo, New York. Department of Audit and Control. *Comptroller's
    Report—1959/1960*.
City of Buffalo. Department of Audit and Control. *Annual Report of the Fiscal
    Year ended* 1961, 1962, 1963, 1964, 1965, 1966, 1967, 1968, 1969,
    1970, 1971, 1972, 1973, 1974, 1975, 1976, 1977, 1978, 1979, 1980,
    1981, 1982, 1983.
City of Cincinnati. Department of Finance. *Financial Report for the Year Ended
    December 31*, 1969, 1970, 1971, 1972, 1973, 1974, 1975, 1976,
    1977, 1978, 1979, 1980, 1981, 1982, 1983, 1984, 1985, 1986, 1987,
    1988, 1989, 1990.
City and County of Denver. Auditor's Office. *Auditor's Annual Report for the
    City and County of Denver for the years* 1968, 1969, 1970, 1971,
    1972, 1973, 1974, 1975, 1976, 1977, 1978, 1979, 1980, 1981, 1982,
    1983, 1984, 1985, 1986, 1987, 1989.
District of Columbia Armory Board. *Annual Reports for the District of
    Columbia National Guard Armory Board and the Robert F. Kennedy
    Stadium*, 1962, 1964, 1968, 1969, 1970, 1971, 1972, 1973, 1974,

1975, 1976, 1977, 1978, 1979, 1980, 1981, 1982, 1983, 1984, 1985, 1986, 1987, 1988, 1989, 1990.

District of Columbia Armory Board. *Final Construction Report on District of Columbia Stadium.* Washington D.C.: GPO, 1973.

City of Los Angeles. Los Angeles Memorial Coliseum Commission. *Annual Report for Fiscal Year 1938–1939.*

City of Los Angeles. Los Angeles Memorial Coliseum Commission. *Progress Report and Financial Data, Four Years Ended December 31, 1949.*

City of Los Angeles. Los Angeles Memorial Coliseum Commission. *Report on Examination of Financial Statements for the Fiscal Year* 1946, 1947, 1948, 1949, 1950, 1951, 1952, 1953, 1954, 1955, 1956, 1957, 1967, 1968, 1969, 1970, 1971, 1972, 1973, 1974, 1975, 1976.

Louisiana Stadium and Exposition District. *Combined Statements of Revenues and Expenses for Fiscal Years* 1977, 1978, 1979, 1980, 1981, 1982, 1983, 1984. Made available through private correspondence with Bill Curl of the Facility Management of Louisiana.

Milwaukee County. *1953 Financial Report for the Year Ended December 31, 1953.*

Milwaukee County. *1954 Financial Report for the Year Ended December 31, 1954.*

Milwaukee County. *Financial Report for the Year Ended December 31,* 1956, 1957, 1959, 1960, 1961, 1962, 1963, 1964, 1965, 1966, 1967, 1968, 1969, 1970, 1971, 1972, 1973, 1974, 1975, 1976, 1977, 1978, 1979, 1980, 1981, 1982, 1983, 1984, 1985.

City of Minneapolis. Department of Finance. *Budget and Financial Statistics for the Fiscal Years* 1974, 1975, 1976, 1977, 1978, 1979, 1980.

State of Minnesota. Financial Audit Division, Office of the Legislative Auditor. *Financial Statements and Management Letter for the Year Ended December 31,* for years 1982, 1983, 1984, 1985, 1986, 1987, 1988, 1989, 1990, 1991.

San Diego, California. City Manager's Office. *Annual Budget Fiscal Year* 1968, 1969, 1970, 1972, 1973, 1974, 1975, 1976, 1977, 1978, 1979, 1980, 1981, 1982, 1983, 1984, 1985, 1986, 1987, 1988, 1989, 1990.

GOVERNMENT PUBLICATIONS

Council of Economic Advisors. *Economic Report of the President.* Washington, D.C.: Government Printing Office, February 1985.

Erie County. County Legislature. *1971 Minutes,* Meeting for 23 September 1971.

U.S. Bureau of the Census. *County and City Data Book.* Washington, D.C., 1956.

U.S. Bureau of the Census. *County and City Data Book.* Washington, D.C., 1962.

U.S. Bureau of the Census. *County and City Data Book.* Washington, D.C., 1972.

U.S. Bureau of the Census. *State and Metropolitan Area Book*. Washington, D.C., 1982.

U.S. Congress. Senate. Committee on the District of Columbia. *Future Use and Financing of RFK Stadium*, 92nd Cong., 1st sess., 1971.

U.S. Congress. Senate. Subcommittee on Antitrust and Monopoly of the Committee on the Judiciary. *Organized Professional Team Sports*. 85th Cong. 2d sess., 1958.

U.S. Congress. House. Select Committee on Professional Sports. *Inquiry into Professional Sports, Part 1*, 96th Cong. 2d sess., 1976, 550.

U.S. Department of Commerce. *Construction Review* (July–August, 1983): 56.

U.S. Department of Commerce. *Construction Review* (September-October 1984): 54.

U.S. Department of Justice. Federal Bureau of Investigation. *Uniform Crime Reports for the United States*. Washington, D.C.: United States Department of Justice, for years 1958, 1959, 1960, 1961, 1962, 1963, 1964, 1965, 1966, 1967, 1968, 1969, 1970, 1971, 1972, 1973, 1974, 1975, 1976, 1977, 1978, 1979, 1980, 1981, 1982, 1983, 1984, 1985.

U.S. Department of Labor. Bureau of Labor Statistics. *Employment, Hours, and Earnings, States and Areas, 1939–1982*. Washington, D.C.: Bureau of Labor Statistics, 1984.

INTERVIEWS AND CORRESPONDENCE

Adams, Charlie. Private conversation with chief financial officer, Oakland–Alameda County Coliseum Complex, 27 July 1992.

Anderson, Rick. Telephone conversation with Atlanta City Finance Department, 4 June and 22 June 1987.

Berkhardt, Ms. (first name is not known). Telephone conversation with Washington, D.C. Armory Board, 25 February 1987.

Brown, Doug. Interview with Department of Finance, City of Baltimore, 26 June 1987.

Campbell, Terrence. Telephone conversation with Orchard Park Tax Assessor, 23 June 1987.

Carlson, Roger. Telephone conversation with Minneapolis Property Tax Assessor's Office, 23 June 1987.

Cavagnaro, Joseph. Telephone conversation with Texas Stadium Corporation, February 1985.

Cunningham, Bill. Telephone conversation with Baltimore city councilman, 24 June 1987.

Dusek, Steve. Telephone conversation with a Minneapolis business leader. June 1985.

Flaherty, Mike. Telephone conversation with director of Mile High Stadium, 23 June 1987.

Gach, Greg. Telephone conversation with the senior accounting analyst, Erie County Finance Department, 23 December 1987.

Gala, Andrew. Telephone conversation with Foxboro city administrator, 4 June 1987.

Galvin, Pat. Telephone conversation with the Mile High Stadium management, February 1985.

Graziano, Robert V. Letter from Los Angeles Dodgers, vice president of finance, 23 October 1992.

Hogan, Charles. Telephone conversation with Fulton County Assessor's Office, 29 May 1987.

Hunigman, Fred. Telephone conversation with assistant manager of Veterans' Stadium, 14 December 1982.

James, Stacey. Telephone interview with public relations representative of New England Patriots, 30 December 1993.

Janette, James A. Telephone conversation with assessor division chief with County of San Diego, 29 July 1987.

Johnson, Bruce. Telephone conversation, May 1982.

Leon, Charles. Telephone conversation with the City of Buffalo Budget Office, 25 November 1987.

Maki, Steve. Telephone conversation with Metropolitan Sports Facilities Commission, 24 June 1987.

McNeill, Nancy. Telephone conversation, 26 January 1984.

"Memorial Stadium, Summary of Direct Expenditures and Revenues, Fiscal 1970 to Fiscal 1980," acquired from Doug Brown.

Milwaukee County Comptroller's Office. Private undated correspondence.

"Pat" (last name is not known). Three telephone conversations with the Civic Center Redevelopment Corporation of St. Louis, 7 February 1986.

Phillips, Dean. Telephone conversation with executive director of the Indiana Convention Center, 15 April 1983.

Quintella, Bob. Private correspondence with executive vice president of the Oaklnad–Alameda County Complex, 29 April 1992.

Riles, Wilson, Jr. Private correspondence with Oakland city council member, 19 June 1990.

Saltwell, E.R. Telephone conversation with the Chicago Cubs office, February 1985.

Smith, Ellis. Telephone conversation with New Orlean's Tax Assessor's Office, 3 March 1986.

Telephone conversation with Foxboro Assessor's Office, 4 June 1987.

Telephone conversation with Foxboro City Administrator's Office, 4 June 1987.

Telephone conversation with Irving, Texas Tax Office, 14 June 1987.

Telephone conversation with Texas Rangers public relations department, February 1985.

Telephone interview with the New England Patriots public relations department, 20 May 1983.

Telephone correspondence with the New York Yankees public relations office, date unknown.

Wachendorf, Robert E. Telephone conversation with downtown reappraisal director, County of Hamilton, Ohio, 24 April 1987.

Ward, Ray. Letter from executive vice president, Oakland Alameda County Coliseum Complex, 27 January 1987.

Wendt, Linda. Telephone conversation with the commercial property division of the Denver Assessor's Office, 3 June 1987.

Wiley, Nancy. Telephone conversation with the State Fair of Texas, 7 January 1986.

JOURNAL ARTICLES

Alchian, Armen A. "Some Economics of Property Rights." *Il Politico* 30 (1965): 817–829.

Baade, Robert A., and Richard F. Dye. "Sports Stadiums and Area Development: A Critical Review." *Economic Development Quarterly*, no. 2 (August 1988).

_____. "An Analysis of the Economic Rationale for Public Subsidization of Sports Stadiums." *The Annals of Regional Science*, 22 (July 1988).

Borjas, George J. "The Politics of Employment Discrimination in the Federal Bureaucracy." *Journal of Law and Economics* 25, no. 2 (October 1982): 271–299.

Coase, Ronald H. "The Problem of Social Costs." *Journal of Law and Economics* 3 (October 1960): 1–45.

Davies, David. "The Efficiency of Public versus Private Firms, the Case of Australia's Two Airlines." *Journal of Law and Economics* 14, no. 1 (April 1971): 149–165.

Demsetz, Harold. "When Does the Rule of Liability Matter?" *Journal of Legal Studies* (January 1972).

El-Hodiri, Mohamed, and James Quirk. "An Economic Model of a Professional Sports League." *Journal of Political Economy* 79 (November/December 1971): 1302–1319.

Fulton, William, "Desperately Seeking Sports Teams." *Governing* I, no. 6 (March 1988).

Hilton, George W. "Milwaukee's Charter Membership in the American League." *Historical Messenger of the Milwaukee County Historical Society* 30, no. 1 (Spring 1974): 2–17.

Hines, Thomas S. "Housing, Baseball, and Creeping Socialism: The Battle of Chavez Ravine, Los Angeles, 1949–1959." *Journal of Urban History* 8, no. 2 (February 1982): 123–143.

Hunnicutt, J.M. "Parking Demand for a Large Downtown Stadium." *Traffic Engineering* 39, no. 10, (July 1969): 48.

Johnson, Arthur T. "Congress and Professional Sports: 1951-1978." *ANNALS of the American Academy* (September 1979): 102–115.

_____. "Municipal Administration and Sports Relocation Issue." *Public Administration Review* 43, no. 6 (November- December 1983): 522–525.

Neale, Walter C. "The Peculiar Economics of Professional Sports." *Quarterly Journal of Economics* (February 1964).

"New Cincinnati Stadium Features Convenience." *The American City* 83 (September 1968): 116.

Okner, Benjamin A. "Subsidies of Stadiums and Arenas." In *Government and the Sports Business.* Edited by Roger Noll. Washington, D.C.: Brookings Institute, 1974.

Okner, Benjamin A. "Taxation and Sports Enterprises." In *Government and the Sports Business.* Edited by Roger Noll. Washington, D.C.: Brookings Institute, 1974.

Quirk, James. "An Economic Analysis of Team Movements in Professional Sports." *Law and Contemporary Problems* 38 (Winter/Spring 1973): 42–66.

Rosentraub, Mark S., and Samuel Nunn. "Suburban City Investment in Professional Sports: Estimating the Fiscal Returns of the Dallas Cowboys and Texas Rangers to Investor Communities." *American Behavioral Scientist* 21, no. 3 (February 1978): 393–413.

Rothenberg, Simon. "The Baseball Player's Labor Market." *Journal of Political Economy* 64 (June 1956): 242–248.

Scully, Gerald W. "Pay and Performance in Major League Baseball." *American Economic Review* (December 1974): 915–930.

Shubnell, Lawrence D., John E. Petersen and Collin B. Harris. "The Big Ticket: Financing a Professional Sports Facility." *Government Finance Review* 10, no. 12 (June 1985): 9.

MAGAZINE ARTICLES

"A Financial Hero in New Orleans." *Business Week,* 18 September 1971, "Names and Faces" column.

"A Geodesic Dome For Brooklyn Dodgers." *Progressive Architecture* 36, November 1955.

Alm, Richard. "Sports Stadiums: Is the U.S. Overdoing It?" *US News & World Report* , 21 May 1982.

"Atlanta Pitches for the Big Leagues." *Atlanta Magazine* 3, November 1963.

"Bids Under $20 Million Signal Stadium's Start." *Engineering News Record* 188, 6 April 1972.

Bingham, Walter. "I Don't Need Money, I Need Points." *Sports Illustrated* 19, no. 19, 4 November 1963.

"Build Stadium Now, Roof It Later." *Engineering News Record* 171, 11 November 1963.

"City Studies Proposal for $51 Million Stadium." *Engineering News Record* 190, 11 January 1973.

"Civic Leadership Scores a Home Run with St. Louis' New Ball Park." *Engineering News Record* 175, 14 October 1965.

"Coming Up: End Runs and Pop Flies on the Ohio." *Progressive Architecture* 43, March 1962.

"Dodger Dome Generates City Center Proposal." *Architectural Record* 119, April 1956, 217–220.

"Giants' Baseball Stadium Called a 'Firetrap'." *The Architectural Forum* 112, February 1960.

"Giants New Park: 45,000 Seats All Empty." *Engineering News Record* 163, October 1959.

"Job Site Casting." *Engineering News Record*, 168, 5 April 1962.

Kirshenbaum, Jerry. "Let Me Make One Thing Clear." *Sports Illustrated,* 7 June 1971.

Lucas, J. Anthony. "Wanta Buy Two Seats for the Dallas Cowboys?" *Esquire*, September 1972.

"Money Offerings for the Gods of Sport." *Economist* 315, no. 7650 (14 April 1990): 23–24.

"New Jersey: Money Problems Plague Builder of $300 Million Sports Complex." *Engineering News Record* 191, 18 October 1973.

"New Jersey's Stormy Land-use Battle." *Business Week*, 9 December 1972.

"New Orleans Superdome Going Up Despite Foundation Arguing." *Engineering News Record* 188, 15 June 1972.

"New York's Stadium Is Over Estimate." *Engineering News Record*, 23 March 1961.

"Owner Gambles $338,000 on Stadium Completion." *Engineering News Record* 190, 7 June 1973.

Powell, Douglas S. "Is Big League Baseball Good Municipal Business." *American City*, November 1957.

Schienseson, Julian. "Public Works Features of Cincinnati's Riverfront Stadium." *Public Works* 102 (May 1971): 82.

Shrake, Edwin. "Thunder Out of Oakland." *Sports Illustrated* 23, no. 20, 4 November 1965.

"Some Home on the Range." *Sports Illustrated*, 14 August 1972.

"State of the Stadium." *Atlanta Magazine* 4, March 1965.

"Steel Dome to Top $85 Million Stadium." *Engineering News Record* 188, 4 May 1972.

"Super Headache." *Newsweek*, 29 April 1974.

"Superdome Battle Stirs New Orleans." *Business Week*, 27 May 1972.

Temko, Allan. "How Not to Build a Stadium." *Harpers* 223, August 1961.

"The Shape's the Thing." *Progressive Architecture* 49, February 1968.

"Underground Activity Supports Above-Ground Action." *The American City* 82, September 1967.

NEWSPAPER ARTICLES

"...and the Cost of Playing Ball." *New York Times*, 5 March 1971.

"Angels, Anaheim in Partial Settlement." *Los Angeles Times*, 6 September 1985.

"Angel Stadium Prospects Grow." *Los Angeles Times*, 7 April 1964.

"Armory Board Reveals Stadium Plan for D.C." *Washington Post*, 23 April 1958.

"Armory Site Is Favored for Stadium." *Washington Post*, 26 January 1958.

"Armory Site OK with Marshall." *Washington Post*, 27 January 1958.

"Change of Stadium Site Could Be 'Kiss of Death'." *Washington Post*, 16 April 1959.

"City's White Elephant Going On Short Rations." *The Baltimore Sun*, 24 August 1933.

Cline, Francis X. "Way to Go." *New York Times*, 12 February 1977.

"Council Resolution for Dodger Baseball." *Los Angeles Times*, 17 September 1957.

"Cronin Says Tom Yawkey Still Opposed to Nats Moving Out of Nation's Capital." *Washington Post*, 22 August 1958.

"Danger of Coliseum Going Broke Seen." *Los Angeles Times*, 17 December 1982.

Dorsey, C. Lee. "Dorsey Wants Nats to Hire a General Manager." *Washington Post*, 19 January 1958.

Downey, Mike "He Was Wrong, He Knows It, and He Should Admit It." *Los Angeles Times*, 8 April 1987.

"East Capitol Loop Site for Stadium Approved by Planning Commission," *Washington Post*, 6 March 1959.

"Engineers Ready Plans, Stadium Cost for Board." *Washington Post*, 29 January 1959.

"GAO Insists on Open Bidding for Stadium." *Washington Post*, 20 August 1959.

"George Marshall Sure of Stadium's Success." *Washington Post*, 18 July 1958.

"Giants' Oakland Move Ripped." *Daily News* (Los Angeles), 3 October 1985.

"Griffith Delay Stuns Official." *Washington Post*, 9 September 1958.

"Griffith Will Not Seek Shift." *Washington Post*, 8 September 1958.

"Grower Demands Fair Price for Stadium Site." *Los Angeles Times*, 3 April 1964.

"Higher Rental Suggested for New Stadium." *Washington Post*, 1 February 1959.

"Ike Signs Stadium Bill." *Washington Post*, 24 September 1959.

"L.A. Council Votes Dodger Deal, 11–3." *Los Angeles Times*, 17 September 1957.

"League Tells Griffith to Stay in D.C." *Washington Post*, 8 July 1958.

Lipstye, Robert. "John McGraw Said Yankees Go Away." *New York Times*, 6 May 1971.

"Los Angeles Council Votes Dodger Deal." *Los Angeles Times*, 17 September 1957.

"Minneapolis Board OK's Plan." *Washington Post*, 3 September 1958.

"Minneapolis No Sure Gold Mine as Big League Town." *Washington Post*, 24 August 1958.

"Money Stadium Cost Would Feed 17,655 Babies for Year." *The Baltimore Sun*, 24 August 1933.

"Murphy's Resolution Defeated and Annual Meeting Is Tranquil." *Washington Post*, 1 February 1958.

"Planners Again Okay Stadium Site." *Washington Post*, 3 April 1959.

Povich, Shirley. "Armory Simply Isn't Right Spotfor (sic) Stadium." *Washington Post*, 5 February 1958.

"President Signs Bill For New D.C. Stadium." *Washington Post*, 29 July 1958.

"Redskins Turn Down Lease Terms." *Washington Post*, 9 April 1959.

"Rockefeller and Mayor Try New Pitch." *Los Angeles Times*, 21 September 1957.

"Senators Must Operate in D.C. under Corporate Law." *Washington Post*, 5 September 1958.

"Signs Point to Dodgers in L.A. by '58." *Los Angeles Times*, 20 September 1957.

"Skins May Eye Stadium at Maryland." *Washington Post*, 2 April 1959.

"Skins Will Pay 10% Rent." *Washington Post*, 4 September 1958.

"Smog Would Halt Bums' Night Games." *Los Angeles Times*, 18 September 1957.

"Stadium Land Leased to Armory Board." *Washington Post*, 13 December 1958.

"Stadium Site Awaits Fine Arts' Approval." *Washington Post*, 17 March 1959

"Stadium Will Be Built If Redskins Sign Up." *Washington Post*, 11 February 1959.

"Webb Ready to Bring A's to L.A. if O'Malley Fails." *Los Angeles Times*, 23 September 1957.

Weyler, John "20th Anniversary...The Big A." *Los Angeles Times*, 19 April 1986.

MISCELLANEOUS

Anaheim Stadium. A souvenir booklet made available by the Anaheim Stadium management.

Ashwood, John E. "Transportation Planning Consideration for New Stadia." Report on the advisability of building a major dome stadium in Phoenix, Arizona.

Coughlin, Robert E., Janet E. McKinnon, and Thomas A. Reiner. *The Economic Impacts of the Spectrum on the City of Philadelphia and the Metropolitan Region.* Philadelphia, PA: Regional Science Research Institute, May 1978.

Cox, Preston, Gary W. Finger, Ronald L. Promboin, James S. Vas Dias. *Financial Evaluation of Los Angeles Rams Football Company and the City of Anaheim Lease Agreements.* SRI International, 1978.

Denver, Colorado. Denver's Mile High Stadium Is "On the Move" in Colorado. Denver, 1980.

Eddystone, C. Nebel, III, Project Director. "The Economic Impact of the Louisiana Superdome (1975-1985)," Economic impact study conducted by the Division of Business and Economic Research, University of New Orleans, 1985.

International Association of Auditorium Managers. *Professional Sports Lease Survey*, Chicago, 1985.

Los Angeles, California. *Los Angeles Memorial Coliseum.* A publication by
    the Los Angeles Memorial Coliseum Commission.
"Louisiana Superdome Quick Facts." A fact sheet distributed by Facility
    Management of Louisiana—Louisiana Superdome. Received in a
    private correspondence from Bill Curl, Facility Management of
    Louisiana.
Maryland Department of Economic and Community Development. *The
    Economic Impact of Professional Sports on the Maryland Economy*
    January 1985.
"Metrodome Statistics." *Greater Minneapolis*, page 52. This was a photocopy
    of a page sent by the Metropolitan Sports Facilities Commission.
Minneapolis, Minnesota, Metropolitan Council. *Recommendations for a
    Metropolitan Sports Commission*, 24 January 1974.
Schaffer, William A., George D. Houser, Robert A. Weinberg. *The Economic
    Impact of the Braves on Atlanta: 1966.* Atlanta GA: Industrial
    Management Center, February 1967.
Schaffer, William A., and Lawrence S. Davidson. *Economic Impact of the
    Falcons on Atlanta.* Atlanta, GA: The Atlanta Falcons, 1972.

Index

Accumulated Net Present Value
(ANPV), 17
Ad Art, 136
Alchian, Armen, 14-15
American Football League (AFL),
41
Anaheim, California, 173
Anaheim Stadium: 75–82, 101,
159, 170, 204, 212, 213, 215,
216; construction costs, 78;
example of volatile ANPV, 166-
167
Arata, Blake, 137
Arlington, Texas, 64
Arlington Stadium, 202, 204, 211,
213, 215, 216
Arrowhead Stadium, 211, 212
Astrodome, 135, 169, 196, 205,
211, 212, 215
Atlanta, Georgia, 22, 83, 173. *See
also* Georgia Dome
Atlanta Braves: contribution to
finances of Atlanta–Fulton
County Stadium, 85; effect on
Atlanta–Fulton County Stadium
cash flows of lease extension
signed in 1990, 87

Atlanta Falcons, contribution to
finances of Atlanta–Fulton
County Stadium, 86
Atlanta–Fulton County Stadium,
83–90, 159, 167, 169, 170, 172,
204, 212, 213, 215, 216;
construction costs, 84
Autry, Gene, 75, 77

Baade, Robert, 177, 178-183, 184,
186
Balboa Stadium, 101, 216
Baltimore, Maryland, 173. *See also*
Oriole Park at Camden Yards
Baltimore Colts, 6, 29, 93
Baltimore Memorial Stadium, 29–
39, 166, 170, 172, 204, 211,
212, 213, 215, 216; construction
costs, 31
Baltimore Orioles, 6, 30, 65,
attendance records effect on
profitability of Memorial
Stadium, 31–32
The Baltimore Sun, 29
Bear Stadium, 47
Blues' Field, 92
Borjas, George, 16
Boston, Massachusetts. *See* Braves
Field; Fenway Park

Boston Braves, 21
Bowron, Fletcher, 56
Bradley, Tom, mayor of Los
    Angeles, 2
Braves Field, 21, 209, 216
Brooklyn, 53. *See also* Ebbet's
    Field
Brooklyn Dodgers, 5, 6, 13;
    attendance 1952–1956, 55,
    world series attendace as
    evidence Ebbet's Field was a
    drag on attendance 54
Buffalo, New York, 173
Buffalo Bills, 6, 41, 43, 127, 168
Buffalo Memorial Stadium, 41–45,
    127, 168, 170
Buffalo Sabres, 6
Buffalo War Memorial Stadium,
    41, 160, 204
Busch, August, 30
Busch Stadium, 196, 210, 212, 215

Cafritz, Morris, 62
California Angels, 203
Cammeyer, William, 1
Candlestick Park, 84, 91, 207, 212,
    213, 215, 216
Carr, Edward F., 62
Carrier Dome, 152
Chavez Ravine, 56
Chicago, Illinois. *See* Comiskey
    Park (new); Comiskey Park
    (old); Soldier Field; Wrigley
    Field
Chicago Cardinals, 41, 203
Chicago White Sox, 22
Cincinnati, Ohio, 173. *See also*
    Crosley Field; Riverfront
    Stadium
Cincinnati Bengals, 110; 1993
    agreement to keep team in
    Riverfront, 110; hostile
    relationship with Reds, 110
Cincinnati Reds, 110; hostile
    relationship with Bengals, 110
City of Atlanta and Fulton County
    Recreation Authority, 83

Cleveland Stadium, 205, 212, 215
Coase, Ronald, 14
Colorado Rockies, 166
Comiskey Park (new), 195, 204
Comiskey Park (old), 209, 211,
    213, 215, 216
Connick, William, 138
Construction costs differences from
    estimated costs, 157-158
Cooke, Jack Kent, 167
Coons, Rex, 75
Cotton Bowl, 216
Crosley Field, 109, 209, 213

D'Alesandro, Thomas, 189
Dallas, Texas, Cotton Bowl, see
    Cotton Bowl
Dallas Cowboys, 41
Davies, David, 15
Davis, Al, 3, 91-94
Demmert, Henry, 9
Demographic determinants of
    stadium subsidies, 164-165
Demsetz, Harold, 8
Denver, Colorado, 173. *See also*
    Mile High Stadium
Denver Bears, 47-48
Denver Broncos, 47, 166
Denver Nuggets, 47
Detroit, Michigan. *See* Tiger
    Stadium
District of Columbia Stadium, 61
Dixon, Dave, 136
Dodger Stadium, 53–49, 75, 76,
    160, 166, 170, 209, 211, 213,
    215, 216
"Doers," 47, 48
Dye, Ricard, 177, 178

Ebbet, Charles, 53, 55
Ebbet's Field, 53, 209, 216
Eisenhower, Dwight D., 62
El-Hodiri, Mohamed, 8
Ellig, Jerome, 10, 22
Erie County, 127

Facility Management of Louisiana
(FML), 139
Factors leading to subsidies, 161
Federal Bureau of Investigation,
187
Fenway Park, 209, 211, 213, 215
Finley, Charles O., 92
Forbes Field, 210
Foxboro Stadium, 121–125, 160,
167, 171, 196, 211, 212;
construction cost, 122, 209
Frank Youell Field, 91
Fuller, Buckminster, 54
Fulton County, 84

Georgia Dome, 84, 195, 204
Giles, Warren, 57
Golden State Warriors, 92
Government in the Sports Business,
9, 11
Greenbay, Wisconsin, Lambeau
Field, see Lambeau Field
Griffith, Calvin, 61-63; reaction to
blacks and reason for leaving
Washington, D.C., 63; request
for a stadium to replace the Met,
151
Griffith Stadium, 63, 210, 216

Hahn, James, Jr., 2
Hahn, Kenneth, 56
Hamilton County, 109-110
Hilton, Baron, 77, 101
*Home Field Advantage: Municipal
Subsidies to Professional Sports
Teams*, 17
Hoosierdome, 152, 169, 216
Hopkins, Samuel, 189
Houston. *See* Astrodome

Indianapolis Hoosierdome, 30, 205
Interior Department, 62
Irving, Texas. *See* Texas Stadium
Irwindale, California, 93

Jack Murphy Stadium, 77, 101–
107, 167, 169, 171, 180, 212,
213, 215; construction costs,
102, 207
Joe Robbie Stadium, 195, 197, 210
Johns Hopkins University, 30
Johnson, Arnold, 92
Johnson, Arthur T., 12, 16, 203
Jozsa, Frank, Jr., 9-10, 163

Kansas City, Missouri: Harry S.
Truman Sports Complex, 169,
206; Municipal Stadium, 206.
See also Arrowhead Stadium;
Royals' Stadium;
Keezar Stadium, 91, 208
Kiam, Victor, 122
Kingdome, 169, 208, 211, 212,
213, 215
Kraft, Robert, 122
Kroc, Ray, 65, 102
Kuhn, Bowie, 138

Lambeau Field, 205, 212
Levy, Bernard, 135
Long Beach, California, 76
Los Angeles, 2, 5, 173. *See also*
Dodger Stadium
Los Angeles Angels, 76
Los Angeles Coliseum, 75, 212,
216
Los Angeles Coliseum Commission
(LACC), 2, 206; and Raider
move to Los Angeles, 92-94
Los Angeles Dodgers, 76
Los Angeles Olympic Organizing
Committee, 93
Los Angeles Raiders, 2
Los Angeles Rams, 77; move to
Anaheim, 92
Louisiana Stadium and Exposition
Commission, 135

Louisiana Superdome, 135–147,
     158, 167, 169 171, 173, 206,
     212; attempt to attract Major
     League Baseball, 138;
     competition with Houston
     leading to cost overruns, 135;
     controversy over defective piles,
     137; effect of 1974 NFL strike
     on cash flows, 140
Louisiana Superdome Authority,
     135

Marshall, George, 61, 62;
     relationship with National
     Armory Board, 63
McKeithen, John, 135
McNicols Arena, 47
Meadowlands, 205, 211, 212, 216
Methods of estimating economic
     impact of stadium investments,
     177-178
Metrodome, 149–154, 161, 166,
     169, 171, 173, 211, 212, 213,
     215; construction costs, 152,
     206; effect of property taxes on
     finances, 154; relationship
     between Twins records and
     financial success of stadium,
     153
Metropolitan Sports Area
     Commission (MSAC), 149
Metropolitan Sports Facilities
     Commission (MSFC), 152, 161
Metropolitan Stadium (the Met),
     149, 206, 212, 213, 216
Miami, Florida. See Orange Bowl;
     Joe Robbie Stadium
Miami Dolphins, 93, 180
Mile High Stadium, 47–52, 160,
     166, 170, 205, 211, 212
Milwaukee Brewers, 22
Milwaukee County Stadium, 21–
     28, 169, 211, 212, 215, 216;
     construction costs, 23, 206; host
     to Green Bay Packers, 22

Minneapolis, Minnesota, 149, 173;
     attracting Washington Senators,
     62-63. See also Metrodome;
     Metropolitan Stadium
Minnesota Twins, 150
Minnesota Vikings, 149
Mizell, Wilmer, 175
Montreal, Canada, Olympic
     Stadium, 625
Moore, Gerald, 151
Moses, Robert, 54, 76
Murdoch, Keith, 77

National Armory Board, 62; failure
     to reach an agreement with
     Padres, 65; financing RFK
     stadium, 67-73; interest income
     from sale of bonds, 67;
     relationship with congress, 65
National Association, 1
National Housing Authority
     (NHA), 56
National League 1993 expansion,
     66
Neale, Walter C., 8
New England Patriots, 121
New Orleans, Louisiana 173. See
     also Louisiana Superdome
New Orleans Jazz, 137; impact on
     finances of Superdome, 140
New Orleans Saints: impact of
     finances of Superdome, 140
New York. See Polo Grounds;
     Shea Stadium; Yankee Stadium
New York Giants (football), 6
New York Jets, 6
New York State Urban
     Development Corporation, 127
New York Yankees, 6
NFL Dallas Texans, 29
Noll, Roger, 9
Nunn, Samuel, 14, 178, 183, 184

O'Malley, Walter, 53, 75, 76;
    reaction to California
    referendum process, 57; reaction
    to Los Angeles' offer to move to
    Los Angeles, 56; view of
    baseball, 53
Oakland, California, 173
Oakland–Alameda Coliseum
    Complex, 92, 159, 167, 171,
    190, 211, 212, 213, 215, 216;
    construction costs, 94, 207
Oakland–Alameda County
    Coliseum, Inc. (OACCI), 91–99
Oakland Raiders, 91, 93, 216
Okner, Benjamin, article on pricing
    of stadiums, 10-12
Orange Bowl, 206, 212
Orchard Park, New York, 127, 173.
    See also Rich Stadium
Oriole Park at Camden Yards, 195,
    204

Philadelphia, Pennsylvania. See
    Shibe Park; Veterans Stadium,
Pittsburgh, Pennsylvania. See
    Forbes Stadium; Three Rivers
    Stadium
Polo Grounds, 210, 216
Pontiac, Michigan. See Silverdome
Poulson, Norris, 5, 56
Princeton University, 54
Proposition B: referendum to
    approve land swap with
    Dodgers, 57

Quirk, James, 8, 9

Redland Field, 109
RFK Stadium, 61–73, 158, 167,
    169, 170, 208, 212, 216
Rich Stadium, 127–133, 168, 169,
    171, 172, 211, 212; construction
    costs, 128, 207; legal issue of
    property taxation, 129
Rickey, Branch, 53; view of
    baseball, 53

Riverfront Stadium, 109–119, 171,
    172, 211, 212, 213, 215;
    alternative property tax
    assumptions, 113; construction
    costs, 110, 205; effect of 1981
    baseball strike on cash flows,
    111; effect of 1974 NFL strike
    on cash flows, 112; fans'
    reaction to opening, 110;
    municipal stadium tax revenues,
    113; payroll taxes, 113
Rockefeller, Nelson, 55
Roosevelt Field (Jersey City, New
    Jersey), 205
Rose Bowl, 93
Rosentraub, Mark, 14, 178, 183,
    184
Rottenberg, Simon, 7
Royals' Stadium, 211, 213, 215

San Diego, California, 173. See
    also Balboa Stadium; Jack
    Murphy Stadium
San Diego Chargers, 77, 101
San Diego City Council, 101
San Diego Management Company,
    102
San Diego Padres, 65, 101
San Diego Sports Arena, 102
San Diego Stadium, 101
San Diego Stadium Authority, 101,
    102
San Francisco. See Candlestick
    Park; Keezar Stadium
San Francisco 49'er's, 91
Schaefer Brewery, 121
Schaefer Stadium, 121. See also
    Foxboro Stadium
Schwegmann, John, 136-137
Scully, Gerald, 8
Seattle, Washington. See
    Kingdome; Sickes Stadium
Seattle Pilots, 22
Shea, George, 63
Shea Stadium, 169, 207, 212, 213,
    215, 216
Shibe Park, 210, 216

Short, Robert, 64; relation with
    National Armory Board, 64
Sickes Stadium, 210
Sigholtz, Robert, 65
Silverdome, 207, 211, 212
Sisk, Bernice: advice to Armory
    Board regarding accepting risk
    in lease arrangements, 65
Smith, Adam, 3, 14
Smith, John, (owner of Pacific
    Coast League San Diego
    Padres), 57
Smith, John, (part owner of
    Brooklyn Dodgers), 53
Soldier Field, 205, 212
Sources of economic growth
    generated from stadium
    investment, 176-177
Special Committee on Sports and
    Cultural Facilities, 150
Sportsman's Park, 29, 210, 216
St. Louis, Missouri. *See* Busch
    Stadium; Sportsman's Park
St. Louis Browns, 29
St. Louis Cardinals, 29
Stadium Realty Trust, 121
Sullivan family, 121-122
Sullivan Stadium. *See* Foxboro
    Stadium
Superdome. *See* Louisiana
    Superdome

Tampa Stadium, 196, 208, 212
Texas Rangers, 64, 202
Texas Stadium, 209, 211, 212
Three Rivers Stadium, 158, 169,
    207, 211, 212, 213, 215
Tiger Stadium, 202, 209, 213, 215
Title I of the Federal Housing Act
    of 1949: refusal by New York to
    use it to keep Dodgers in
    Brooklyn, 54-55; use by Los
    Angeles to attract Dodgers to
    Los Angeles, 56
Toronto, Canada, Exhibition
    Staium, 215

Union Grounds, 1, 53
University of California, Los
    Angeles (UCLA), 93
University of Maryland, 30
University of Minnesota, 153

Veeck, Bill, 30, 65, 92
Venable Park, 29
Veterans Stadium, 169, 207, 212,
    213, 215

Wagner, Robert, 56
Washington, D.C., 173. *See also*
    Griffith Stadium; RFK Stadium
Washington Redskins, 61;
    permission to build luxury
    boxes, 66; plans to move to
    Washington suburbs, 66
Washington Senators (old), 6, 61;
    contribution to RFK Stadium
    finances, 68
Washington Senators (new), 64,
    102
Webb, Del, 77, 92
Wilson, Lionel, 94, 189
Winter, Max, 150
Wood, Bob, 201
Wrigley Field (Chicago), 209, 211,
    213, 215
Wrigley Field (Los Angeles), 55,
    75

Yankee Stadium, 158, 169, 207,
    210, 211, 212, 215

About the Author

DEAN V. BAIM is an Associate Professor of Economics and Finance at Seaver College, Pepperdine University, where he has been on the faculty since 1983. Dr. Baim was named Pepperdine University Professor of the Year in 1990, and Pepperdine University Society for the Advancement of Management's Professor of the Year in 1984, 1989, 1991, and 1992. He has served widely as a consultant and as an advisor. He has written numerous journal articles and contributions to books.

ISBN 0-313-27816-4

90000>

EAN

9 780313 278167

HARDCOVER BAR CODE